Becoming

George Orwell

Becoming
George Orwell

Life and Letters, Legend and Legacy

John Rodden

PRINCETON UNIVERSITY PRESS

PRINCETON AND OXFORD

Copyright © 2020 by Princeton University Press

Published by Princeton University Press

41 William Street, Princeton, New Jersey 08540

6 Oxford Street, Woodstock, Oxfordshire OX20 1TR

press.princeton.edu

All Rights Reserved

LCCN 2018946113

ISBN 9780691182742

ISBN (e-book) 9780691190129

British Library Cataloging-in-Publication Data is available

Editorial: Ben Tate, Hannah Paul, and Charlie Allen

Production Editorial: Natalie Baan

Text Design: Carmina Alvarez

Jacket Design: Matt Avery/Monograph

Production: Jacquie Poirier

Publicity: Jodi Price and Katie Lewis

Copyeditor: Sarah Vogelsong

Jacket illustration by Lauren Nassef

This book has been composed in Minion Pro

Printed on acid-free paper. ∞

Printed in the United States of America

10 9 8 7 6 5 4 3 2 1

Rose Gallagher Rodden
1928–2018
with undying gratitude

Contents

Acknowledgments

First I must acknowledge the extraordinary pleasure I have had in the company of the remarkable man and writer who has once again sat patiently for this portrait. Among his invaluable legacies to me has been to bring me into contact with many wonderful people who have played an important role in my life and work, and I welcome the opportunity to thank them here.

At Princeton University Press, the shrewd advice of Ben Tate has improved the book substantially. From its earliest stages, Ben has been a robust advocate of this book and encouraged me to approach it with an eye toward the informed general reader.

I also owe a large debt of gratitude to my old friend Peter Dougherty, former director of Princeton University Press, for his faith in this project since its infancy. At a later date, assistant editor Hannah Paul, editorial assistant Charlie Allen, production editor Natalie Baan, and copy editor Sarah Vogelsong were most generous and understanding as they shepherded the book through the production process. Natalie and Sarah devoted care and consideration to the manuscript and its author far beyond the duties of professionalism, extending to kindness and personal interest.

This book took much longer to complete than I had originally imagined when I first embarked on it. Throughout the decade of its gestation, I was assisted by personal friends and valued colleagues who shared their research with me, commented on portions of the manuscript, arranged public lectures, or otherwise stimulated my thinking.

In England, I have benefited from the generosity of Ian Angus, Ian Willison, Sarah Gibbs, Quentin Kopp, D. J. Taylor, Masha Karp, Richard Keeble, Tim Crook, Roger Howe, Sarah Gibbs, Peter Davison, and Dione Venables. At the University of Texas at Austin, Thomas Staley, former director of the Harry Ransom Center (HRC), and W. Roger Lewis, director of the Program in British Studies at the HRC, have been valued allies. Roger invited me to deliver an HRC lecture that came to form the basis of a chapter in this book and, quite beyond the scope of this project, has been gracious with my many queries and requests for help.

As many other scholars can confirm, one of the most enjoyable little adventures in the course of long hours of research involves the discovery of a long-stalked datum pursued merely to adorn a humble footnote. In this book the zaniest escapade was my tracking down information about the exact Washington hotline number of the John Birch Society during the Cold War, and I thank the long-suffering research staff of the Library of Congress for their good humor in checking tattered phone books, dusty newsletters, and forgotten correspondence from the 1950s onward as they stayed on the hunt at the behest of their obsessive client.

During the last decade, I have also been graced with the good fortune of regular dialogues or correspondence with a few friends who have shared their immense knowledge about British history in general and Orwell's writings in particular: Scott Walter, Alan Munton, Henk Vynkier, Vincent Kling, and Jeffrey Meyers. Two other old friends, William Cain and Paul Cantor, helped me recast the book during its formative stages.

Another pair of cherished friends, Gorman Beauchamp and Jack Rossi, not only spent long hours on the phone in conversations about our shared intellectual passions but also volunteered to read sections of the manuscript. They furnished me wise and much-appreciated counsel. Two of the chapters emerged from articles coauthored with Professor Rossi, and I thank him for generously allowing me to draw on them for this book.

Several other mentors and teachers from my early years continue to occupy a large role in my life, among them Dave Efroymson, Jim Butler, Michael Levenson, and Michael Dillon. All of them have been edifying and indeed inspiring presences in my life across the decades.

Going even further back in time, I thank my first teacher-hero, my high school debate and English teacher, John Buettler, with whom I began to discuss Orwell's *Nineteen Eighty-Four* as a 14-year-old schoolboy. Although John raised his eyebrows more than once at that teenager's chutzpah (or immaculate innocence), he steadfastly stood close by as I sallied forth and tilted at every windmill on my path. My quest extended to writing long letters to the FBI requesting information about their "Orwellian" surveillance policies and even conducting after-school telephone "interviews" with Bureau agents, who regularly called (to my mother's consternation) our (wiretapped?) phone for "updates on my work"—and who proved eager to obtain a copy of my oratorical address denouncing them, a speech widely (and passionately) delivered at weekend forensic tournaments throughout Philadelphia.

A wide circle of comrades have provided support of still other kinds. Caleb Upson, James B. M. Schick, Jonathan Imber, Parker Thayer, Olivia Schultz, and Adam Bourenane have given me invaluable editorial assistance. Thomas Cushman, Bill Shanahan, Ethan Goffman, Erica Walter, Robert Boyers, Morris Dickstein, Gene Goodheart, and Alan Wald have shared their insight on a broad range of political and intellectual issues. The infectious good spirits of Raphael and Jack Bemporad, Lynn Hayden, Jud Smith,

Mitch Baranowski, Zachary Cameron, and Anna Thibodeau have buoyed and bolstered me, as have the ministrations of a pair of good friends since ancient times, Kathleen O'Connor and Greg Sokoloff, both of whom have reached out repeatedly across the miles and decades. Closer to home, so too have Ruth Maxwell, whose Christian charity has been exemplary, and Lance Harris, my co-conspirator of yore and the fairest of foul-weather friends. Lance has saved me from myself on countless occasions, tossing yet another custom-made life preserver into my sea of troubles and—*voilà!*—ending them.

Family members on both sides of the Atlantic have been kind to me with their constant expressions of interest and encouragement. Among those in Ireland are Kathleen Fegan; Annie, Anne, Nuala, and Liz Gallagher; Brian Rodden and Brigid Rodden Gallagher; Brid Crumlish and Sean, Molly, and Kate Curran; and Evelyn McGinley.

Meanwhile my three younger brothers—Edward, Thomas, and Paul—have been blessedly tolerant of "My Life with George," as I once titled an open letter to Orwell. Acknowledging him (albeit with occasional sighs and rolled eyes) as their big brother's (intellectual) big brother, they have provided me unsolicited yet (belatedly) welcome advice and comic relief as they have accepted him into our family life with gentle sarcasm yet unfailingly good grace. That fraternal spirit even extended to Paul's search through the book for stylistic infelicities and Thomas's scrutiny of a passage at a moment's notice, whereby he would invariably zap yet another cowering typo with his laser-beam delete button.

This book was largely composed during the declining years of my mother, Rose Gallagher Rodden, whom I assisted as her at-home caregiver. (Or rather the reverse, as she would surely maintain.) She passed away suddenly as the book neared completion. A lady of steely determination born of the struggles of her hardscrabble youth in County Donegal, Ireland, she mellowed considerably during her sunset decade. Toward the end she often struck me as a delightful 80-something girl with wrinkles. Her abiding confidence, charming nonchalance, good cheer, and newly acquired forbearance with her head-in-the-clouds son as she listened patiently to my ramblings during our long wheelchair rides through the streets, all the while nodding politely and humming an Irish folk tune—begorrah, that was pure maternal love.

In gratitude for her serendipity and stamina as we rolled along in that sea of song, warmed by wave after lilting wave of seemingly endless sun-drenched afternoons under the vast Texas sky, I dedicate this book to my wild Irish Rose.

Becoming

George Orwell

FIGURE 1. In January 2017, just days after the presidential inauguration of Donald Trump, *1984* was again topping American best seller
lists. This cartoon captures that moment, charging that Trump is keeping tabs on the *New York Times* (or some other purveyor of allegedly
left-slanted "fake news"). The cartoon mocks Trump as an "Orwellian"
leader who is keeping an all-seeing eye on any "enemy of the people."

Is the cartoon also a veiled critique of George Orwell himself for
compiling his controversial "list" of "crypto-Communists"—and thereby
suggesting that Orwell and Trump are quite alike?

Unlikely. But Orwell did keep a notebook in which he listed various
writers and public figures whom he did not trust to promote the British
government's best interests in Cold War propaganda campaigns. As he
lay on his deathbed in 1949, Orwell shared his list with Britain's spy-
masters in the Information Research Department (IRD), the postwar
British equivalent of the CIA. A department of the British Foreign Office,
the IRD was closed down in 1977.

It warrants mention that this was not the first time that a headline
such as "*1984* Sales Zoom" had appeared in newspapers. Thirty-four
years earlier, as the countdown to 1984 neared completion and the
new year approached, *1984* was topping best seller lists throughout
the world. The novel stayed at No. 1 for almost six months, between
October 1983 and April 1984, an unprecedented feat for a book originally published 35 years earlier.

PROLOGUE

Donald and Winston at the Ministry of Alternative Facts

Big Brother, Welcome to Broadway!

It was a bright cold day in January, and the keyboards were clicking $$$$$$$$$$$$$$.[1] In a deliciously fitting historical irony, the first full day in office of the new American president, Donald Trump, commenced on January 21, 2017—the sixty-seventh anniversary of George Orwell's death—just as Orwell's grim novel of a dystopian future, *Nineteen Eighty-Four*, began its ascent once again to No. 1 on the best seller lists.

Such is Clio's caprice.

In hindsight, the Orwellian countdown to Inauguration Day started even before Election Day on November 8. Trump's startling victory triggered an unexpected explosion of popular interest in the novel, however, as sales of the Signet paperback edition jumped tenfold in the next six weeks. On the eve of the inauguration, the book hovered between No. 5 and No. 7 on the Amazon.com best seller list. Following the inauguration, a series of controversial public statements by senior officials in the new administration catapulted it to No. 2. And by the morning of January 25, it stood at No. 1.[2]

Fast-forward six months: Welcome, Big Brother, to Broadway!

Opening on June 22 as the first major entry of the 2017–18 Broadway season, a British production of *1984* was staged at the newly refurbished Hudson Theater. Jointly arranged by London producer Sonia Friedman and New York producer Scott Rudin, this stage version had been mounted in London in 2013–14 and has most recently starred Andrew Gower as Winston Smith. Co-created by writer-directors Robert Icke and Duncan Macmillan, *1984* had toured to sold-out houses—and rave reviews—throughout England. The production had featured a giant video wall from which Big Brother looked down on his party members to make sure no one was committing "thoughtcrimes." Critics hailed the lighting, sound, and video design as a provocative assault on the mind and senses—like a trip to Room 101—and compared the production to movies by Stanley Kubrick and David Lynch. The London production was performed for a few regional American audiences in 2016, most notably at the American Repertory Theater in Cambridge, Massachusetts, and at the Shakespeare Theatre in Washington D.C. The Broadway show featured an all-American cast.

The Broadway staging of *1984* succeeded months-long efforts to satirize and protest the policies of Trump and his administration. For example, on April 4—the date on which the fateful events that open Orwell's novel occur—a Hollywood-based political advocacy group (dubbing itself the United States of Cinema) arranged the return screening of Michael Radford's film adaptation in American theaters. Originally released in 1984 and starring John Hurt as Winston and Richard Burton as O'Brien—in Sir Richard's last film appearance before his death—160 art house movie theaters across the country in 148 cities and 42 states (plus five locations in Canada and one in England) screened *1984* as part of a larger political campaign against the decision by the Trump administration to cut funding from artist grant programs, including the National Endowment for the Arts, the National Endowment for the Humanities, and the Corporation for Public Broadcasting.

The Oprah of the Oval Office, or
Doubleplusgood Dystopianism?

How did all this come to be? Several related news events that exemplified what has come to be known as the "post-factual world" account for the meteoric rise and final breakthrough of *Nineteen Eighty-Four* to the top of the best seller lists in January 2017. Within hours of Trump's swearing in, White House press secretary Sean Spicer heatedly insisted that the inauguration had been the best attended ever—"period"—regardless of what the photo and statistical evidence might indicate. Two days later, on the Sunday morning television show *Meet the Press*, Kellyanne Conway, a close advisor to the president, defended Spicer by "explaining" that his false claims were merely "alternative facts." Alarms rang out across the globe that Winston Smith could not have come up with a better line in his cubicle at the Ministry of Truth, where all fabrications are merely what could be termed "alternative facts." Within minutes of the novel's historic reconquest of first place on the best seller list—as had already happened during September 1983 to April 1984, 34 years after its original publication in June 1949—staffers from news organizations such as CNN and PBS were in touch with me for comments about "what Orwell would say."

I dubbed Conway, whose inadvertent masterstroke of euphemistic Newspeak suddenly made her the darling of the publishing industry, the "Oprah of the Oval Office," a wonder woman who could immediately turn serious books (above all, dystopian classics) into best sellers, even if they had been selling poorly (or had been out of print) for years. Her notorious phrase immediately went viral and was translated into numerous languages.[3] Not that the Fourth Estate abuses language any less than does the administration—or is any more unlikely to be ignorant of the

English language. After my own interview with PBS, I read the following sentence in its published report on the Amazon best seller story: "Born in 1903, Orwell lived through two world wars and saw the rise of totalitarian regimes on an unpresidented [*sic!!*] scale." (Unfortunately—yet predictably—this was not deliberate irony, as I later ascertained.)

Signet regarded the entire development as "doubleplusgood." Its edition of the novel soared even higher in the two months following the inauguration, enjoying a 10,000 percent increase in sales, whereupon the publisher immediately announced a new print run of 100,000 copies, including an additional 25,000 of *Animal Farm*. In Britain, sales of the Penguin edition of *Nineteen Eighty-Four*, which had been selling approximately 5,000 copies per week in the run-up to January 20, multiplied following the January news events, inducing Penguin to print 75,000 more copies immediately. Random House also printed an extra 175,000 copies of the novel based on sales forecasts.

Obviously, the sales of *Nineteen Eighty-Four* have risen in response to Trump's audacious attempts to manipulate facts throughout his long presidential campaign and since his November 2016 election victory. His tall tales grew, if anything, even more Bunyanesque during his first week in office. For instance, besides outlandish claims of mass voter fraud and his contention that he had lost the popular vote in the November election because 3 million votes had been cast "illegally," Trump maintained that the science behind climate change is a hoax perpetrated by the Chinese.

In his personal manifesto, *The Art of the Deal* (1987)—which some critics regard as a self-revealing statement of his life philosophy à la Hitler's *Mein Kampf*—Trump discusses his style of "bravado" and penchant for "truthful hyperbole," which he considers "an innocent form of exaggeration—and a very effective form of promotion." Unsurprisingly, among the other postelection best sellers on Amazon.com was Trump's *The Art of the Deal*. By late January, it had consistently secured a place in the top 15.

Sanity Is Statistical—Not?

It is interesting that the connection between "alternative facts" and Orwell's dystopia was first made by a reporter who dubbed it "a George Orwell phrase"—as if Orwell himself might have been a Winston Smith who crafted his lies in clever-sounding language or even a version of Donald Trump. As I hope to show in the succeeding chapters, this confusion about and conflation of the author George Orwell with such "Orwellian" locutions is a common occurrence. Is "Orwellian" language the limpid, direct style of the author? Or is it the diabolical doublespeak of Big Brother? Certainly in the public mind—and in common usage—that proper adjective mainly signifies the latter. And this sinister meaning of the man's name in adjectival form reflects the rise of what can be called the "Orwell legend," that is, the development of an individual into an icon. I discuss throughout the book the difference between Orwell and "Orwell," with the latter representing the towering totem invoked by ideologically motivated (or ill-informed and careless) observers to bolster whatever arguments they seek to advance.[4]

Scandals galore and internecine warfare notwithstanding, Trump has proven a master at dominating the airwaves. It is as if he based his entire campaign strategy and governing outlook on the famous party slogan in *Nineteen Eighty-Four*: "Who controls the past controls the future: who controls the present controls the past." The point is this: whoever controls the present controls both the past *and* the future. Such a tremendous power to command headlines and dictate the public conversation of the moment—exemplified by his direct connection to the wider public via his ever-active Twitter account[5]—is a terrifying demonstration of what Orwell termed the "mutability of the past." The phrase refers to the so-called rectification of history by *Minitru* bureaucrats such as Winston Smith, whereby facts are indeed "mutable," that is, all kinds of "alternative facts" can be invented that allow various scenarios to be accepted as reality. After all, Winston Smith is brainwashed in Room 101 to believe that $2 + 2 = 5$. His efforts to maintain that "sanity is not statistical" fail utterly, leading to the novel's final line of despair: "He loved Big Brother."

Yet one caveat is necessary. The rise of the Internet and sound bite infotainment industry in our ADD culture make the kind of activity that Winston performs in the Ministry of Truth unnecessary. There is no need for the Trump administration to rewrite already published articles to make them retroactively match some new alternative reality or draft backdated articles about these sham events; it just needs to repeat its "alternative facts" incessantly so that they dominate the airwaves and people accept these mutable "facts" in the way that Julia in *Nineteen Eighty-Four* simply accepts that Oceania had "always been at war with Eurasia"—or was it Eastasia? Newscasters have no more command over Oldspeak precepts than does the president himself. In the age of endless spin and limitless cyberspace—not to mention avatars and Internet addiction—the lines between virtual reality and "objective truth" (a concept cherished by George Orwell) fade and blur into $2 + 2 = $.[6]

Of course, none of this obfuscation of language or "rectification" of history is new (or "unpresidented") with Donald Trump or with a Republican administration. Trump's predecessor, Barack Obama, was the only president in history to have officially been at war for every single day of his eight years in the White House—

FIGURE 2. Calls to "impeach Big Brother" did not begin with Donald Trump and the aftermath of the 2018 midterm elections in the U.S., which witnessed control of the House of Representatives shift to the Democrats and the start of congressional investigations to impeach him. "Big Brother" Ronald Reagan also witnessed scattered calls for impeachment from his political opponents, as Ziggy learns in this February 1982 cartoon. (Attempts to impeach Reagan never gained strong congressional support. In 1999, however, the case turned out quite differently for Democratic president Bill Clinton, who was impeached by a Republican-led House in December 1998, though not convicted by the U.S. Senate two months later.)

and let us not forget that he was awarded the Nobel Peace Prize after only eight months in the White House, the only political leader ever to win it during his very first year in office. "War Is Peace," anyone? President Bill Clinton too was adept at denying objective truths and proclaiming "alternative facts," famously insisting that the truth of his testimony under oath regarding his affair with "that woman" (Monica Lewinsky) was fully understandable if one grasped "what the meaning of the word 'is' is."

How's that for a "George Orwell [*sic*] phrase"?

FIGURE 3. Orwell Man? Or "Orwell" Man?

George W. Bush is depicted here as an "Orwellian" tyrant, the Big Brotherish autocrat who not only defends wiretapping but also—through a virtuoso feat of doublethink and doublespeak—demonstrates that freedom is slavery. His logic? If "terrorists" hate America, the Land of the Free, then the only logical solution for all (double)thinking people is to abolish all freedoms through wiretapping, waterboarding, and other security "measures."

This cartoon appeared in April 2006, as the quagmire of the American occupation of Iraq was deepening.

INTRODUCTION

Orwell, My "Orwell"

Rationale of the Book

Becoming George Orwell: Life and Letters, Legend and Legacy pursues the bizarre saga of a leitmotif: the posthumous pilgrimage of author into apocrypha. What concerns us is the metamorphosis of a man of letters, the writer George Orwell, into a titanic totem, the icon "Orwell." Throughout the following dozen chapters, I draw a distinction between Orwell's "work" and his "Work." That distinction emerged vividly in our account in the Prologue of how the media's feeding frenzy about "alternative facts" eclipsed and elided the writer Orwell into the *bête noir* "Orwell." (Recall that one reporter dubbed the Trump spokeswoman's now-famous euphemism "a George Orwell phrase.")

This same distinction between Orwell and "Orwell"—between the work and the Work—is also captured in my subtitle. Essentially, the book is divided into two sections. The first half-dozen chapters address the "Life and Letters" of Orwell. The subsequent pages ponder the "Legend and Legacy" of "Orwell," with the concluding chapters meditating on "Orwell, *My* 'Orwell,'" in which I speak in a very personal way about Orwell's patrimony in terms of my own inheritance. I call Orwell "my intellectual big brother," and I can jest that I could have subtitled this book "Scrivener and Soul Brother."

As it proceeds to discuss in detail all these topics sequentially, *Becoming George Orwell: Life and Letters, Legend and Legacy* begins with a consideration in Part 1 of Orwell's personal life and literary achievement, spotlighting variously the eccentricities of the English Quixote, his lifelong disputatious debate with a schoolmate acquaintance, his little-noticed transition from apprentice writer "Eric Blair" into prose laureate "George Orwell," and both the fictional masterpieces of his last years and his accomplishments in nonfiction.

The chapters in Part 2 explore diverse aspects of Orwell's colossal reputation and checkered heritage. Here the scope broadens further as the narrative ranges across Orwell's ambiguous afterlife. An opening pair of chapters addresses Orwell's uncanny resemblance to a pair of *engagé* leftist French contemporaries, illuminating aspects of his stature both as a *littérateur* and *intellectuel* and as a figure of world literature. As we shall see, he bears comparison in striking respects with a fellow odd fellow, the little-remembered novelist Jean Malaquais, and with a famous odd man out, the heterodox radical Albert Camus. (Orwell's mother was partly French, and France was the only European nation outside Britain in which Orwell spent any substantial length of time—except for his months as a militiaman on the Catalonian front in the Spanish Civil War—having lived as a young man in Paris during his late 20s and returned there as a war reporter for the *Observer* in 1945.)[1]

Succeeding chapters explain the how and why of Orwell's posthumous fame and, in particular, the astonishing apotheosis of "the Orwell legend" and the birth of the canonical figure of mythic proportions, "St. George" Orwell. Those developments have resulted in a strangely silhouetted afterlife, one both radiantly shining and ruthlessly smeared, as the next pair of chapters discuss. The outcome is an image ever oscillating between light and darkness. First he is exalted as a "pious agnostic" and religious fellow traveler (indeed a near-saint for many Catholic intellectuals despite his anti-Catholic animus). Moments later he is the Big Brother bogeyman, the "Orwellian" doomsday prophet of endless warfare, whether cold or cyber.

As the book presents these episodes in Orwell's controversial afterlife, we witness the interplay of legend and legacy in world history. Our gaze then lowers from these scenes on the international stage and the study closes on a personal note, concluding with a meditation about Orwell's influence on my own political and moral outlook and, in a final contemplation, with a speculation on the future of his heritage, "Whither Orwell—and 'Orwell'?"

"Double" Trouble

But who—or what—*is* this haunting, spectral presence "Orwell"? And what indeed *is* the relationship between Orwell and "Orwell," work and Work?

"Orwell" is a half-sibling of the man and author Orwell. Forever in stealthy, shadowy pursuit of Orwell, the apparition "Orwell" frequently impersonates Orwell; conversely, Orwell is commonly mistaken for "Orwell" in public discourse. Locked in a *Blutsbrüderschaft*—indeed a death embrace borne in the dying writer's throes of fathering *Nineteen Eighty-Four*—the pair have come to share numerous (elective) affinities that all too often render them easily confused doubles. The *doppelgänger* motif in general and the issue of mistaken identities in particular is a recurrent theme of this book, but it is less a question of the historical George Orwell meeting the apparition "Orwell" than a matter of us twenty-first-century citizens lighting upon "Orwell" and—with a shock of recognition—glimpsing ourselves in the Other. Our encounter with the *doppelgänger* "Orwell" is an uncanny experience of the strange (*das Unheimliche*). Abruptly we glimpse ourselves in an unfamiliar way—not unlike Dr. Frankenstein beholding himself with awed horror in the fantastical creature to whom he has given life.[2]

Throughout the following chapters, I draw attention to the diverse manifestations of the *doppelgänger* "Orwell" and its complex relation to Orwell the man and writer. To remain alert to such matters keeps us poised on the precipice of mass psychodrama, for "Orwell" is typically perceived as a Frankenstein monster—or a Mr. Hyde—who disturbs and dims our proud personae as fair Children of Light. "Orwell" holds up the mirror to ourselves, tilting it so as to provoke us into endless rumination and self-interrogation: Are we really the grand heirs of Enlightenment liberalism, deputized to advance Liberty, extend Equality, and foster Brotherhood?[3] It is a sign of our cultural neurosis that such an examination necessarily exposes the precariousness of identity for us postfactual postmoderns.

Let us return to the relation between the man and author Orwell and "Orwell." From one angle, it is of course unfortunate that George Orwell is doubled with the dark and often dastardly phantasm "Orwell." Yet, in another sense, the pairing points to the doubleness within the writer Orwell himself, who was the author not only of the limpid, plain prose of the fine essays, but also of Newspeak and the party slogans of *Nineteen Eighty-Four*. As a result, the literary artistry of Orwell brilliantly enables us to recognize the "Orwell" within ourselves, even as we might hear him say: "*Nineteen Eighty-Four, c'est moi!*"[4]

And yet, even as we concede that point, we may imagine that if Orwell met his spectral double in a Fleet Street pub, he might well not recognize himself in the Other—any more than we tend to recognize ourselves in "Orwell" either. The distance between the Prose Laureate of English and the quacking duckspeaker of Newspeak is so great as to seem incommensurable. The Orwell

"Hello——ORwell 1984?"

FIGURE 4. As this Cold War cartoon attests, the language and imagery of *Nineteen Eighty-Four* were already being used to satirize wiretapping in the 1960s, long before the twenty-first century. Moreover, not only Republican presidents such as George W. Bush (and Donald Trump, Ronald Reagan, Richard Nixon, etc.) have been deemed "Orwellian." Here the famous political cartoonist Herblock mocks the administration of a Democratic president, John F. Kennedy. The cartoon depicts a citizen of the (Amerikan?) Empire picking up the phone, only to realize that the Thought Police agents of "Little Brother" (aka the president's younger brother, Attorney General Robert F. Kennedy) are on the line.

The cartoon's title, "Hello—ORwell 1984," reflects the characteristic blurring and conflation of the bogeyman behemoth "Orwell" and George Orwell, the author renowned for intellectual integrity, encapsulating the Frankenstein "creature vs. creator" motif that we have highlighted throughout this book. (Was Herblock's "ORwell 1984" title also meant to imply that the last four digits of the Justice Department's hotline are 1-9-8-4—and thus perhaps to allude to the John Birch Society, which had by this time adopted those digits in the phone number of its Washington office?)

avatar appears at a glance to bear no relation to the noble Defender of the King's English. Nonetheless, given its multifarious
low-toned hues and somber shadings, *Nineteen Eighty-Four* may
stand as Orwell's truest autobiography—as well as a most revealing biography of the post–World War II age.

As I have repeatedly discovered throughout my work, this im-
ponderable figure, "Orwell," contains multitudes. In this respect
Orwell/"Orwell" invites us to approach him as a character in a
novel—a novel co-authored, as it were, by Orwell himself and
by the literary acquaintances who have memorialized him. Their
memoirs make it clear that the greatest character that Orwell
(and Eric Blair) ever invented was in fact George Orwell.

His Ever-Living Voice

These figurative pairs—Orwell and "Orwell," work and Work—
function as personified metaphors to guide local argument and
furnish global structure in this book. As such, they mark a new
and exciting departure from my previous studies of Orwell and
his heritage. Never before have I devoted so much attention to
matters of biography and literary criticism, the "Life and Letters"
of Part 1. Nor have I ever dared to broach at such length the issue
of Orwell's complex heritage in terms of my own personal legacy—
or pondered how my intellectual life and scholarship have unfolded in and through my engagement with him.

To address how the interpretive frame of Orwell/"Orwell" and
work/Work configures Western cultural politics and current
events of social consequence, let me share here a pair of questions
I am often asked: Is George Orwell as important today as he was
a few decades ago? Is Orwell's work still pertinent to and powerful for a new generation of readers and intellectuals?

I shall return to these subjects in the Conclusion, but my immediate response is this: the work is arguably not as important today, but the Work indisputably is. The distinction mirrors that between Orwell, the writer and man on the one hand, and "Orwell," the literary figure, political icon, and cultural talisman on the other hand. Given this kind of distinction, I would say that his Work, that is, the work of "Orwell," is not only as important today, but almost as timely as it was during his lifetime and in the later twentieth century. So too is the work represented by widely anthologized essays such as "Why I Write" (1946), which shows how an engaged citizen speaks out and maintains moral and intellectual integrity. And to no small extent because it flowed from the pen of a committed writer who was himself perceived to have exhibited a high degree of literary and ethical integrity, such prose has resonated deeply with successive generations of readers. For it is the work of a man and author, George Orwell, who possessed an artistic power and moral credibility borne of writing from the bones, whereby you live what you write and write from the depths of your experience.

This capacity to *speak* so compellingly on paper represents one of the vigorous and enduring strengths of Orwell's prose style, the perception that readers gain of an ever-living voice and of an honest human being expressing difficult truths. It is a plain, unadorned style, empowered by a voice so fresh, direct, and clear that we feel we are holding audiobooks of our own making, what the Germans call *sprechende Bücher*. And it is an artfully simple (deceptively so!) style through which we encounter a very humanizing portrait of the intellectual.

Ultimately, Orwell's work has given rise to the Work of "Orwell," and this latter pair is as important and timely as ever. That is the case not only because of the fact that *Nineteen Eighty-Four* has become a generic metaphor in the war of words—given its warnings against excessive government power, invasions of privacy, abuses of freedom, violations of human rights, bowdlerization of language, and on and on. As I have emphasized, it is also because Orwell's own life exemplifies how to be an outspoken citizen generally and how to be an intellectual in particular. As magnificent as some of Orwell's literary essays are, he was not first and foremost an armchair critic pronouncing his views about high culture and the classics, but rather an intellectual who wrote for the age, not the ages. Ironically, he has managed to speak powerfully to his time and our own.

Although I have written books on American and European public intellectuals, the English novel, the politics of culture in Germany, Latin American fiction, the literary interview, human rights abuses, comparative communist and capitalist education, and other topics, I have always returned to Orwell. His life and letters, his legend and legacy, have all preoccupied me. I have felt a powerful connection with him and with particular aspects of his thought and literary personality or persona.

Much of a person's response to anyone has to do with his or her generational relationship. This is also true with respect to a writer, as I discovered in conducting numerous interviews both with Orwell's old friends and acquaintances and also with several of his immediate intellectual contemporaries who responded to him as generational coevals in his own life. By contrast, I am two or three generations removed not only from Orwell's era but even from the posthumous publication of his writings, most of which appeared by the mid-1950s, before I was born. As a result, by the time I embarked on a serious inquiry into Orwell's *oeuvre*, the scholarly ground had already been well tilled. By the mid-1980s, more than three decades after his death, his books had sold in the tens of millions in five-dozen languages, and I beheld a Brobdingnagian spectre ("Call me 'Orwell'") straddling the planet and dwarfing (and overshadowing) the now-famous man of letters. The writer George Orwell had become a world-historical figure, but the ever-lengthening ("Orwellian") shadow of "Orwell" had become far more visible and widely known. And so the critical task was at least as much to make sense of his Work, of the unique phenomenon of "Orwell," as it was the investigation and interpretation of his writings themselves.

My point here is that historical timing induced me to make "Orwell," even more so than George Orwell, the focus of my work decades ago—and the media attention riveted ever after on this spectral presence has continued to direct my own critical inquiries during the last 30-odd years. For if the analysis of his writings had already reached a very sophisticated and, in certain areas, near-definitive status by the early 1980s, this was not at all true of "Orwell" as a literary icon, cultural symbol, and political talisman. No scholar or intellectual had closely investigated his outsized reputation. In my first book, *The Politics of Literary Reputation*, published in 1989, I set myself this challenging task. My aim was to discuss not only Orwell's writings, but also the phenomenon of "Orwell."

"If you want to understand Orwell," Richard Rees once remarked, "you have to understand Blair." Even more so, I would contend: If you want to understand "Orwell," you have to understand Orwell. And so, while much has been written about the process of "Eric Blair" becoming "George Orwell" (one biography refers to it, in its subtitle, as *The Transformation*), the following pages discuss what might be called the transmogrification of Orwell into "Orwell." This is a much bigger, more far-reaching, and more nebulous matter, virtually unbounded in scope, as a series of studies I have conducted about the history of Orwell's reputation and impact in the modern world attest. Indeed, I might title them *Orwell Unbound,* or rather *"Orwell" Unbound,* thereby highlighting the immense, incalculable, and seemingly measureless character of the reception and influence of "Orwell."

And yet: Might it be that the genius of Blair/Orwell is not to be found, at least not chiefly, in his writings, whether fiction or nonfiction? A case can be made that the greatness of Orwell was in the man, whose originality and uniqueness inspired a wide circle of friends and acquaintances to apotheosize him almost immediately upon his death. This is another sense in which we can speak of "Orwell." In this characterization, the quotation marks refer not to a bogeyman, but to a literary figure "transfigured" by those who met him, the figure of "George Orwell" in all of his endearing eccentricities (his love of schoolboy papers such as boys' weeklies), odd-man-out oddities (his acrid shag cigarettes that he proudly rolled himself), and outlandish proclamations ("All tobacconists are fascists!").

In saying all this, I reverse the judgment of Bernard Crick in his biography of Orwell: "The work is greater than the man." Certainly a touch of genius is there in the books, especially in *Animal Farm* and *Nineteen Eighty-Four,* and arguably in *Homage to Catalonia* and several of the brilliant essays. Yet it strikes me forcefully, on turning from the books to the memories of those who met Blair/Orwell, whether they loved or hated him, that his literary gifts represent only a fraction of his curriculum vitae.[5] Orwell stands, as A. N. Wilson once wrote of a very different writer and thinker, Hilaire Belloc, "at the opposite end of the spectrum from Shakespeare, a genius wholly subsumed in his work and who, by all accounts, 'gave' little in actual meeting." Orwell was much more like Dr. Johnson, whom Wilson also places at the Belloc pole as a man who was mythologized "by his intimates" even though he too composed "no one literary work by which this belief could be sustained."[6] Perhaps to an extent even greater than that of Johnson, the enduring power of this figure "Orwell" consists not so much in what he wrote as in what he was—or rather "became." Or still better: is *perceived* to have become.

So "Orwell" is not just a matter of haunting catchwords and horrifying nightmare visions. It is equally, if not more so, about the man whom we have caricatured and canonized. In this sense "becoming George Orwell" is also fundamentally about the process of what could be called "figuration." Or, as his friend Malcolm Muggeridge wrote in a diary entry shortly after Orwell's death, marveling at the memorial tributes to and growing reputation of "George," the story of Orwell's afterlife is also about "how the legend of a human being is created," about how a man "becomes" a myth. It is both fortunate and unfortunate that Orwell was memorialized not by one Boswell, but by several well-intentioned yet partial memoirists—among them Muggeridge, Julian Symons, George Woodcock, Tosco Fyvel, Cyril Connolly, Bertrand Russell, Stephen Spender, and Richard Rees. They have all bequeathed us vivid portraits of the author as a middle-aged man.

Freelancing in the Footsteps of "St. George"

Not only for me but also for many of my peers and elders, Orwell seemed, as I titled a later book, "every intellectual's big brother." Decades earlier I had already discovered that I was simply following in a long line of impassioned readers, whether enthusiasts or enemies. In *Every Intellectual's big brother: George Orwell's Literary Siblings* (2006)—the lowercase usage is meant to specify Orwell rather than "Orwell"—I described how other intellectuals have responded to Orwell and how we are all part of a literary family. My own stirring and powerful attraction to Orwell, both his life and his *oeuvre*, eventually led me to study the writing of his admirers and even his antagonists. I found myself ardently drawn to those who esteemed Orwell, albeit often at a different historical moment and for different reasons than myself, such as the group of New York intellectuals associated with *Partisan Review* between the 1930s and 1990s, one of whom (Dwight Macdonald) became personally acquainted with Orwell through extensive correspondence. I began to interview and write about many of these generational peers of Orwell, who were my own American intellectual elders. If I could not meet Orwell personally, I could at least get to know them. I could in fact visit and get to know them far more easily than I could Orwell's aging British colleagues across the Atlantic.

On a more personal (or more visceral) level, I feel a special affinity with Orwell because I identify with his battle, like my own, to become an independent writer and intellectual. That struggle has never been easy, but it is even more difficult today than it was in Orwell's time, because the Western academy has swallowed up intellectual life and regurgitated academic specialists, most of whom do not write for the public or in an accessible idiom. There is no institution—whether in the form of Ph.D. or creative writing programs or law schools or think tanks—that forms intellectuals.

Today as ever—all the certification bodies, credentialing institutions, MFA workshops, and graduate and postgraduate fellowship programs notwithstanding—the vocation of the intellectual can only be pursued and practiced in the time-honored way that, assisted by his generational ancestors, Orwell also followed. What way is this? Sustained by yearning and will, you immerse yourself in the work of those who have gone before you and have become serious writers and intellectuals themselves.

Or, as I put it in *Every Intellectual's big brother*, you "adopt" an intellectual big brother or big sister. You ingest his or her work as a way of realizing your own best self as a writer and human being.

Orwell had the advantage of belonging to a large London literary community supported by numerous little magazines and intellectual quarterlies. Nowadays these urban communities, whose hubs were typically literary reviews or cultural quarterlies, have almost vanished. The university has replaced them with remunerative employment that is far more comfortable yet forms a very different creature than the traditional intellectual. I have written about this shift in my forthcoming book *The Intellectual Species: Evolution or Extinction?*, in which I describe how the "species" of the traditional literary intellectual, who addresses the broader public on issues of common national and international concern, is gravely endangered today. The rise of the adjective "public," as in "public intellectual," has coincided with the death of the species. Decades ago, one never needed to distinguish between a "public" intellectual and other kinds of intellectuals. But now that the academic or the policy intellectual—the resident species of the higher education institutions or Washington think tanks—dominates the scene, a sea change has occurred: a loose fish swimming freely against the nets that would hold him (such as in Melville's *Moby Dick*) and speaking out to the wider public on diverse issues of common interest is all too uncommon.

I have embraced Orwell warmly, if also gingerly and cautiously, as an intellectual big brother. I once wrote an open letter to voice my debt to him and explain why I have devoted such a substantial part of my life and intellectual energy to him and his heritage. I began to realize in the 1980s that I had adopted Orwell as my intellectual big brother as a way of discovering and resolving my own issues of personal identity as a writer and aspiring intellectual. Orwell came into my life at a moment when my needs and dreams could be clarified by glimpsing the Orwell in myself, that is, by seeing how we were indeed brothers of a different generation, elder and (very) junior men of letters.

If I have also devoted myself to "Orwell" and to his Work—and thus to the author's literary and political legacy—I discern that this decision also has had to do with his influence on me—or rather on my wider worlds of culture, society, and politics. Orwell lends himself to this purpose in a distinctive way, because he has become a world-historical individual, what Jean-Paul Sartre referred to as a "singular universal," a rare being whose existential trajectory (inadvertently?) situates him at a historical crossroads where he somehow manages to touch on universal concerns through his singular life.

The Effluence of His Influence

Orwell is the most important writer since Shakespeare and the most influential writer who has ever lived. Quite a bold claim! Let me clarify it, if not qualify it. I do not say that he is the greatest imaginative writer, nor even the leading novelist of his generation. I do not even mean that he is the best-selling writer of all time. I make no exalted claims for the intrinsic quality of his work versus that of other writers.

Rather, I'm speaking simply about cultural impact and the effluence of his influence.[7] No English-language writer in recent generations has aroused so much controversy and inspired so many younger writers and intellectuals. Certainly no one before or after Orwell has contributed so many incessantly quoted words and phrases to our cultural lexicon. "Big Brother is watching you!" is the most famous and frequently cited line in twentieth-century literature—and no runner-up is even close.[8] Indeed his very name as a proper adjective is quoted in numerous languages tens of thousands of times per year. His appeal both to serious readers and to academics and intellectuals—his "literary bandwidth," as it were—knows no comparison. It is in these respects that I use the phrases "most important" and "most influential."

Undeniably, I was not alive either when he lived or when most of his posthumous work was published in the first post–World War II decade. As the year 1984 crept ever nearer and the "countdown" mentality took hold, however, I witnessed with fascination the rise of the world-historical "Big O," that ever-looming leviathan that incarnated the severely abridged, sensationalized Work and came to be represented by the master sign "Orwell" and mobile-missile-metaphor "Orwellian."

Of course, "Orwell" is a double-edged sword. This is the bogeyman behemoth, the "Orwellian" spectre of *Nineteen Eighty-Four*, the Big Brother who is quoted and misquoted in legions of contexts.[9] Both the Work and "Orwell" (or "Orwellian") have been invoked *ad nauseam* in contemporary discussions about the invasions of Afghanistan and Iraq, Saddam Hussein and Vladimir Putin (and Donald Trump—and Barack Obama), and so forth. "Orwell" possesses a dark, sometimes raven-black, side, but I have been concerned with both the darkness and the light, that is, the full palette of the literary legacy—the iridescent, multicolored portraits as well as the sketches in sepia gracing the gallery in all their wondrous variety and ambiguity. "Orwell" can be used for positive ends, but typically he has been abused for ends that the man and writer would never have endorsed and perhaps never even have imagined. Surely George Orwell would have objected to the monochromatic view of him as a Cold Warrior and even more fiercely, as he did late in his lifetime, to his reputation in some quarters as an antisocialist.

I have sought to clarify with scholarly accuracy his legacy and not to indulge in the practice of robbing his grave or moving his coffin to the left or to the right for my own political purposes. I readily grant, however, that every person has his or her blind spots and biases. And so I have aimed here again in the present study to declare my own interests and convictions, thereby to render my "color filter" discernible so that the reader may know: *Caveat lector!* And so forewarned may you perceive how I inevitably, inescapably (re)construct my storied Orwell—and "Orwell"—through the lens of my own history and subjectivity.

PART 1

Life and Letters

FIGURE 5. Eric Blair, 1920. As a 17-year-old, Blair was a big, strapping boy. His body was not yet emaciated and laid waste from the pulmonary tuberculosis that would destroy his health within two decades and claim his life by his mid-40s.

CHAPTER 1

The Quixotic, Adamantly
Unsainted Life He Lived

The Edwardian Eric

Eric Arthur Blair was born on June 25, 1903, in Motihari, India, where his father, Richard Walmesley Blair, 46, was stationed. Blair was employed in the Opium Department of the Indian Civil Service and resided with his half-French wife, Ida Mabel Limouzin, 28. Eric was the lone boy of three children. A sister, Marjorie, was five years older; another sister, Avril, was almost five years younger. Orwell would later write in a tone of pedantic irony that his family was among the "lower-upper-middle-class" ranks that dotted Edwardian society.

As an infant, Eric was taken by his mother to be raised in England, in the area around the Thames Valley. Surrounded by women—his mother, two aunts, and two sisters—he was indulged as a child. Save for a few weeks in 1908 when Avril was conceived during Richard Blair's home leave, Eric had no contact with his father until he was nine. Their relationship always remained strained. Orwell later described his memories of his father as a "gruff-voiced elderly man, forever saying 'don't.'"

A bright, chubby little boy, as his early photographs show, Blair suffered from poor health, particularly bronchitis, which foreshadowed the lung disease that would plague him throughout his life and eventually kill him. Young Eric loved nature—birds, flowers, animals. He also possessed a lively imagination and re-called that he was forever "making up stories and holding con-versations with imaginary persons." At four he wrote his first poem, in which he compared the rungs of a chair to a tiger's teeth, an impressive image that he later speculated might have been in-spired by hearing William Blake's poem "The Tyger."

From 1908 to 1911 Blair attended a day school staffed by Ur-suline nuns. In 1911 he won a partial scholarship to St. Cyprian's, a preparatory school in Eastbourne that specialized in gaining its pupils admission into England's most prestigious public schools. His life at St. Cyprian's, portrayed in his posthumously published and ironically titled (after another Blake poem, "The Echoing Green") essay "Such, Such Were the Joys," was a grim one, marked by the routine tortures—bad food, frequent beatings, poor hygiene—that English children often experienced in these schools. Orwell came to hate the headmaster and his wife, called "Flip" and "Sambo" in his essay, for their snobbish pretentions and shame-less catering to the sons of the rich. (Originally composed in 1947, the essay provoked legal concerns about libel of still-living per-sons, which led Orwell to alter their names and ultimately shelve the essay during his lifetime.)

For all his complaints, Blair received an excellent general edu-cation in prep school. Nonetheless he left St. Cyprian's with a sense of guilt and failure that he would carry for the rest of his life, regardless of his successes. After earning a scholarship to at-tend Wellington College, he left that school after a few weeks in the fall of 1917 for a place at Eton, the most famous English pub-lic school. As a scholarship student, Blair was given wide latitude in his studies. He rarely applied himself and won no awards, but he used his freedom to master French and to read widely in En-glish literature, including the leading authors of the day: George Bernard Shaw, H. G. Wells, and Rudyard Kipling were among his favorites. He was an iconoclast, with few friends and a reputation as a cynic. His main tutor, Andrew Gow, told Orwell's biographers that he was "always something of a slacker." Yet unlike his attitude toward his prep school, Orwell harbored no lasting ill will toward Eton. In fact, decades after graduation, he signed up his adopted son, Richard, for his alma mater within weeks after obtaining him in 1944.

From Eton to Empire

His checkered academic record at Eton notwithstanding, Blair might have qualified for Oxford or Cambridge, but he was encouraged neither by Gow nor by his family. So instead Blair followed in the footsteps of his father and, in 1922, sat for the qualifying entrance examination to the Indian Civil Service. He passed seventh out of 26 candidates, doing exceptionally well in Latin and history. His professional choice to train as a policeman was surprising. So too was his selected preference for a posting to Burma. It is not clear why he made these decisions—one reason he gave was that his mother had relatives in Burma. Regardless of his motive, in October 1922, the 19-year-old Blair set forth on an odyssey that would unexpectedly veer into a career as a writer.

The five years that Blair spent in Burma, 1922 to 1927, would constitute his unsentimental higher (self-)education. While his old schoolmates were going up to university, Blair served the Empire, one of only 90 police officers charged with overseeing a nation of 17 million Burmese across 260,000 square miles. He would later describe his experience as "five boring years within the sound of bugles." Orwell left no record of his life in Burma except for scattered snatches of material in his essays and letters, as well as his novel *Burmese Days*, which draws from Blair's personal experiences there. Addressed as Assistant Superintendent of Police Blair, the 20-year-old junior officer was sent to a primitive village in the Irrawaddy Delta for his first posting. He had 30 to 50 policemen under his command, a mark of the high value that the Indian Civil Service accorded its recruits. Later during his service, Blair took charge of a district with a population of more than 200,000 people and supervised nearly 300 men, quite a responsibility when one considers that his Oxbridge peers were still at their studies.

Like his antihero John Flory in *Burmese Days*, he was not regarded by his colleagues as very clubbable. He did not frequent the colonial officers' club. One fellow officer later described him as "rather shy, retiring ... someone who did not mix well." Blair came to abhor the life of a sahib, with its racism, its sadism, and its smugness. Above all, Blair loathed the sahib ethos of white privilege. He never forgot the cruelties that he witnessed in the Far East. When his outbound ship stopped over in Ceylon, he watched a sergeant violently kick a coolie for not unloading cargo properly. For Blair, that image summed up the relations between the ruler and ruled. The sight of rickshaws drawn by men loaded down like donkeys sickened him.

Burma made a deep impression on the gangly youth. Mesmerized by the country's wild terrain, jungles, and cities, with their exotic mixture of races and traditions—Chinese, English, Indian, and Burmese—he had a sharp eye for cultural detail and registered all the contradictions of colonialism, the perversities that mutually corrupt both sides when one race rules another. With his gift for languages, he mastered Burmese dialects and was able to converse with well-educated Burmese, a rarity within the English settler class, who proudly separated themselves from the native population.

Blair's Burmese experience transformed him into a strong anti-imperialist. Readers have never ceased to wonder since his death "what Orwell would say" about such topics as the Third (or Fourth) World, the checkered course of decolonization, and the responsibility (or perceived White Man's Burden?) of the West (or G-7 members) to narrow the still-yawning gap between the rich and poor nations. Today the question, "If Orwell were alive today ..." continues to be posed. How would Orwell conceive international relations between more and less developed nations in the twenty-first century? Would Orwell the anticolonialist regard the war in Iraq as an instance of American imperialism? Or would he condemn the postcolonial nations, often tyrannized by autocrats such as Robert Mugabe in Zimbabwe, as even more unjust than the British Empire? Might Orwell, who died before the African and most Asian colonies gained independence, have distinguished between what neoconservative thinkers such as Lewis Feuer have termed "progressive" and "regressive" colonialism, or between (putatively ameliorative, reformable) "authoritarian" regimes and (intrinsically fixed) "totalitarian" regimes, per the formulation of Jeane Kirkpatrick? Such are the conjectures.

At some point early in his service, despite his excellent pay—at 24 he was making approximately £700 a year, the salary of a successful middle-class manager—Blair realized he had no stomach for being a servant of Empire. Did he nonetheless stay five years in Burma because he was too embarrassed to throw over a "good career" and return home? Perhaps. It is clear from his writings during the decade after his departure that he had despised what he was doing and was appalled by the behavior of the English sahib in the East. Apart from *Burmese Days*, the only evidence for his state of mind at that time about his life as a policeman must be adduced from two short prose works, "A Hanging" (1931) and "Shooting an Elephant" (1936). Each of them highlights the quotidian depravities of the British officer class under imperialism, whether the inhumanity of the so-called masters during the hanging of a wretched native or the cowardice of the sahib that drives him to shoot a rogue elephant because the natives expect it. Facing the elephant, the autobiographical narrator sums up the lesson Blair learned in the East in a self-admonitory statement about the master-servant relationship that also serves as the moral of the latter story: "When the white man turns tyrant, it is his own freedom that he destroys."

Becoming a Writer

Transferred to the town of Katha in northern Burma in the spring of 1927, Blair contracted dengue fever, took leave, and departed Burma for England in July 1927, never to return. While staying with his parents in Southwold, a coastal town in Suffolk, he told them his decision to resign his Empire commission and become a writer. They were shocked and dumbfounded as to why he would abandon such a promising and honorable career. Relations with his father, never warm, cooled considerably. Years later Orwell wrote in "Shooting an Elephant" that Burma taught him that "oppression" was the fundamental evil of colonialism and that he "had to escape not merely imperialism but from every form of man's domination over man." For Orwell that education took shape through an urge to understand the oppressed, to live with the poor and the downtrodden and "to be one of them and on their sides against the tyrants."

Blair resided with his parents for a few months and then moved into cheap rooms on the Portobello Road in the Notting Hill section of London. He did some writing but spent much of his time dressed as a tramp wandering in the area around the East End of London and for a time lodging in the doss houses, home to the poorest of the poor. He went hop picking to see what it was like to do hard peasant labor. In order to experience what it was like to be oppressed, he went about his explorations of the dark side of London with an attention to detail that would characterize his later reportage.

In "Why I Write" (1946), Orwell stated that Blair "wanted to write enormous naturalistic novels with unhappy endings, full of detailed descriptions and arresting similes, and also full of purple passages." Yet it remained unclear to him what he would write about. In the spring of 1928 he moved to Paris to join the thousands of young men and women who flocked there in search of literary fame. Speaking fluent French, he never felt limited to the expatriate community and mixed easily with native Parisians. He wrote one or two novels that he destroyed and a few short stories and essays, a couple of which he preserved and would later rework. Written under the name "E. A. Blair," his first publication appeared in October 1928 in the French newspaper *Le Monde* and dealt with censorship in England. He made his debut appearance in England in *G. K.'s Weekly* several months later, in December 1928. He also published a few other pieces in French magazines but was soon running low on funds. As a result, he took odd jobs, including tutoring students in English, and then for 8 to 10 weeks worked in various restaurants as a dishwasher. In March 1929, he became ill and spent two weeks in the Hôpital Cochin in Paris with a bad case of bronchitis, coughing up blood in a ward for the poor, the fearful weeks of which he later recalled in a gripping essay, "How the Poor Die" (1946).

After spending 18 months in Paris, Blair returned to his parents' home in Southwold just before Christmas 1930. He would live with them intermittently for the next four years. During this time he continued writing while occasionally exploring the depths of London, again mixing with the poor and downtrodden. He tried teaching, first in April 1932 at a boys' school in Hayes, Middlesex, near London called The Hawthorns, and then conducting

French classes at Frays, a small college in Middlesex, in the autumn of 1933. At Frays, his salary was £70 per term. Right away he bought a motorbike and drove it with a certain recklessness throughout the countryside, catching severe pneumonia that December after a jaunt in torrential rains. Most of the time, however, he tried to polish a semifictional account of his risqué Paris adventures and sordid London tribulations in what would become his first book, *Down and Out in Paris and London,* released in January 1933 by the left-wing publisher Victor Gollancz. It was at this time that Blair adopted the name George Orwell, apparently because he disliked his first name and didn't want to embarrass his parents: "George" as a gesture to England's patron saint (as well as to one of Orwell's favorite writers, George Gissing); "Orwell" after a small river in Suffolk. Blair actually proposed a number of alternative pseudonyms to his publisher in rather casual fashion, including H. Lewis Allways. (What might his legacy have been if he had adopted that name? Imagine this possible alternative to the frequent headline speculating about George Orwell's possible stand on issues decades after his death: "If H. Lewis Allways Were Alive Today." Somehow it rings a bit flat!)

Down and Out was a moderate success and convinced Orwell to become a full-time writer. By the time that it appeared, Orwell had already begun working on a novel dealing with his experiences in Burma. *Burmese Days* would appear in the fall of 1934, the first of four realistic novels that Orwell would publish in the 1930s. Concerned that its satirical portraits of colonial police officials might run afoul of the libel laws in England, Gollancz turned down the novel, but it was soon picked up by Harper Brothers and published in November 1934 in the United States, where it was positively reviewed and sold 3,500 copies.

By this time Orwell had given up his teaching position at Frays College because of a severe bout of bronchitis. He spent the latter weeks of 1934 living with his parents in Southwold, where he finished his next novel, *A Clergyman's Daughter*, which was published in March 1935 shortly after Orwell had moved to London. Meanwhile, the success of *Burmese Days* in America led Gollancz to bring out an English edition in July, which the *New Statesman and Nation* cited as one of the "Best Books of 1935."

On leaving Southwold in the fall of 1934, Orwell went to work as a part-time clerk at Booklovers' Corner, a secondhand bookshop located in the Hampstead section of London and owned by a couple active in the Independent Labour Party (ILP), a radical offshoot of the Labour Party. He was paid a small wage and given a room over the store where he could live and work. His 16 months there from October 1934 to January 1936 witnessed a number of major developments in his life. He met his future wife, Eileen O'Shaughnessy, wrote his novel *Keep the Aspidistra Flying*, and received an assignment from Gollancz to investigate poverty in the north of England for a book that would gain him broader recognition than all his previous literary work.

Eileen O'Shaughnessy was "the nicest person I have met in a long time," Orwell told one of his friends. She was studying psychology at University College, London, when they encountered each other and was an educated, sophisticated young woman. He proposed marriage after only a few weeks, but she put him off. They married in June 1936 and rented a modest two-storey house in Wallington, Hertfordshire, a tiny village near Cambridge, for the lowly sum of 7s, 6p per week.[1] The couple's new home had two small rooms on each floor, a little sweetshop in the front, and a privy at the back of the yard. Orwell started a garden, bought a goat for milk, and adopted a dog (whom he named Marx). He thoroughly enjoyed his domestic circumstances despite the spartan conditions. He and Eileen would remain in Wallington until 1940.

Keep the Aspidistra Flying was published in April 1936 to good reviews, and Gollancz expressed the belief that Orwell had a promising future, predicting that he was "likely in years to become one of the half dozen most important authors" in England. Given his confidence, he commissioned Orwell to visit the most depressed areas of England to report on the social and economic conditions found there. It was a brilliant idea, because Orwell's vivid, documentary prose was ideally suited to publicize the Depression-era miseries endured in the industrial Midlands.

Becoming a Socialist

Orwell spent February through March 1936 traveling through the north of England surveying labor conditions and interviewing the unemployed, especially in the coal mining districts around the town of Wigan. He resided in slum housing with the poor, went down a coal mine despite his six-foot, three-inch height, and attended trade union meetings and political rallies.

On his return he composed a prose documentary, *The Road to Wigan Pier*, which showed his gift for sociological analysis and graphic descriptions. Written in an evocative first-person voice, the book was featured by Gollancz in his popular Left Book Club series. Published on March 8, 1937, it sold well (more than 50,000 copies alone through the Left Book Club) and won Orwell wide recognition for the first time. Orwell had found his métier as a controversialist and writer of provocative reportage. Although he had flirted with socialist ideas in the past, he had not clearly thought out what he believed politically. The Midlands trip, his "road to Wigan," represented a major step on his journey toward becoming a socialist.

The Spanish Civil War, which broke out in July 1936, would complete his political education. Because he wanted to go to Spain to take an active part in supporting the Republican camp, Orwell rushed to complete *The Road to Wigan Pier* for Gollancz. He first tried to join the International Brigade but was rejected by the leader of the Communist Party of Great Britain, Harry Pollitt, as politically unreliable. Through contacts in the ILP, Orwell went to Barcelona in December 1936 and joined the Workers' Party of Marxist Unification (POUM), a uniquely Spanish amalgam of anarchism and Trotskyism. The party was broadly Marxist yet stridently anti-Stalinist, a blend that suited Orwell's developing political ideas. Deeply touched by Barcelona's climate of revolutionary fervor and egalitarian spirit, Orwell regarded his weeks there as a magnificent example of socialism in action: no tipping, no aristocratic titles, no fancy hotel suites, no house servants, no rigid class hierarchy. Everyone was addressed as "comrade"—even the prostitutes. Orwell would later write that he "was breathing the air of equality."

Orwell stayed nearly seven months in Spain, a period he remembered as a mix of confusion at the front and boredom behind the lines. In the main he went to fight, not write. ("Eric Blair: grocer" was entered in the rolls of foreign enlistees, one of his commanders, Georges Kopp, was intrigued to notice.) Learning of Orwell's experience as a policeman, POUM leaders promoted him to corporal (or "cabo"). He was a good officer and popular with his troops. Orwell was sent to the Aragon front, joining the 29th Division, which was stationed in a quiet sector between Saragossa and Huesca. He spent 80 days at the front, with only three brief leaves. When he later wrote about his time there, he recalled the cold, the smell of the latrines, and the poor military equipment—his troops were largely equipped with pre–World

War I era weapons. Fighting was intermittent, prompting one of Orwell's friends to refer to the war near Orwell's sector as a "comic opera with an occasional death."

Eileen Blair arrived in Spain in mid-February to be close to her husband and to work as a secretary in the ILP office in Barcelona. She managed to visit him at the front in mid-March and found him "almost barefoot, a little lousy, dark brown and looking really very well." Shortly after her visit Orwell suffered a cut on his hand that became infected. He spent 10 days in the hospital, where almost all his valuables were stolen. When he returned to the front, he learned that his POUM unit was planning a night attack on the fascist position outside Huesca. Despite recently having his arm in a sling, he led a charge that seized the fascist trench. Ultimately, Orwell's unit had to withdraw when enemy forces counterattacked, but his first taste of fire left him wanting more action.

At the end of April, Orwell was granted leave and returned to Barcelona to visit his wife and fight on the more active front around Madrid. He was shocked to discover that the POUM had now been branded "Franco's Fifth Column" by the Stalinist-dominated Republican forces. In the first week of May, battles broke out in Barcelona between POUM and Communist militias. The combat lasted four days, during which Orwell spent most of his time guarding Republican headquarters from the roof of a nearby cinema. He was becoming disillusioned by the internecine warfare between Republican factions and was growing outraged by the Stalinist campaign to wipe out the POUM.

He returned to the Huesca front on May 10 and was promoted to lieutenant. Ten days later, he was shot in the throat by a fascist sniper. The bullet missed his carotid artery by millimeters. Orwell's comment on his near-fatal wound was typical: his initial thought was for his wife, and his second thought was "a violent resentment at having to leave the world, which, when all is said and done, suits me so well."

After stays in the hospitals of Siétamo, Barbastro, and Lérida, Orwell was sent on May 29 to a POUM sanatorium on the slopes of Mount Tibidabo near Barcelona. He spent two weeks recuperating and then decided to return to England to tell the truth of what he had witnessed in Spain. While he was convalescing, the revolution suddenly took a grim turn. The Barcelona government, now dominated by Communist Party officials closely allied with Stalin's Russia, declared the POUM an agent of the fascists and had its Castilian leader, Andrés Nin, tortured and killed. Orwell was unaware of what was happening when he returned to Barcelona on June 20 to meet Eileen and set out for England. He soon had to go into hiding because the police labeled him a "known Trotskyist" and a dangerous POUM "agent," having been tipped off by a British communist spy (an appropriately named Mr. Crook) who reported directly to the NKVD in Moscow. Crook had infiltrated the POUM, inveigled his way into a desk job at the ILP headquarters in Barcelona (where he "worked" alongside Eileen Blair), and snuck out thousands of POUM documents that Russian embassy officials quickly photographed. (In the 1990s, documents were discovered in the recently opened Soviet archives indicating that, if captured, Orwell and his wife were slated to be shot as Trotskyist spies.)

On June 23 Orwell and his wife left Barcelona by train. Carrying papers that listed them as casual English tourists, they crossed into France with no trouble. They spent a few days resting on the French Mediterranean coast, where Orwell began preparing, in his words, to "spill the Spanish beans" about the Stalinist treachery in Catalonia and the campaign to wipe out the POUM. (Later in the summer he published a series of articles in the *New English Weekly* under just this title.)

Spain did indeed serve as the arduous finishing school of Orwell's political education. He "now truly believed in Socialism"—or, as he would later specify, "democratic Socialism," with a sharp emphasis on "democratic." Orwell believed that the antifascist revolution had been betrayed by the Communists, who prolonged the fighting to divert attention from the purges in Stalin's Russia and to weaken the West. They were chiefly beholden to Stalin's aim to wipe out potentially rival socialist groups rather than interested in a Loyalist victory. The Spanish Communists had acquired "more points of resemblance to Fascism than points of difference." For the British Left, this was heresy. Orwell soon found that he couldn't get his reportage on Spain published in left-wing organs. Commissioned to write an article on Spain by Kingsley Martin, editor of the *New Statesman*, Orwell's work was rejected on the grounds that it was politically unacceptable. To "sugar the pill," as Orwell described it, Martin asked him to review a book on Spain, Franz Borkenau's *The Spanish Cockpit*. That too Martin refused to publish, explaining that Orwell's firm endorsement of Borkenau's anti-Stalinist critique "was against editorial policy."

Disgusted by Martin's contemptible hypocrisy and determined to tell the story of what he had seen in Spain, Orwell began writing almost immediately on his return to England what he regarded as one of his most important books, *Homage to Catalonia*. In it, he accused the English newspapers and magazines of lying about what was happening in Spain and of parroting the Soviet-dictated party line that the POUM and the fascists were allied in betraying the revolution. Written in the white heat of righteous anger, the book was completed by December 1937. Meanwhile, Orwell's health, further damaged by his wound in Spain, broke down completely. He began coughing up blood, and his weight dropped to just 159 pounds on his six-foot, three-inch frame. He entered a tuberculosis sanatorium in Kent, where doctors suspected that he had suffered at least four previous bouts of pneumonia. He spent six months there, slowly recovering from his illnesses and polishing his manuscript.

Just as Orwell expected, Gollancz refused to publish his book. Like Martin, he would have nothing to do with anything that contravened what Orwell would deride a few months later in a much-admired essay on Charles Dickens (doubtless with Marxists like Martin and Gollancz in mind) as "the smelly little orthodoxies" of the Left. Instead Orwell submitted *Homage to Catalonia* to a newly founded, receptive small press, Secker & Warburg, which brought it out in April 1938. It was a commercial failure, selling only 867 copies of 1,500 printed during his lifetime. Yet this elegiac account enshrined in moving prose the unforgettable saga of his Spanish Civil War experience, the decisive event that transformed Orwell into a fearlessly outspoken anti-Communist for the rest of his life.

No discussion of Orwell's months in Catalonia is complete without mention of the amusing anecdotes about him that his fellow soldiers reported, which also reflect "how the legend of a human being is created" and have contributed to the eccentric, mythic figure of "Orwell" the man—and specifically "Orwell" the man of La Mancha, the English Quixote. For instance, Stafford Cottman, an 18-year-old soldier in Orwell's unit, recounted how Orwell "rejoiced" over his "luck" in being so tall after a sniper's bullet hit him in the throat (i.e., not in the head). (Other comrades pointed out, however, that if Orwell hadn't been so tall, his head would not have stuck out over the parapet.) Bob Edwards, Orwell's company commander, recalled two hilarious stories of Orwell's knight-errantry on the Aragon front, either one of which could have made his reputation as Quixote. Gallantly holding a bleeding soldier on a donkey through the night, Orwell and Edwards accidentally wandered into a fascist-held village instead of the designated Loyalist one—and then had to sneak out. (Meanwhile the wounded man had stopped bleeding, "due to either fright or natural causes.") In another episode, Orwell, who reportedly hated rats as much as Winston Smith, shot one and caused the whole militia to begin firing at supposed fascists. Machine-gun nests and night patrols flew into action. The end result was the destruction of the cookhouse and two buses. None of this, however, should obscure the fact of Orwell's genuine bravery in battle, to which both his English and Spanish comrades have attested.

Orwell's own reports of his war experiences are evidence aplenty that he had an endearing, quixotic side to his character— he refused on principle to shoot at an escaping enemy soldier struggling to hold his trousers up; he required size 12 boots that could not be gotten in Spain and had to be shipped from England ("that Trotskyite with big feet," H. G. Wells later tagged him[2]); he was accepted by the Spaniards as a commanding officer only after "the big Englishman" had drunk them under the table. It is, without question, fitting that Spain—the land of Don Quixote—always fascinated Orwell.

"Sergeant Blair" on the Home Front

In late September 1938, just as the Munich crisis peaked, Orwell and Eileen sailed to Morocco with money loaned anonymously by the novelist L. H. Myers, who gave them £300. (Orwell never learned the source.) They hoped the mild climate would enable him to recover his health. During the couple's seven months in Morocco, Orwell completed the last and best of his realistic novels, *Coming Up for Air*, which unfortunately failed to attract much notice, partly because it appeared in mid-June 1939, with Europe on the brink of a new war.

Orwell's experience in Spain convinced him that a major war was inevitable, and that it would result in some form of fascism. Temporarily believing that no real difference existed between the capitalist democracies and the fascists, he formally joined the ILP, which espoused a blend of anarchism and pacifism. He had moved in ILP circles for years, not only at Booklovers' Corner but also as a contributor to John Middleton Murry's *Adelphi* (edited in the 1930s by Orwell's good friends Max Plowman and Richard Rees, his eventual literary coexecutor along with Sonia Orwell). But Orwell's support for the ILP didn't last long. On the night before the Nazi–Soviet pact was signed on August 23, 1939, he dreamed that not only would war soon come but that he would register to fight. "The long drilling in patriotism which the middle classes go through had done its work," he wrote. "Once England was in a serious jam it was impossible for me to sabotage" the British war effort.

Orwell was certainly antiwar for several months in 1938–1939. With the war's outbreak in September 1939, however, he became strongly antipacifist—and, in fact, an English patriot entranced by the possibility that World War II might become a revolutionary war that would usher in democratic socialism and spell the end of the Empire and British imperialism. He was quite explicit that his form of English patriotism had nothing to do with nationalism or imperialism, carefully distinguishing between them in "Notes on Nationalism" (1945). Patriotism is a matter of cultural sentiment and in no way involves imposing one's values on other peoples, whereas nationalism features aggressive politics and cultural domination. Patriotism is a feeling of home: a social, literary, and artistic matter that expresses a sense of community and represents a commitment to the maintenance and enrichment of the social fabric. Whereas "Englishness" for Orwell had much to do with patriotism (he proudly cast himself as a left-wing patriot), British imperialism and the crude promotion of Empire did not—and nothing aroused his ire more than the right-wing pro-imperialist arguments of Conservatives echoing Joseph Chamberlain that subsumed nationalism to patriotism.

So Orwell's wartime politics represented no defense of British colonialism. Rather, he hoped that Britain would suffer a series of defeats sufficiently minor to still ensure victory over Hitler and yet sufficiently major to remove Churchill from power and introduce a Labour government. That hope became reality in the July 1945 elections. Yet what could Orwell do for the war effort specifically? That was his problem after hostilities broke out. Eileen took a job in London working for the Censorship Department in Whitehall and only went down to their home in Wallington on weekends. Orwell was rejected for active military service in October 1939 for health reasons. He tried again and again to find some kind of war service during the winter but found nothing worthwhile.

Meanwhile, he published a collection of well-received essays, *Inside the Whale*, on March 11, 1940. The writer Inez Holden, a friend and lover (whose liaisons with him lasted more than a decade, from the mid-1930s on), noted in her journal the sharp growth in Orwell's critical and public reputation during the three years between *Wigan Pier* and *Inside the Whale*: "It's strange the way a writer's fame begins slowly creeping up to him and then racing so that after a while he seems to be a poor relation of his own fame," she observed. "People of taste and sensitiveness, writers, political workers and actors (who now show signs of being extremely left-wing), socialist doctors, factory workers and technical instructors in touch with their Labour organisations are all well aware of Orwell."[3]

Holden was the first to record what could be said to be the transition from Blair becoming Orwell to Orwell becoming "Orwell." Already in 1940, if only within a select circle of London writers and intellectuals, Orwell had gained notoriety as a champion of the down-and-outs, as a heterodox socialist scourging his fellow socialists in the first part of *The Road to Wigan Pier*, as a courageous Spanish Civil War militiaman, and as a superb literary essayist—all of which would contribute to the grandly inflated image of the legendary "Orwell" just a decade later.

The spring and summer of 1940 witnessed significant changes in Orwell's daily round. He closed up his house in Wallington in May and moved to a house in Dorset Gardens near Regent's Park. He began reviewing plays and films for the middle-class magazine *Time and Tide*, many of which seemed to him nonsensical in the face of the worsening military situation. (He taught himself to write his reviews in one sitting so as to have time for more serious work.) After the fall of France in June 1940, he joined the newly formed Local Defense Volunteers, better known as the Home Guard. Orwell hoped that the Home Guard would become a revolutionary force on the home front and help transform England democratically, serving as a true "people's militia," as he described it in *The Lion and Unicorn*, which appeared as part of the Searchlight Books series published by Secker & Warburg on February 19, 1941.

Here again, the eccentric, wonderfully human dimension of Orwell's quixotic days on the home front have been recalled by his friends. V. S. Pritchett has recounted Orwell's preference for top-floor flats because one could more easily get out on the roof to put out firebombs. Malcolm Muggeridge and Fredric Warburg have joked about how "Sergeant Blair" in the St. John's Wood Company of the Home Guard posed a greater threat to England than did the enemy.

An eyewitness account of "Sergeant Blair" in action by Orwell's handpicked corporal justifies this gentle mockery. "Corporal Fred Warburg," Orwell's publisher by this time, has recalled with bemusement that Orwell viewed the Home Guard as the "ideal" fighting force: it was "unprofessional," "volunteer," "inefficient," "anti-fascist and anti-Nazi," and "animated above all by a deep affection for the England he loved above all else." Fittingly, Orwell and Warburg, a veritable Don and Sancho, were put in charge of what became known as the Home Guard's "Foreign Legion," the foreign refugee recruits, most of whom were unable to perform correctly even the simplest movements of close-order drill and whose "love of indiscipline amounted to genius." Among Warburg's favorite memories of Sergeant Blair was the day Orwell, forgetting to make sure that an inert, nonfiring charge was in place for a routine drill, ordered "Fire!"—whereupon a practice (though nonexplosive) bomb went whizzing past dozens of men. No one was badly hurt, though one man lost all his false teeth, top and bottom, and another was unconscious for 24 hours. Appearing before a court of inquiry a few weeks later, Orwell was not disciplined, though he was informed that a new set of dentures had cost £100. He was not charged the money but was nevertheless angered. The cost of new dentures, he told Warburg, was altogether excessive.

Orwell tried again to join the army in 1941 but was once more classified as unfit for military service. On June 25, 1941, three days after the German attack on the Soviet Union, he was offered a job as a broadcaster to India by the British Broadcasting Corporation (BBC), a position classified as "essential war work." The pay was £640 per year, comparable to what he had made while in the police force in Burma 13 years earlier. He took the job and began serving in August 1941.

Orwell stayed at the BBC for 27 months, but he keenly felt that he was wasting his talents on a job that didn't suit him and was irrelevant to the course of the war. Nonetheless, he developed imaginative programming, featuring influential writers and poets such as E. M. Forster, T. S. Eliot, and Dylan Thomas. On learning that virtually no one was listening, however, Orwell became frustrated and angry. He deeply desired to do something more important for the war effort.

On November 24, 1943, Orwell resigned from the BBC to become literary editor of *Tribune*, taking a pay cut to £500 per year. *Tribune* was a left-wing weekly edited by Aneurin Bevan and George Strauss, and its stance matched Orwell's position on the war—leftist yet anti-Stalinist. Whereas Orwell had been frustrated at the BBC, he felt fulfilled at *Tribune*. He was a good editor, though with a weakness for accepting reviews and articles all too readily, perhaps because he remembered his own struggles as a writer. He began writing an idiosyncratic column, "As I Please," in which he wrote about anything that caught his interest—books, Christmas feasting, cigarette prices, war guilt, amusing epitaphs, American fashion magazines, shortages of watches and clocks, the dirtiness of snow, or (un)printable four-letter words. He also contributed to the American independent left-wing journal *Partisan Review* and reviewed books for the *Manchester Evening News*. According to biographer Bernard Crick, Orwell wrote an impressive 100,000 words of essays and journalism between the time he left the BBC in November 1943 and January 1945.

Shortly after he started at *Tribune*, Orwell and Eileen decided to adopt a child. It was their way of saying that they believed in

FIGURE 6. George Orwell, autumn 1945, at his Canonbury Square apartment in London. Note the gauntness of his frame and hollowed-out face, a shocking contrast to Eric Blair's appearance as an Eton schoolboy still unravaged by tuberculosis.

This photograph was taken by the Anglo-Italian Vernon Richards (Vero Recchioni), an anarchist friend in the Freedom group, a circle formed around the journal of that title and including libertarians such as Richards's lover Marie-Louise Berneri and George Woodcock, who became one of Orwell's closest friends. Orwell contributed to *Freedom* and served as vice chairman of the Freedom Defence Committee, chaired by his friend Herbert Read, the only formal office in a political organization that he ever accepted.

the future. In June 1944, they took home a three-week-old boy, naming him Richard Horatio Blair, just days before their home was hit by a V-1 bomb and destroyed. After staying a short spell in the country with the baby, they moved in September 1944 to a fifth-storey flat on Canonbury Road.

Orwell and Eileen didn't have much time to enjoy life together as a family. Orwell wanted to get to the front before the war ended. Through his friendship with David Astor, owner of the *Observer*, he was accredited as a war correspondent both by that paper and by the *Manchester Evening News*. In mid-February 1945, he flew to Paris to stay with other foreign correspondents at the Hotel Scribe. Traveling through liberated France and Allied-occupied Germany, he reported on wartime events for three months. Meanwhile, Eileen became ill and was told that her health condition necessitated a hysterectomy. On March 29, 1945, while undergoing the operation, she died at the age of 39. Orwell received the news by telegram in Paris and flew back to England. Soon he would begin what would turn out to be the final phase in his own shortened life.

Fulfillment and Finale

While working at the BBC, Orwell had begun writing what would become his breakthrough book, *Animal Farm*. He finished the book, a bitter parody of the Russian Revolution, in February 1944 and circulated it among London publishers for more than a year without success. No press wanted to publish a book critical of a wartime ally and thereby potentially disrupt the war effort and even endanger the campaign against Nazi Germany. Finally, Secker & Warburg accepted *Animal Farm*, but wartime paper shortages and other delays postponed its release (in a modest edition of 4,500 copies) until August 17, 1945, just days after the official end of World War II. Selling 140,000 copies in Britain by the year's close, *Animal Farm* was a stunning success. A year later it became a runaway best seller in the United States, where it was chosen as the Book-of-the-Month Club selection for September 1946. During the next four years, *Animal Farm* sold a half-million copies in the United States alone. Orwell was financially secure for the rest of his life.

Alas, it was all too late to save him. Orwell's tuberculosis flared up once again, this time more seriously. Still, he used the money from *Animal Farm* to rent a farm, Barnhill, on the island of Jura, part of the Inner Hebrides, off the west coast of Scotland. He had grown to dislike London and wanted a quiet place to raise his son and write. He went to Barnhill for the first time in the spring of 1946, staying for four months to make the house habitable. He would return to London for a time, but after 1946 Barnhill was his formal residence. He loved its isolation, its surprisingly mild climate—the Gulf Stream flowed close by—and its fishing.

His health nevertheless deteriorated steadily. Beginning in December 1947 Orwell spent seven months in Hairmyres Hospital near Glasgow coping with a bout of tuberculosis. A second, more serious episode occurred in December 1948, after which Orwell spent eight months in the Cotswold Sanatorium in Gloucestershire trying to recover. But the damage to his lungs was too far advanced. He was transferred to University College Hospital, London, on September 3, 1949, just weeks after the June publication of his last book, his towering and terrifying masterpiece, *Nineteen Eighty-Four*. Between bouts of illness, he had labored over the manuscript for three years, even typing a draft himself in Barnhill when he couldn't secure a secretary.[4] Finally published in June 1949 in England and the United States—where it was the Book-of-the-Month Club choice for July—it received glowing reviews and elicited comparisons between its author and utopian satirists ranging from Swift to Dostoyevsky, Shaw, and Wells.

Desperate for a companion who would rejuvenate him and share his life, Orwell had been searching for a wife since Eileen's death. He proposed to four young women, possibly more, but was rejected. On October 13, 1949, however, he married Sonia Brownell, 29, a secretary at his friend Cyril Connolly's literary magazine *Horizon*. Three months later, on January 21, 1950, Orwell died of pulmonary tuberculosis at the age of 46 years and seven months.

The "what ifs" of Orwell's tragic, premature, untimely death have been irresistible to biographers, critics, and avid readers of Orwell:

- What if Orwell had not been so impatient to complete *Nineteen Eighty-Four*?
- What if he had not overstrained himself to produce a cleanly typed version of the manuscript in the winter of 1948–1949 on the secluded island of Jura in the Scottish Hebrides?
- What if he had simply traveled to London during that winter and worked there with a typist?
- What if he had waited patiently in Jura until the following summer, when it is likely that a typist would have been willing to spend several weeks with him there?

His publisher and friends could find no secretary to travel to and reside on Jura to type the book. So he rashly decided to do the job himself—and suffered on its completion his last and fatal hemorrhage of the lungs, a development that landed him in sanatoria in Scotland and later in London, from which he never emerged.

On the other hand, let us reframe these questions and shift our attention from the life to the afterlife …

- What if he had delayed completing *Nineteen Eighty-Four* until he found a London secretary?

- What if his health had not broken down from the exertion and exhaustion of pushing himself to type *Nineteen Eighty-Four*?
- What if he had relocated to London and been under constant medical care as he supervised a typist's progress on the manuscript?
- What if the novel had appeared in print even just a year later rather than detonating on the cultural front just as the Cold War was approaching its height in June 1949— only a dozen weeks before the explosion of the Soviet Union's first atomic bomb in August 1949?

If any of these scenarios had come to pass, perhaps both Orwell and the novel never would have become so famous and controversial. After all, the Cold War would have already entered an even deeper phase by mid-1950, with both the Red Scare and McCarthyism fully underway in the United States since February 1950. If so, perhaps its impact as the "prophetic" work of a dying "visionary" might have been much attenuated (or even seemed anticlimactic). For its publication date would then have followed—rather than preceded and "forecast"—the alarming events of fall 1949 to spring 1950: President Harry Truman's reluctant announcement on September 23 of the Soviet Union's successful atomic test; the victorious Mao Zedong's proclamation forming a communist People's Republic of China on October 1; the perjury conviction of Alger Hiss, a former State Department official turned Soviet agent, on January 21 (Orwell's last day); émigré German scientist Klaus Fuch's confession that he had spied for the Soviet Union as a researcher for the Manhattan Project on January 24; Truman's declaration that the United States would build a "super-bomb" (later known as a thermonuclear or "hydrogen" bomb) on January 31; Wisconsin junior senator Joseph McCarthy's incendiary speech denouncing "the traitorous actions" of those like Hiss with "the finest jobs in government" on February 5; and on and on, arguably culminating in the outbreak of a new war, one that would soon engulf the United States, the Soviet Union, and China, when North Korea invaded South Korea on June 25, roughly a year after *Nineteen Eighty-Four*'s release (and, in a fittingly ironic twist, Orwell's birthday).

Yet if such events had intervened, perhaps *Nineteen Eighty-Four* would never have exploded so thunderously on the cultural front. Perhaps Orwell's incredible posthumous fame would never have developed or the disputes about his legacy never have arisen. Perhaps Clio would have never secured the alchemical raw materials— that is, the requisite admixture of historical events—out of which she would brew the all-too-human Orwell into the mythic, monstrous "Orwell." Was this the crafty handicraft of the Hegelian cunning of reason in History? From the vantage point of Clio's inscrutable aim to contrive this unique phenomenon—"Orwell"— did the deadly decision to complete the novel on Jura prove opportune, even auspicious? A *felix culpa*? Orwell's fortunate fall ... into "Orwell"?

And yet still again, even if we grant that he remained on Jura and typed the novel himself ...

- What if he had not received such a strong dose (i.e., an overdose, with awful side effects) of streptomycin, the new miracle drug for tuberculosis that had been smuggled in for him from the United States?
- What if his doctors (among them Andrew Morland, who had also handled the case of D. H. Lawrence) had experimented with the doses that they administered to Orwell?

- What if he had recovered—or even just become "a good chronic" (in Morland's phrase) and survived a few more years?

If he had lived ...

Perhaps the "Orwellian" ideological graffiti smeared by decades of screeching sound bites and scarifying headlines, as it were, across Eric Blair's headstone and George Orwell's heritage—which has both defaced and served to conflate Blair/Orwell and "Orwell"—would never have occurred, since Orwell would have been able to contest claims to his name and novel. Irony of ironies: the side effects Orwell suffered while being treated with streptomycin were so horrible that he stopped taking it and donated his unused medicine to two tuberculosis victims, both of whom recovered under the reduced dosages.

The "what ifs" are legion.

The moments of entrance and exit are adventitious.

The contingencies of repute are incalculable.

So it is all impossible to say.

*Un*saintly George

George Orwell—or rather "Eric Blair"—was buried at Sutton Courtenay, Berkshire, on January 26, 1950. The latter name not only was engraved on his tombstone ("Here Lies Eric Blair," it reads), but was also the one he used in legal circumstances all his life.[5] (Oddly enough, Sonia Brownell used the married name "Orwell.") Thus Eric Blair remained the identity of his personal life, whereas Orwell became the literary personality. And so, in a final irony, this incarnated *nom de plume*—the only fully rounded, three-dimensional character that the novelist ever created—would live on in his books. And he would do so not just in a leather-bound *Collected Works* that Blair had fantasized as an adolescent would be published, but in a magisterial *Complete Works* about which he never remotely dreamed. Nor could he even have dared to fantasize that his last book might become his *monumentum aere perennius*, exist in dozens of languages, and be found in virtually every city throughout the globe.[6] No, the name "George Orwell" would not need to be etched in stone.

So ended his life. His remarkable and utterly unprecedented afterlife thereupon commenced. Just a word about it here is apposite. Let it be understood that Eric Blair, aka George Orwell, the man of clay exalted today as "St. George" Orwell—the radiant literary personality apotheosized by acclamation and canonized in curricula—was no "saint." Perhaps he was not even the "virtuous man" whom Lionel Trilling memorialized or the "social saint" honored by John Atkins. He was a great writer, a decent man, and reportedly a good and faithful friend. At the same time, this quixotic, adamantly unsainted man had an anti-Semitic streak, an ambivalence toward homosexuals, and a dislike of feminism. He led a somewhat conflicted personal life, as his numerous infidelities during his marriage to Eileen attest. He was a mortal like all of us, with all of the foibles and flaws of a fallible human being.

"Saints should always be judged guilty until they are proven innocent," wrote Orwell just a year before his death in "Reflections on Gandhi." Orwell certainly would have applied that standard first and foremost to himself if the thought (which would have seemed to him bizarre) had ever crossed his mind that he might some day be exalted as an exemplar of virtue. He would have entered a plea of *nolo contendere* if his own personal life had ever come under the inquisitional gaze of the Thought (and

Behavioral) Police. Taking him at his own word, we should accept his plea of "guilty." The task for us readers in the twenty-first century is neither to prostrate ourselves before a canonical "St. George" nor to deface his gravesite. Rather, it is to read his often challenging, sometimes half-baked writings closely, distinguish his fine work from his "good bad books" and occasional tripe, and aim to see his life clearly and see it whole. At his best, he himself did exactly that; let his own example as a critic and intellectual inspire us by its virtues and both enlighten and restrain us by its failings.

So this opening chapter devoted to "the unsainted life he lived" should remind us that Eric Blair *became* George Orwell, just as Orwell *became* "Orwell." We need to see beyond our presentist bias and glimpse the origins, emergence, and development of such a process—and never forget that Blair/Orwell was a man of his time and led a writer's life, a London literary life of the 1930s and 1940s filled with personal friendships and rivalries, encounters with book publishers and magazine editors, marriages and love affairs, travails with physical health, and the upheavals of war and family tragedy. He was no "classic" Author dwelling in a literary firmament of canonized "stars," no "monument" of *Collected Works* (let alone a 20-volume *Complete Works*), no gargantuan "Orwell" bestriding the twentieth century. He *became* all this—and that "becoming" was to no small degree *our* doing.

Today only the texts remain. But the texts alone are inevitably misread if we remain inattentive to or incognizant of the daily round of the man's material existence, the dense texture of the writer's life experience from which they arose. Absent this context, the texts are engorged by "Orwell"—the canonical "St. George"— and willy-nilly then both exalted as classics ascribed to a monumental Figure and rocketed into the celestial statusphere. Thereupon fixed in the cultural firmament, it is as if they and their reception (and production and distribution) somehow exist apart from the social processes of reputation-building and canon formation, indeed as if they exist (and have always existed) above and beyond the quotidian realities of the life of the man who composed them.

All this is as well to remind us—myself, above all—of a dictum I first expressed in a study of Orwell decades ago: "Reputations are made, not born."[7]

FIGURE 7. Christopher Hollis, 45, during his first term in the British parliament as a Conservative M.P. for Devizes in Wiltshire. This official portrait from the National Gallery in London was done by the distinguished portrait photographer Walter Stoneman in 1948.

CHAPTER 2

Frenemies at Fisticuffs?

The Debate Rounds of Two Cordially Contentious Old Etonians

Reconsiderations, Revaluations

Largely absent from the excellent biographical and critical studies of Orwell is sustained attention to his unusual relationship with a schoolmate and writer who had known him as "Eric Blair" during his schooldays and to the equally unusual book he wrote about him, the first acquaintance or colleague familiar with those early years to do so. The recent republication of Christopher Hollis's critical-biographical study of George Orwell—originally published in 1956 (by Hollis's own firm, Hollis & Carter) and out of print for more than a half century—furnishes an occasion not only to reconsider the conservative streak in the socialist Orwell, but also to examine the tense yet mutually rewarding lifelong relationship between these two Old Etonians.

When I first read Hollis's *A Study of George Orwell: The Man and His Works* around 1980, not long after Hollis's death, I regarded it as a well-written, provocative, and serious examination of an author who had already become a political icon and leading figure in twentieth-century English literature. Nonetheless, I expressed strong reservations about Hollis's "shadowboxing" proclivity to jump into the ring with Orwell and counterpunch his way through round after round of argument on practically every single issue that separated the two men, with unceasing blows directed against Orwell's deviations from Hollis's orthodox Catholicism and political conservatism. One Catholic historian later wrote that I was "indignant" about Hollis's approach to Orwell. Yet it was much more that I, as a fellow Catholic layman who shared Hollis's admiration for Orwell, felt rather chagrined by Hollis's aggressive, no-holds-barred proselytism—as if Hollis were obsessed with posthumously converting his old schoolmate into a pious churchman or, at minimum, into what I termed a "religious fellow-traveler."

Rereading Hollis's *Study* decades later—and it is indeed a close "study" by a masterful polemicist who scrutinizes his debating opponent's positions, weighs the evidence thoughtfully, and counts up the ayes and noes of the "case" carefully—I am much more impressed by its frank and forthright style of presentation. Especially in the current political climate of disinformation campaigns, "fake news," endless spin control, and utter disrespect for and blatant distortion of adversaries' statements, I would now emphasize much more that Hollis pays Orwell the deep respect of appraising his positions with full seriousness. And that decision—to which Hollis brings literary clarity, political candor, and even moral courage—warrants our respect.

Hollis's "study" is not a biography. Rather, it is a critical assessment and biographical portrait, as its subtitle—*The Man and His Works*—reflects. Hollis's *Study* appeared just six years after Orwell's death, when the latter's reputation was just beginning to skyrocket. The book played a major role in defining Orwell as a man of "common decency," the signature phrase of his *oeuvre*.

In hindsight, Hollis's *Study of George Orwell* represents the most substantial, lively, and thorough analysis of Orwell's life and work in the first two post–World War II decades, the best—if highly debatable, let us say—work on Orwell among the first five book-length assessments of him. Until George Woodcock's *The Crystal Spirit* (1966), written by an anarchist thinker-activist and man of letters who befriended Orwell during the last decade of his life, Hollis's *Study* was the most influential book on Orwell. Today it still stands as a vintage showpiece of the 1950s, the most comprehensive eyewitness account of Eric Blair during the Eton and Burma years. In a trim 200 pages, Hollis (1902–1977) combines intellectual biography and personal reminiscence of Blair in an engrossing, combative engagement with the man and his works.[1]

The Man

Born just eight months before Eric Blair in December 1902, Hollis was one of four sons of an Anglican bishop. He attended Eton on a scholarship. Another scholarship took him to Balliol College at Oxford University, where he carved out a distinguished career, including a term as president of the Oxford Union Society. In 1924 he converted to Catholicism and soon became a well-known figure in Catholic intellectual circles. After graduation Hollis traveled with the Oxford debating team on an international tour that included Australia and New Zealand, a trip that provided him the opportunity to stop off and visit Blair in Burma for a week in 1925. During the next decade, Hollis taught at Stonyhurst, a Jesuit secondary school in Lancashire, and then spent five years teaching and doing economic research at the University of Notre Dame in the United States, returning to serve the British war effort as an intelligence officer in the Royal Air Force after the war broke out in 1939.

Elected as a Conservative Member of Parliament for Devizes in Wiltshire in 1945—against the liberal-left political tide that swept the Labour Party to victory over Winston Churchill and the Conservatives that July—Hollis gained reelection twice before retiring undefeated in 1955. As chairman of the educational publishing house Hollis & Carter and a contributor to and member of the board of directors of the *Tablet*, Britain's foremost Catholic magazine, for three decades, Hollis was one of England's most prominent postwar Catholic laymen.

Hollis's *Study of George Orwell*, published just after he left Parliament, is probably his best-known work. It received an enthusiastic reception in English Catholic circles, within which it exerted a significant shaping influence on the Catholic intelligentsia. Hollis's detailed report of Blair's schooldays at Eton was received as authoritative, even more than Cyril Connolly's class portrait in *Enemies of Promise* in the 1930s had been. Except for Connolly, "no one knows more of [Orwell's] early years than I," said Hollis, noting that only he among Orwell's memoirists had met Blair in Burma and had read Orwell's work in the order it had appeared, uninfluenced by the distortions of Orwell's later fame. Until Peter Stansky and William Abrahams's *The Unknown Orwell* (1972), their book-length biography of the Blair years, Hollis's personal account of Blair's Eton and Burma periods was generally accepted as the final word. In fact, it reads today as a miniature version and rich foretaste of Stansky and Abrahams's book—"the Unknown Orwell," as it were, before *The Unknown Orwell.*

Both the elective affinities and sharp contrasts between Hollis, the Conservative Catholic apologist, and Blair/Orwell, the adamant atheist and heterodox democratic Socialist (he always uppercased the noun), are notable. As near-contemporaries, Hollis entered the famed Eton College in 1914; Blair arrived two years later. Sharing a similar social and economic background—the rising middle classes of late Victorian and early Edwardian England—both Blair and Hollis came from families of modest means and were "scholarship boys" at prep school. Blair's father worked in the Indian Civil Service; Hollis's father was vice principal of the Wells Theological College and later Bishop of Taunton.

Although both Hollis and Blair underwent the prevailing preparatory school rigors of the English upper classes, they responded to them in utterly different ways. Blair's miserable experience at St. Cyprian's at the hands of the headmaster and his wife, above all the sadistic beatings that he recalled with still-seething anger in his posthumously published essay "Such, Such Were the Joys," scarred him for life.

Hollis attended the more fashionable Summer Fields, located in the attractive meadows on the northern fringes of Oxford. Possibly the most prestigious prep school in Edwardian England and certainly the top choice of the era's intellectual elite, Summer Fields was reputed to foster more public school scholarship boys than any other British prep school. Despite its strict code of conduct and occasional privations, Hollis felt forever blessed to have attended Summer Fields, where he enjoyed the benefactions of his headmaster, C. H. ("Doctor") Williams, to whom he expressed lifelong gratitude (both in his Orwell study and in his autobiography, *Along the Road to Frome*) for accepting him as a transfer pupil from a mediocre Leeds grammar school, fully waiving his fees, and personally guiding and grooming him ("Doctor" was an "an excellent coach") to win an Eton scholarship.[2]

As young Etonians, both Hollis and Blair read and esteemed G. K. Chesterton, who defended Christian and Catholic orthodoxy aggressively and formally converted to Catholicism in 1922. His adroit apologetics and personal example influenced Hollis's own conversion two years later; in contrast, Blair/Orwell prized instead the literary gifts of "G.K.C." and his patriotism while lamenting (and lambasting) his religious views.

Hollis's biographical chapters on Blair at Eton and in Burma in 1925 are the most authoritative in the book. Nevertheless, his views on Blair at Eton are opinionated and disputable—and much disputed. Hollis argues that Blair's "grievances"—that he was a poor boy among the rich, that he was unpopular and branded "ugly"—were nonsense. Rather, Blair was "a natural solitary" who enjoyed the fact that Eton allowed him to pursue his own interests and read whatever he wished and otherwise largely left him alone. Even though Hollis seldom crossed paths with Blair at Eton and knew him only slightly there, his *Study* does not hesitate to draw conclusions about Blair's schooldays. Hollis notes, for example, that in contrast to his lengthy critique of his prep school and despite his complaints about English public schools, Orwell wrote virtually nothing about his time at Eton. Here again, Hollis believes the reason owes to the simple fact that Blair "was little interfered with" at Eton. As to Orwell's later evaluation of his Eton years, notes Hollis, when Orwell and his wife Eileen adopted Richard, they promptly enrolled him there.

Hollis also contests the widespread assumption that Blair applied to enter the civil service because his mediocre academic record prevented him from attending Oxford or Cambridge. Hollis believes that Orwell rejected Oxbridge in an act of defiance. Nor did economic issues have anything to do with Orwell's decision, he contends, because Blair could have probably won a university scholarship (as Hollis himself did). Blair missed much by spending five important years of his youth in the Indian Imperial Police in Burma instead of at Oxford or Cambridge among his intellectual peers, Hollis argues, adding that despite passages in his writings criticizing Oxford and Cambridge, Blair/Orwell came to regret and resent his exclusion from those circles. Such speculations are difficult to confirm or refute. But a letter to Jacintha Buddicom, Blair's childhood friend (and adolescent sweetheart), suggests that Blair may have decided to join the Indian Civil Service after she spurned his proposal of marriage.[3]

Whatever the reason, Hollis went up to Oxford while Blair followed in his father's footsteps and joined the Indian Civil Service as a policeman in Burma. During their two meetings in Burma in 1925, Hollis describes Blair as behaving like the stereotypical sahib and imperialist, exhibiting "no trace of liberal opinions" such as he had paraded at Eton. "At pains to be the imperial policeman," Hollis recalled, loneliness had embittered Blair, who sermonized that "theories of no punishment and no beatings were all very well at public schools but they did not work with the Burmese." Blair harbored a special animus for Burmese priests—not for religious reasons, but rather "because of their sniggering insolence."

Hollis writes that he maintained this view of Blair until years later, when he read Orwell's superb autobiographical story/essay "Shooting an Elephant" and discovered how much Blair had hated his role in policing the natives. Is it possible that Blair was pulling Hollis's leg and merely play-acting the cartoonish sahib? Orwell's first biographer, Bernard Crick, argues that Blair/Orwell considered Hollis "a glib and priggish liberal, Oxford Union to boot; so he probably gave him the 'realist' line" with satiric tongue in cheek.

After Eric Blair started to establish himself in London as a writer and adopted the pen name "George Orwell" in 1933, the two men reconnected. They met occasionally during the last 20 years of Orwell's life, and Hollis visited Orwell in the hospital just a few weeks before Orwell's death in January 1950. Acquaintances rather than confidants, they shared, in Hollis's phrase, "years of continuing friendly argument."

Or perhaps not so friendly, at least to Orwell's mind. When Orwell was having difficulties securing a publisher for *Animal Farm* in 1944 because of its political implications—its satire of wartime ally Russia, its indictment of the Bolshevik Revolution, and its scorn for Joseph Stalin—Orwell's literary agent Leonard

Moore suggested approaching Hollis's firm, Hollis & Carter. Orwell's reaction in a letter to Moore (March 23, 1944) discloses the ideological gulf that separated these two cordially contentious Old Etonians and points up Orwell's ambivalent relationship with Hollis. Orwell told Moore "on no account" to offer the book to Hollis because his firm was pro-Catholic and had "published some of the most poisonous stuff since he set up business. It would do me permanent harm to be published" by him.

Frenemies at fisticuffs? Or was the relationship much warmer on Hollis's side? Either may have been true. Their considerable differences of opinion and divergent religious, social, and political convictions notwithstanding, the two middle-aged Etonians did agree on one burning question of the day: the travesty of capital punishment. Blair spoke out against this "unspeakable" crime as early as 1931 in his short story "A Hanging," while Hollis played a prominent role in the campaign (not popular with his party in the 1940s and 1950s) that led eventually to the abolition of capital punishment soon after his exit as a Conservative MP.

The Works

A recurrent theme of Hollis's *Study of George Orwell* is that, despite his atheism, Orwell possessed a religious sensibility, even a spiritual hunger or yearning for the kind of meaning that Hollis himself had sought when he became a Catholic. What makes Hollis's account of Blair/Orwell fair-minded and yet incendiary is that, despite his own deep Catholic belief, he looks beyond Orwell's anti-Catholicism and finds in him what he calls "a naturally Christian soul" whose thought rested on a subconscious Christian foundation.

Left-wing critics have charged Hollis with attempting to "press-gang" Orwell for "the papists." Hollis's portrait of Orwell as some kind of crypto-Christian has also outraged other readers. Kingsley Amis observed that Hollis "cannot resist drawing Orwell in his own image." True enough, for the book at times reads like a dual biography, with Hollis carrying on a spirited argument with his absent debate opponent on a range of religious and political issues, all the while keeping track of Orwell's likely ayes and noes, coaxing and cajoling him to concede a point, explaining away his atheism, and translating their opposing ideological outlooks into partial agreement.

And yet, as we shall discuss in greater detail in Chapter 10 regarding the progressive, sympathetic stance of American Catholic liberals toward Orwell in the 1950s, it attests to Hollis's intellectual integrity that he could insist, as *Commonweal*'s lay editors also did, that respect for the authority of the Church's hierarchy and teachings must be balanced with the duty of responsible dissent when conscience dictates. In fact, he could concede that strident, aggressive Catholic apologetics brooking "no word of criticism of authority" represented a "disease within" the Church damaging to "the health of Catholicism [and] as potent as any of the attacks on it from without." Hollis adds:

> Indeed the most obedient of Catholics must agree that there has grown up in modern times in certain Catholic circles a contention that it is a failure in loyalty not to champion wholly the side in every passing controversy of anyone who takes the Catholic name.... Orwell was only one of many in the modern world who was prevented from a proper examination of Catholicism's claims by the conduct of Catholics.

His biases notwithstanding, Hollis's role in the shaping of Orwell's posthumous reputation as a man of decency and "virtue"—the basis for the canonization of Orwell as a secular "St. George"—is undeniable. Proceeding from Orwell's view that scientific advancements had steadily exploded the dogmas and doctrines of religious belief, rendering it no longer credible in the contemporary world, Hollis notes that Orwell vaguely acknowledged (though never explicitly admitted) that no earthly faith—whether historical materialism or democratic Socialism or any other "ism" or ideology—could ever fill what he called the "gap" left behind by the crumbling of this foundation. Orwell disclosed his own lifelong struggle with this yawning gap, contends Hollis, when he granted that one of "the major problems of our time is the decay of the belief in personal immortality." Hollis adds: "He was a deeply religious man who, for reasons both temperamental and cultural, could not accept any religion ... a believer without a religion, a man full of convictions, full not only of a moral sense but of metaphysical assumptions."

Whatever the excesses of his enthusiastic apologetics and defense of the Church, Hollis is always direct and pulls no punches. *A Study of George Orwell: The Man and His Works* amounts to a running, spirited commentary on Orwell's writings, including his fiction, prose documentaries and reportage, and essays and journalism. Hollis's sharp analysis shows an appreciation of the complexity of Orwell's thought even while the biographer searches relentlessly for the religious dimension in his literary *oeuvre*. Casting Orwell in his own image, Hollis claims that Orwell resembled the kind of old-fashioned cultural conservative for whom tradition, decency, patriotism, and love of nature were important. He believes Orwell shared his own views opposing nationalists, jingoists, and other Conservatives who championed colonialism and Empire—that is, that Orwell despaired of modern "Conservatives because they despaired of Conservatism."

Hollis also has a good critical eye. He was the first to point out the autobiographical attributes of Orwell's fictional antiheroes, especially John Flory in *Burmese Days* and Gordon Comstock in *Keep the Aspidistra Flying*, describing the latter as Orwell with all the fun left out. Like Blair/Orwell, the two protagonists are both public school boys thrown into an atmosphere for which they are unprepared.

Hollis's verdict on Orwell's nonfiction reportage is mixed. Although these works gained Orwell literary prominence for the first time in the mid-1930s, Hollis does not have a high opinion of *The Road to Wigan Pier*, which addresses the terrible conditions of northern English miners during the worst years of the Depression. He finds unimpressive Orwell's denunciation of soulless industrialism, his call for social justice, and even his biting derision of the failures of socialism because Orwell conceives these issues exclusively in sociopolitical terms, failing to grasp them more deeply as questions only "soluble within a religious framework." Furthermore, given the nature of the modern state, Hollis argues, the destruction of existing class distinctions would lead not to equality but to the emergence of a more ruthless ruling class.

Even though they stood firmly in opposite political camps on the issue of the Spanish Civil War, with Hollis and most English Catholics supporting the fascists under General Francisco Franco and Orwell on the Republican side in defense of the Loyalist government, Hollis generously praises *Homage to Catalonia* as Orwell's most attractive book and concedes that Franco's defeat would have been a blow to Hitler's prestige and might have changed the course of history. What most impresses and gratifies Hollis is Orwell's realization that the ceaseless stream of lies spread by both sides in the Spanish war exemplified the decay of objective truth in the modern world. Catalonia turned Orwell into an implacable foe of Stalinism and of the English leftists who parroted its line; the political outlook expressed in *Animal Farm* and *Nineteen Eighty-Four* is traceable to his experiences in Spain. As Hollis forthrightly acknowledges, it was in Catalonia that Orwell "for the first time came face to face with organized religion as a strong force. He disliked it intensely," and after this encounter he invariably treated Catholicism as "an evil political force."

Orwell's journalism during World War II is of particular interest to Hollis because of their shared patriotism and sense of "Englishness." Hollis applauds Orwell's severe criticism of the British pacifists who opposed the war effort, especially the naïve, sentimental pacifists who imagine goodness will always triumph over evil. Orwell's critique includes religious pacifists like Gandhi, a man whom both he and Hollis otherwise admired for his moral courage. Gandhi's argument that the Jews should have committed collective suicide as a way of arousing the world against the Nazis was flawed, Orwell and Hollis concur, because Gandhi's pacifism could only succeed in liberal societies like Britain that gave his campaign for social justice a public hearing, not in totalitarian tyrannies like Hitler's Germany that snuffed out dissenting voices, leaving them unknown and unheard.

Hollis lauds Orwell's last two indictments of totalitarianism, the fable *Animal Farm* and the dystopia *Nineteen Eighty-Four*. Hollis extols *Animal Farm* as a stellar work of art—literary genius united with a good cause—that combines Lord Acton's bromide that "power corrupts" with James Burnham's claim that revolutions lead not to classless societies but instead to new ruling classes.

Nineteen Eighty-Four is more problematic for Hollis, who finds it ultimately too bleak and negative. The despotic superstate of Oceania emerged not from the degeneration of communism, but rather as the inevitable outcome of a trend toward totalitarianism after a half-century of war, argues Hollis, insisting still again that Orwell's atheism contradicted his emotional and spiritual awareness. According to Hollis, Orwell saw yet could neither affirm nor refute the Christian answer to the pessimism and despair of *Nineteen Eighty-Four*: the embrace of religious faith and the corollary that this life is a preparation for the next. Orwell could not, therefore, resolve a dilemma that he once expressed as the paramount challenge for the modern age: how to "restore the religious attitude while accepting death as final."

CHAPTER 3

The Literary Breakthrough, or When Blair Became Orwell

Blair in Burma

Let us transition here from the man to the emerging man of letters, that is, to an in-depth consideration of when—and how and wherefore—the transformation of Blair into Orwell began. We mentioned in Chapter 1 that one of Eric Blair's early essays derived from his experience in the Indian Imperial Police and sheds light on his revulsion toward imperialism in the 1920s. As Britain entered the "low, dishonest decade" of the 1930s, Blair—still a little-known aspiring London author—published that essay, a powerful piece of short prose entitled "A Hanging." Soon he would become better known as a truth-teller under the pen name "George Orwell." As we also noted in our discussion of his struggle to "become George Orwell," he used that *nom de plume* for the publication of his first book, *Down and Out in Paris and London*. Blair adopted the pseudonym in order to avoid embarrassing his family with his forthcoming Jack London–style book on experiencing Depression-era poverty with the East End tramps.

"A Hanging," which appeared in the *New Adelphi* in August 1931, is regarded as a classic today, even if it is seldom anthologized in literature textbooks or taught in introductory rhetoric and composition courses to undergraduates. Published little more than two years after he returned from what he called "five wasted years" as a policeman in British-occupied Burma, it is derived from Blair's experiences in the Indian Imperial Police.

It is worth reviewing again briefly Blair's years in Burma, for they had a defining influence on the tone and thrust of his now-famous essay—and on how "Blair" became "Orwell." When Blair chose after graduating from Eton not to go on to university but instead to join the Burmese section of the Empire's Indian sub-continental police force, he was probably the first Etonian ever to do so. The experience matured him quickly. Between the ages of 19 and 24, while his peers back in England were attending under-graduate seminars and enjoying nights out on the town, Blair was supervising matters of life and death in Burma, in charge of a vast geographical district whose population equaled that of a medium-sized European city. He also had an experience uncommon for literary Englishmen of his generation: he served under Burmese officials, giving him both insight into how a provincial region of the British Empire functioned and deeper understanding of na-tive sensibilities.

Blair served in Burma (now Myanmar) during 1922–1927, of-ficially resigning his commission in January 1928 during his leave home. Burma proved traumatic for Orwell. Perhaps motivated by pride, he stayed there five years but came to hate the work he had to do and suffered guilt and shame from ruling over a people who hated him and on behalf of an empire whose ethos he rejected.

At some point during his service in Burma—he never specified when—Blair concluded that he had to leave. He came to recog-nize that he wanted to be a writer. Blair had tried to deny this truth, but in doing so he believed he "was outraging my true nature."

Back in England, as he later wrote in *The Road to Wigan Pier*, all doubts about his future ended. "I was already half-determined to throw up my job, and one sniff of English air decided me,"

Orwell wrote. He believed that his time in Burma had coarsened him, nearly turning him into a brute. He "was conscious of an immense weight of guilt that I had got to expiate." When Blair informed his parents of his plans to leave the Imperial Police and to become a writer, they were shocked, particularly his father, whose life had been spent in service to the Empire.

Blair/Orwell never returned to Asia. But his first successful publications in England drew on his Burmese experiences. Furthermore, like Winston Churchill, who used his time in India as a soldier to educate himself by reading widely, the autodidact Blair also completed his education in Burma. He kept up with his reading and carefully studied the Burmese people and their ways. Unlike most Englishmen there, he avoided the white man's club, with its billiards, its whisky and soda, its false bonhomie, its expat hauteur, and its ersatz upper-class pretensions and arrogant contempt for Asians, a milieu that he would later savage in *Burmese Days*.

Narrative Structure and Literary Strategy

"A Hanging" tells the story of the execution of an unidentified Indian man. We learn neither his name nor anything about his background. Nor do we know his crime. He is an Everyman, described only as "a brown, sullen, puny wisp of a man with a shaven head and vague liquid eyes." He could be anyone—and that is the point: he could be you or me.

The first-person narrator also remains unidentified. Blair (he had not yet adopted his *nom de plume* Orwell) does not want to limit the reader's sympathies by diverting us with details that may distract from the essay's punch. "I watched a man hanged once," he writes simply. "There is no question that everybody concerned knew this to be a dreadful, unnatural action." The narrator rein-

forces this point by drawing attention to the prisoner's humanity, as he—a dead man walking—diligently sidesteps a puddle.
"He and we were a party of men walking together, seeing, hearing, feeling, understanding the same world and in two minutes,
with a sudden snap, one of us would be gone—one mind less, one
world less."

"A Hanging" is a prose gem, a brilliant 2,000-word burst of
arresting insight and poignant feeling. Blair is both the narrator
of "A Hanging" and a detached observer of the event, an objective third-person narrative voice that calmly drives home his message. The essay begins with a direct descriptive opening: "It was
Burma, a sodden morning of the rains. A sickly light, like yellow
tin foil, was slanting over the high walls into the jail yard. We
were waiting outside the condemned cells, a row of sheds fronted
with double bars, like small animal cages. Each cell measured
about ten feet by ten and was quite bare within except for a plank
bed and a pot of drinking water."

The opening contains some of the touches for which the mature work of Orwell would become known: original images, vividly descriptive prose, and specific details that highlight a scene.
The simile of the morning light "like tin foil," the inclusion of the
precise dimensions of the bleak cells, and the latter's comparison
with "animal cages" exemplifies the clear, crisp prose that his documentary works and journalism of the 1930s would soon feature.
Blair's intuition about the importance and timing of literary detail is impeccable throughout "A Hanging." When the condemned
man is told that he is to be hanged, he urinates on the cell floor.
This too anticipates Orwell's later essays and reportage, in which
an often understated happening suddenly generates sympathy in
or paints a dramatic portrait for the reader. Within a few lines,
Blair forges an emotional identification between the reader and
the condemned man.

After sketching the background for the reader, Blair carefully divides his essay into three distinct parts in order to convey the sheer futility and wrongness of taking a human life. First, as the prisoner is led to the gallows, Blair introduces an incident designed to humanize the scene: "A dreadful thing had happened—a dog, come goodness knows whence, had appeared in the yard." It came "bounding among us with a loud volley of barks, and leapt round us wagging its whole body, wild with glee at finding so many human beings together. It was a large woolly dog, half Airedale, half pariah. For a moment it pranced round us, and then, before anyone could stop it, it had made a dash for the prisoner, jumping up to lick his face. Everyone stood aghast, too taken aback even to grab at the dog."

The prisoner's reaction is revealing. Blair writes that "he looked on incuriously, as though this was another formality of the hanging." Blair here humanizes the prisoner, who is no longer a condemned man but someone with whom a friendly dog wants to frolic. It is as if the narrator challenges the reader-onlooker: How bad can someone be if a happily skipping, dancing, woolly half-Airedale wants to play with him?

In the second section, the prisoner approaches the gallows. An incident then occurs that gives the essay its most memorable moment. The prisoner "walked clumsily with his bound arms, but quite steadily, with that bobbing gait of the Indian who never straightens his knees. At each step his muscles slid neatly into place, the lock of hair on his scalp danced up and down, his feet printed themselves on the wet gravel. And once, in spite of the men who gripped him by each shoulder, he stepped slightly aside to avoid a puddle on the path."

This apparently casual *en passant* event precipitates a small epiphany by the narrator that makes "A Hanging" conscience-pricking for us readers. "It is curious," Blair writes, "but till that moment I had never realized what it means to destroy a healthy, conscious man. When I saw the prisoner step aside to avoid the puddle, I saw the mystery, the unspeakable wrongness of cutting a life short when it is in full tide."

Having carefully, subtly humanized the prisoner, Blair nimbly describes the other participants in the execution. The hangman, "a grey-haired convict in the white uniform of the prison," quickly places the rope around the prisoner's neck. The Indian guards in attendance are uneasy; they "suddenly changed color and had gone grey like bad coffee." With the rope around his neck, the prisoner "began crying out to his god. It was a high, reiterated cry of 'Ram! Ram! Ram! Ram!'" The execution itself is described only briefly—"a clanking noise" as the trap door opens, "and then silence."

The gathering power of this tableau owes to the artful narration, whereby the point of view gradually and ingeniously shifts: its final paragraphs generate a perspective that ultimately induces us to consider ourselves guilty parties—as executioners bereft of any moral high ground. When the dog leaps up to lick the Indian convict, the prisoner's execution proceeds despite the distraction. The scene closes with the dog howling in a corner as the prisoner hangs lifeless before the crowd. The narrator then nonchalantly delivers a remark that makes the reader's hair stand on end. Blair does not mince words about his view of capital punishment: "When a murderer is hanged, there is only one person at the ceremony who is not guilty of murder."

As the narrative reaches this climax in its third and final section, Blair pivots sharply away from a description of the execution itself and toward the reactions of the executioners—and toward "us," the readers. He describes the superintendent poking the hanging man with his stick, saying, "He's all right," and then checking the time as though the execution represents just a tiresome inconvenience for everyone. No sense of sadness at the taking of another life emerges, but again something quite self-indulgent: "relief," "now that the job was done," expressed in a forced, Kiplingesque heartiness punctuated by a (dim)wit who labors uneasily to relieve the tension. The narrator and his fellow officers are representatives of the Raj, "executing" their duties, gulping whiskeys, and kidding (among) themselves. As the scene winds down, Blair writes:

> All at once everyone began chattering.
>
> The Eurasian boy walking beside me nodded towards the way we had come, with a knowing smile: "Do you know, sir, our friend (he meant the dead man), when he heard his appeal had been dismissed, he pissed on the floor of his cell. From fright...."
>
> Several people laughed—at what, nobody seemed certain. Francis was walking by the superintendent, talking garrulously.... "Well, sir, all has passed off with the utmost satisfactoriness ... I have known cases where the doctor was obliged to go beneath the gallows and pull the prisoner's legs to ensure decease. Most disagreeable! ... One man, I recall, clung to the bars of his cage when we went to take him out. You will scarcely credit, sir, that it took six warders to dislodge him, three pulling at each leg. We reasoned with him. 'My dear fellow,' we said, 'think of all the pain and trouble you are causing to us!' But no, he would not listen! Ach, he wass very troublesome!"
>
> I found that I was laughing quite loudly. Everyone was laughing. We went through the big double gates of the prison, into the road. "Pulling at his legs!" exclaimed a Bur-

mese magistrate suddenly, and burst into a loud chuckling. We all began laughing again.

Blair closes "A Hanging" with a single, terse, ironic, collectively self-accusatory sentence: "The dead man was a hundred yards away."

America the ~~Beautiful~~ [*sic*] Barbaric?

If the reader will permit me to digress for a moment here and speak personally, I will also add that this self-accusatory sentence rings especially powerfully for me. "A Hanging" pricks my own conscience as an American, most especially as a Texas resident. I have visited prisons and am a long-time correspondent with prisoners as part of a national pen pal program headquartered in Philadelphia. So I have some small awareness of what inmates suffer, especially those on death row. Moreover, with recent advances in DNA research, everyone today is familiar with the numerous shocking cases of prisoners unjustly incarcerated years or decades ago whose innocence was finally established through DNA evidence. True, public hangings are no longer conducted here. Yet capital punishment remains a regular part of American life—and our execution figures vastly exceed those of Myanmar.

According to official figures of the Texas Justice Department released in early 2019, my own home state of Texas has conducted 560 executions since 1982. With a mere 7 percent of the national population, Texas accounts for more than 40 percent of the nation's capital punishment cases. (The U.S. total now numbers 1,493 since 1976, when capital punishment resumed after a four-year moratorium during which it was suspended in all 50 states.) In Texas alone, 221 citizens, predominantly black men, sit on death row.[1]

Whereas Britain and the rest of Europe—and in fact virtually all of the developed world, with only a couple of exceptions, such as Singapore—outlawed capital punishment decades ago, the United States still practices it with a vengeance. We do so despite the fact that capital punishment has proven sorely lacking as a deterrent—the usual rationale for its continued practice. (And also despite the fact that, in Texas alone, recent DNA research has enabled forensic scientists to determine that at least a half-dozen executions carried out over the last decade were mistakes. A couple of Texans on death row were released in 2017 after the introduction of new DNA evidence.)

We Americans above all, therefore, need to approach Blair's sole impressive essay as something more than a literary event. We need to reread Eric Blair's "A Hanging" for political and moral reasons. We need to be reminded that the guilty are not necessarily—or only—those who are convicted of crime.

We should pause and consider Orwell's ending whenever we presume to sit in judgment and take another's life.

Blair's Literary Breakthrough ...

Let us now return to the narrative and stylistic aspects of "A Hanging" and to its overlooked status as the watershed event in Blair's literary development. First we should address the issue of genre. Is "A Hanging" nonfiction or fiction? "Essay"? Or "short story"?

It is difficult to believe "A Hanging" is sheer fiction, simply a precociously brilliant story. The detail is too precise, the descriptions somehow too lifelike for us to suppose that such an incident didn't happen. Blair simply hadn't reached a level of literary skill able to create a story of such quality from sheer imagination. Moreover, the mature Orwell was less a creator than a craftsman.

Even in Orwell's best works of fiction written years later—particularly *Animal Farm* and *Nineteen Eighty-Four*—his gift was not literary creation, whereby the artwork emerges seemingly *ab ovo* from the pure imagination. Rather, his bent lay in literary invention, whereby Orwell drew on his life and times to craft a pair of classics that stand as the stellar exemplars in modern English prose of the satiric fable and the dystopia, respectively.

Yet those achievements of Orwell still lay far in Blair's future. As we shall presently discuss, nothing else he wrote around this time possesses the naked, overwhelming emotional power of "A Hanging." In this short piece of 1931, Blair momentarily exhibits the literary talent that would blossom in mid-decade. The struggling journeyman somehow accesses the prose gift that would soon mark his literary signature and distinguish him as a master of crystalline prose, "The Crystal Spirit," as George Woodcock memorializes him in his book of that title. Orwell's essay "Looking Back on the Spanish Civil War" ends with a poem featuring that image. In "A Hanging," England's Prose Laureate—"The Crystal Spirit"—is already visible on the horizon.

Scholars have disputed for years whether or not "A Hanging" is straight autobiography. Certainly it bears similarities with other tales written about the strange customs of the East—notably, some of W. S. Maugham's stories. One of Orwell's biographers, the late Sir Bernard Crick, expended enormous effort in his pioneering study, *George Orwell: A Life* (1980), to find out whether Blair had ever witnessed or participated in a hanging during any of his numerous postings in Burma. Crick managed to establish the exact number of executions that occurred during this period, and to specify their type, in every location in which Orwell worked as a policeman. Yet he could find no biographical evidence, either in official correspondence or from any witnesses, to verify whether or not Orwell personally attended or officially participated in the executions. Given the fact that, according to one estimate, between 1923 and 1927 more than 600 people were hanged in Burma, including dozens per year at or near Blair's postings, it is overwhelmingly likely that he witnessed some of them.

The consensus today is that "A Hanging" is "faction," an autobiographically based essay in which Orwell employed fictional techniques and unleashed his imagination to transform a (probable) real-life event (or a composite of events) into an enduring work of art. (Similar scholarly debates have raged for years over whether Orwell ever shot an elephant in Burma, given that the precise genre of his other prose work about Burma, "Shooting an Elephant," is also ambiguous.)

"A Hanging" represents an astonishing performance by an unknown 28-year-old writer. It also demonstrates the first signs of the prose style showcased in Orwell's widely anthologized essays of the 1940s (such as "Politics and the English Language" and "Such, Such Were the Joys"), writings that make him seem "Every Intellectual's big brother," as I often call him. Characterized by acute observation, telling description, and pointed commentary, the essays of his last years also exhibit an economy and directness that makes them unforgettable.

It all began with "A Hanging," which marks Eric Blair's breakthrough both in artistic and in professional terms, when he "overreached" himself, as it were, in an exceptional artistic flight to the higher plateau where his artistic paraclete, the Crystal Spirit, presided, through whom he fleetingly accessed "George Orwell," the writer whose fiction and essays of the later 1930s and 1940s would revolutionize English prose. "A Hanging" was really his first publication that deserves the name "literature." Until this point, Blair had published nothing more than a few book reviews and a couple of newspaper articles, along with a pedestrian piece of expository prose about his experience with the tramps of London.

Nothing prepared literary London for this essay, and it strengthened his resolve to persist in his exertions to complete "Lady Poverty," his work-in-progress on lowlife in London and Paris. It was that manuscript that he revised and completed the following year under the title *Down and Out in Paris and London*, which was published in January 1933.

... Or "Mere Nonfiction"?

The foregoing biographical context of "A Hanging" is crucial to remember in order to appreciate fully the degree of literary growth that this short work represented for Eric Blair. "Blair/Orwell" never showed his greatness as a novelist during the 1930s, even though most of his literary energy was poured into the writing of fiction. He published four traditional novels between 1934 and 1939, which achieved modest success and gained him some recognition in English literary circles. Yet before his death Orwell regarded only *Burmese Days* (1934) and *Coming Up for Air* (1939) as worth reprinting. He dismissed as failures two other novels, *A Clergyman's Daughter* (1935) and *Keep the Aspidistra Flying* (1936). Although *A Clergyman's Daughter* has never found a following, most critics today judge Orwell more generously than he did himself, noticing positive qualities in all four novels, as Loraine Saunders does in her revisionist study of Orwell's novels of the 1930s, *The Unsung Artistry of George Orwell* (2008).

So "A Hanging" is a masterpiece that Blair/Orwell probably did not immediately honor as such. Why? Precisely because it was to him "merely" nonfiction. It is the "faction" that Blair wrote while he was still trying to find himself, a work that foreshadows the mature Orwell's work—which would consist in the 1940s of his landmark essays (such as "Politics and the English Language") and his essayistic fantasias in the forms of the fable (*Animal Farm*) and anti-utopia (*Nineteen Eighty-Four*), which Alex Zwerdling has felicitously dubbed his "didactic fantasies."

Not only does "A Hanging" represent Blair's first major publication in England, but it is also the only example of his best writing published under his real name. When Orwell published "A Hanging" in the *New Adelphi* in 1931, the journal was coedited by John Middleton Murry and Max Plowman. It was an exotic mix of radicalism and modernism. It would serve as Blair's major outlet for the next few years, until he switched to the *New English Weekly* because of a dispute among the *New Adelphi*'s owners. Orwell felt comfortable writing for the *NEW* editor, Philip Mairet, who gave him considerable freedom to write and review what he liked.

Becoming "George Orwell"

We have noted that "A Hanging" tells the story of the execution of a man for a crime never specified. As we have seen, he is an Everyman, merely described as "a Hindu," "puny," and a couple of other physical details. Probably the reason for such descriptive minimalism is that Blair does not want to wrangle with the reader about "justified" or "unjustified" grounds for execution, which would risk blurring the focus of his story-essay—and the purity of his moral critique—by directing attention to the state's judicial arguments or the victim's personal background.

The payoff from Blair's literary economy in terms of artistic power and polemical force is clear: "A Hanging" reads as a formidable indictment of the whole concept of capital punishment. Blair does not advance an abstract, impersonal argument consisting of philosophical speculation or legal hair-splitting, let alone theological reflection. (As we saw in Chapter 2, Christopher Hollis, who knew Blair and visited him in Burma, maintained that his opposition to capital punishment is only tenable on the basis of some religious belief, a view that runs counter to Orwell's well-known atheism.) Rather, "A Hanging" grabs the heart, pressing a moral-affective appeal that aims to arouse the reader's revulsion against what the taking of a human life entails. Another reason why its details lodge uneasily in our hearts and minds owes to its spectacle of intimacy—or rather the (violent, violated) intimacy of spectacle, which presents us with a voyeuristic close-up of a macabre exhibition. Indeed, the guilt-churning paradox of "A Hanging" is that this public spectacle is staged via a language that is severe rather than showy. This paradox represents a brilliant complementarity of form and function, for, as Alex Woloch notes, "the language itself is stunted and corroded," so that the "starkness emerges as a disturbing echo of . . . urgency and deprivation."[2] To a Christian, it might even suggest the scene of Christ crucified at Golgotha: an austere *horreur* capturing the paradox that the shame of the world is the glory of God. Blair's "bare" title, "A Hanging," with its indefinite article, spare yet universalizing, possesses an understated power that makes it seem to apply to all hangings.

"A Hanging" marks the moment when Blair/Orwell marshaled for the first time his full resources as a nonfiction writer—clarity, plain speaking, concision, simplicity, and directness—to bring forth compelling, pellucid prose. Largely neglected in comparison with Orwell's more famous essays, "A Hanging" has rarely been anthologized—unlike, say, "Shooting an Elephant" or "Politics and the English Language." Nonetheless, "A Hanging" has generated considerable discussion, including, as mentioned earlier, questions about whether it is a work of fact or imagination. Crick refers to it alternately as one of "his great essays" and a "short story"—even though Orwell's friend Mabel Fierz claims that he told her that he never witnessed a hanging during his police service in Burma. Her testimony has long been discounted by critics who find the work possessed of such imaginative power that they conclude that Orwell must have experienced such a historical event.

We return now to examine that issue in greater detail. Crick had reservations about the authenticity of "A Hanging," labeling it "a compound of fact and fiction, honest in intent, true to experience but not necessarily truthful in detail." When pressed for information, Crick notes, Orwell told some friends that "A Hanging" was just a story. After his death, his friend Malcolm Muggeridge was approached by Orwell's second wife, Sonia, to write his biography. Although Muggeridge eventually gave up, believing that the task was beyond him, he concluded that "A Hanging" and Orwell's other autobiographical writings were largely fictionalized.

Other biographers have been more inclined to accept the work's authenticity. Gordon Bowker, for instance, says it "most likely" happened. Others avoid the issue. Jeffrey Meyers simply says it is a "confessional" piece of writing. In his "authorized" biography, Michael Shelden concludes that "A Hanging" was based on a real experience. Sonia Orwell took a straightforward view unimpeded by a scholar's probing or a biographer's duty-bound skepticism. When Crick, whom she had commissioned to write Orwell's biography, expressed doubt about whether the incidents in "Shooting an Elephant" took place, she exploded: "Of course he shot a fucking elephant. He said he did. Why do you always doubt his fucking word!"

Are "A Hanging" (and Orwell's other Burma essay, "Shooting an Elephant") "authentic"? On two separate occasions, Orwell claimed that he had attended executions. In *The Road to Wigan Pier*, he wrote that he "had watched a man hanged once; it seemed to me worse than a thousand murders." Eight years later, in one of his idiosyncratic "As I Please" columns in *Tribune*, he made the claim in almost identical words, adding a typical aside: "There was no question that everybody concerned knew this to be a dreadful action."

Perhaps the most suitable word for "A Hanging" is the appropriately ambiguous "sketch," which is the term Orwell himself used to describe "Shooting an Elephant" in a letter to the editor of *New Writing*, John Lehmann, in 1936. Properly speaking, a "sketch" is simply a short narrative, which is not to say a "short story," but rather any brief literary piece with some degree of narrative line—a feature compatible with the essay form. On the other hand, the case for "A Hanging" as a "storied" experience—that is, an actual experience embroidered and enlivened by literary imagination—has gained more support in the last two decades. The likelihood of its "authenticity" has been heightened by discoveries of evidence that other Orwell writings, long believed to be fictional, were based on real experiences. For instance, a copy of *Down and Out in Paris and London* that Orwell sent in the mid-1930s to his then-girlfriend, Brenda Salkeld, contains notes attesting to some of the incidents mentioned. Furthermore, some passages in Orwell's 1936 diary, which he kept during his research trip to the north of England, confirm that many of the events mentioned in *The Road to Wigan Pier* really took place. Orwell may have used creative imagination in these documentaries, but they appear to be firmly rooted in fact.

Flight of Passage, or the Prose Laureate Uncocooned

If "A Hanging" does represent a sudden leap of accomplishment by Blair—one that he did not immediately and fully assimilate or have under control (or perhaps even recognize)—what else did he write of a supposedly "inferior quality" at that time? The only substantial published pieces near coincident with "A Hanging" were his essay on his days in a tramp's hostel, "The Spike," and his brief report of his weeks as a farmhand, "Hop Picking." Published in the *New Adelphi* four months before "A Hanging" in April 1931, "The Spike" is a pedestrian effort that utterly lacks the sophistication of the former. Blair published "Hop Picking" in the *New Statesman and Nation* in October 1931, two months after "A Hanging." Even more so than "The Spike," it is a modest, lackluster article, little more than a description of piecework labor, a selection written up from his diary that remains hardly more than undigested experience.

When Blair wrote "A Hanging," he was trying to convince himself that his real talent lay in imaginative fiction. He persisted in this conviction and strove to write fiction because he firmly believed, as Orwell expressed it in "Why I Write," that a writer had to produce "enormous naturalistic novels with unhappy endings." As a result, he composed only a single other fully successful essay during the period from 1931 to 1936, "Shooting an Elephant," which he did not pen until five years after "A Hanging." So Orwell "fell back," as it were, in his nonfiction prose, content to toss off competent yet unstrenuous book reviews. He challenged himself in his fiction alone.

As a result, scholars (and anthologists) have usually overlooked that "A Hanging" is written with the same economy of style, direct approach, and attention to detail characteristic of Orwell's best later writings. It represents a sublime, isolated, Elysian isle in the otherwise forgettable Dead Sea of Blair, demonstrating that he had fleetingly gained command of his mature literary style years before most critics have acknowledged. Most Orwell scholars believe that the writings that fully reflect the mature Orwell can be dated from "Shooting an Elephant" and *Homage to Catalonia* (1938). Both these works reveal Orwell at his best, as a master of narrative and exposition, a gifted controversialist, and a skilled practitioner of documentary prose. The Orwell of the splendid essays and the two iconic works of imagination of the 1940s, *Animal Farm* and *Nineteen Eighty-Four*, is frequently on display in his prose writings of the later 1930s.

Indeed "A Hanging" recommends itself to us as a literary breakthrough not only in stylistic terms, but also thematically. Its subject matter finds its way not just into relevant topics in *Animal Farm* (e.g., the satirical treatment of Stalin's show trials), but also into the related, more fully developed themes of *Nineteen Eighty-Four*. The nightmare of authoritarian power, the brutal tyranny of the state, the hypocrisy and cruelty of respectable "authority," the ruthless exploitation of the powerless: it is all there in "A Hanging." Moreover, it is fair to say that the process of Eric Blair "becoming George Orwell" was activated and catalyzed by returning to these issues again and again. From that standpoint, "A Hanging" represents not only Blair's literary but also his political and intellectual breakthrough, given that these leitmotifs, all of which are present in "A Hanging," would become the signature governing themes of Orwell's outstanding achievements in prose fiction (and nonfiction).

So we may pivot here and fast-forward in the next two chapters to Orwell's twin masterpieces in fiction, *Animal Farm* and *Nineteen Eighty-Four*, before returning to close Part 1 with an assessment of the man of letters who became "England's Prose Laureate."

CHAPTER 4

Orwell's Twin Masterpieces, *Animal Farm* and *Nineteen Eighty-Four*

The Seismic "Squib"

What havoc "a little squib" can cause! Subtitled "A Fairy Story," *Animal Farm*, or the "little squib"—Orwell's modest term for the book in a letter to the Russian émigré scholar Gleb Struve—was only 30,000 words, a brilliantly original hybrid of Aesopian fable, Menippean satire, and historical allegory. Its publication date in the U.S. was August 26, 1946, almost exactly a year after its appearance in England.

Animal Farm hit a nerve at the right psychological moment in America, just when the pro-Soviet fellow-traveling movement was beginning to decelerate. Published to reviewers' kudos and good sales in the United Kingdom in August 1945, it nevertheless gained attention principally from the English literary-political elite, especially the left-wing London intelligentsia and serious literary-minded readers, and had only a moderate impact on the wider British public. Its full impact was not felt until it crossed the Atlantic a year later, and some of the long-term consequences proved highly ironic. Indeed the circumstances shaping the American reception of this Englishman's "squib" generated cultural and intellectual tremors that contributed decisively to the decades-long ideological fault lines that surfaced between the United States and the Soviet Union.

Fault Lines in the Transatlantic Terrain

Communism was never a powerful political force in either the United States or England, despite broad popular support for the USSR against Nazi Germany during World War II. Both countries, however, contained groups of prominent and influential fellow-travelers whose sympathy, if not primary loyalty, was to the Soviet Union and its communist principles. In the United States, such fellow-traveling peaked during the war, when the Russians became the darlings of the American progressive Left and Joseph Stalin acquired the image of the affable pipe-smoking "Uncle Joe." Unlike in the United Kingdom, however, by the time *Animal Farm* landed on the desks of most American readers, the gloss was already beginning to fade from this rosy picture of the Soviet Union. With the Cold War on the horizon, even liberal-minded Americans' affections for the avuncular wartime ally had cooled. It would take another decade for a similar feeling of estrangement to engulf the left-wing intelligentsia in England—a rising tide of alienation that crested when Nikita Khrushchev's so-called Secret Speech exposing Stalin's crimes shocked the West in February 1956.

Numerous other differences between postwar Britain and America also accounted for the growing transatlantic fault lines. For example, whereas the English were preoccupied with the devastation caused by the war, including postwar rationing and an economy in shambles (not to mention the July 1945 defeat of the Conservatives under Churchill and the societal upheavals wrought by the first Labour government in decades), America was enjoying an unprecedented level of prosperity and global influence—the apogee of the "American Century."

Specific to *Animal Farm*'s reception in the United States was a series of events that disillusioned all but the blindest admirers of the Soviet Union. First, the Russians began clamping down on Communist-controlled governments in Poland and other Eastern European countries. In February 1946 Winston Churchill struck a mortal blow at the Communist cause in his famous Iron Curtain speech, significantly delivered in the United States rather than Great Britain. His purpose was to warn the Americans of the inescapable reality of Soviet imperialism in Europe.

Around the same time, a Soviet agent serving as a minor code clerk in Canada, Igor Gouzenko, defected to seek refuge in the West and revealed that the Russians had been spying on their Western allies throughout the war and had gained valuable information on the construction of the atomic bomb. To make matters worse for progressive defenders of the USSR, Orwell's "squib" arrived soon thereafter, offering the clever and convincing reminder that the West's Soviet "comrades" had been allied with Nazi Germany during the opening two years of the war and only switched sides after Hitler double-crossed and invaded them. The fable also delivered a persuasive and easily understood indictment of the Russian Revolution itself, the centerpiece of much left-wing and progressive praise.

So *Animal Farm* appeared in the midst of an escalating controversy in the United States over how to deal with the Russians. The "Fairy Story" engendered Orwell's Cold Warrior reputation with the wider American public. That reputation would broaden and heighten much further with the publication of his better-known indictment of Soviet communism, *Nineteen Eighty-Four*, three years later. Little known outside certain intellectual circles in England before the war, Orwell became, along with Arthur Koestler, the outstanding popularizer of the perils of Soviet totalitarianism in the postwar years. Orwell's success and credibility, even more so than Koestler's, was linked to the timing of the Cold War and to his radical credentials as an independent socialist who was leftist yet non-Marxist. His unorthodox stance—a freethinking Tory radical who was also an anti-Stalinist critic of the progressive Left—transformed him into a cult hero among American conservatives after his death.

Familiar in the United States only to a narrow band of Trotskyists in New York until *Animal Farm*'s publication, Orwell entered the American scene as a blank slate—and soon became touted as the leading literary Cold Warrior. Only after the American publication of *Animal Farm* and the much louder applause for *Nineteen Eighty-Four*, released on both sides of the Atlantic in June 1949, did many of Orwell's writings from the 1930s and 1940s appear in the United States. His essays, especially "Shooting an Elephant" and "Politics and the English Language," embellished his reputation for limpid, direct, crystalline prose. The image of Orwell in America was simple, clear, powerful—and politically useful. He was welcomed as the outspoken, even belligerent Cold Warrior, the writer who could spearhead the campaign on the linguistic and cultural front.

Toward the end of World War II, as Orwell began to castigate the Soviet Union as something less than a noble, gallant ally of the West, he became suspicious in the eyes of those American leftists who sympathized with the Soviet Union and the cause of communism. By contrast, intellectuals such as Dwight Macdonald and Philip Rahv regarded him as an honest man and not an apologist for either Stalinism or capitalism. Orwell was one of the first writers to recognize that the real threat to Western society was from totalitarianism, not simply from fascism. In an essay on Arthur Koestler in 1946, he made this point with characteristic directness: "The sin of nearly all left wingers from 1933 onwards is that they wanted to be anti-Fascist without being anti-totalitarian." The American Left would not reach this stage in its thinking until long after the war.

The Beast Fable as Political Countermyth

Although Orwell achieved popular success in the United States in 1946 with *Animal Farm*, he had conceived the idea for it after fighting against General Franco's forces in the Spanish Civil War. After joining the non-Stalinist, antifascist POUM militia in Catalonia, he was disgusted on his return home to discover how the popular press had distorted the war. What keenly disturbed him was that the Stalinists and their sympathizers had managed to get their view of the war accepted by knowledgeable leftist groups in England. During his stay in Spain Orwell had watched with growing repugnance the adroit way in which the Stalinists had destroyed the power of other popular left-wing forces opposing Franco. He thus discovered what other European and American leftists were not to discern until after World War II: their ideological pose *au contraire*, the Stalinists subordinated everything to Soviet national interests.

For Orwell, the essence of socialism was that it championed "justice and liberty," as he wrote in *The Road to Wigan Pier*. The Spanish Civil War convinced him to puncture the pretense that the USSR—the Union of Soviet Socialist Republics—was a "socialist" country. Indeed Stalin's totalitarian regime was no more "socialist" than its Janus-faced counterpart on the right: Nazi ("National Socialist") Germany. The Second World War put a temporary halt to any work on Orwell's part to demythologize the USSR. But midway through the conflict he became even more determined to unmask the Soviet system because Russia's heroic opposition to Hitler had further blinded people to the real nature of Communism. In "The Prevention of Literature," (1946), written just a few months after the British publication of *Animal Farm*, Orwell elaborated on his reasons for wanting to expose Communist tyranny. Fifteen years earlier, he noted, when one defended intellectual freedom, one had to do so against the attacks of fascists, conservatives, and Catholics: "Today one has to defend it against Communists and 'fellow-travelers.' One ought not to exaggerate the direct influence of the small English Communist Party, but there can be no question about the poisonous effect of the Russian *mythos* on English intellectual life. Because of it, known facts are suppressed and distorted to such an extent as to make it doubtful whether a true history of our times can ever be written." This attitude dominated Orwell's work in the postwar period. While he continued to assail tyranny and totalitarianism as he had before the war, now his principal object of attack became Russia specifically.

Another factor that convinced Orwell to unmask the Russian Revolution as the betrayal—rather than fulfillment—of the socialist dream of freedom and equality was his intense dislike of avowed Stalinist intellectuals and fellow-travelers in England. Orwell was disgusted with the way "fashionable" leftists—his own inveterate descriptor—swallowed and belched out Communist propaganda. His struggles to get his Spanish Civil War reports and other anti-Communist writings published deepened this sense of disgust. Orwell found it hard to forgive those who had censored him in the 1930s. These personal and political resentments conjured a powerful brew of rage in his mind, firing his commitment to trumpet how Comrade Napoleon's ideology, besmeared throughout the West by smug cadres of well-trained pigs in Britain and elsewhere, had duped most leftists outside the USSR.

By November 1943, his thinking had ripened and he began work on a short political tract aimed at demonstrating how the Bolshevik Revolution had been corrupted by the revolutionaries themselves. After considerable experimentation he hit upon the idea of using the form of the beast fable: a myth to fight a myth. He would destroy the Soviet myth with an even more powerful countermyth.

Within a matter of weeks he had finished the first draft of *Animal Farm* and began trying to find a publisher. Since the Anglo-Russian alliance was still strong, his manuscript found no home. Both conservatives concerned above all to support Churchill and leftist enthusiasts of Stalin united in their opposition. On the Left, Victor Gollancz turned down *Animal Farm* on the grounds that it was "extreme" and "hysterical." At least four other publishers rejected *Animal Farm* (among them Faber's editorial reader, T. S. Eliot, a Tory Anglican[1]), usually on the grounds that, whatever its merits, it was playing into the hands of the Nazis, a charge that Orwell found specious and that angered him bitterly.

Temporarily despairing of seeing his work in print—and even considering having it published at his own expense—Orwell found a small English press, Secker & Warburg, that agreed to put out a limited edition. So *Animal Farm* appeared in 1945 and won immediate critical acclaim. The cordial relations between Russia and England were just beginning to fray, rendering the political-intellectual climate more tolerant of a work condemning the Soviet Union.

The Dawn of George Orwell's Fame

Animal Farm's positive reception in Great Britain was far exceeded by its smashing success in the United States. The initial American reaction to Orwell's allegorical fable came in the form of a favorable review in *Time* in May 1946. Shortly thereafter, the Book-of-the-Month Club announced that *Animal Farm* would be its choice for the month of September, thereby guaranteeing Orwell a large audience in the United States for the first time.

The Club's selection of *Animal Farm* is the often-overlooked key for understanding the origins in the publishing industry of Orwell's worldwide fame today. It represents the single most significant event in the expansion of Orwell's reputation in his lifetime and the most important event in the entire history of his reputation in America. "The *Uncle Tom's Cabin* of our time," one member of the Club's selection committee labeled the work. Extolling the fable's "worldwide importance," Club president Harry Scherman issued a special statement: "Every now and then through history, some fearless individual has spoken for the people of a troubled time.... Just so does this little gem of an allegory express, perfectly, the ... inarticulate philosophy of tens of millions of free men.... Wherever men are free to read what they want, this book and its influence will spread." As if to guarantee that outcome, Scherman also asked subscribers to pick *Animal Farm* rather than any alternate Club choice. The fable sold 460,000 copies through the Club between 1946 and 1949 and soon became a runaway best seller.

After the Book-of-the-Month Club's red carpet treatment, *Animal Farm* received a rapturous welcome throughout most of America. The popular magazines—including *Time, Newsweek*, and the *New York Times Magazine*—were all enthusiastic in their admiration. Some effusive reviewers, however, were less insightful about the fable and its targets. Edward Weeks, writing in the *Atlantic*, concluded an otherwise favorable comment by noting that *Animal Farm* showed a "clever hostility if one applies the analogy to Soviet Russia."

If? To what else could the "analogy" possibly have applied? After all, it took the form of an allegory, with precise, ingenious correspondences to historical actors and events. Today, of course, a prime reason for the enduring relevance and popularity of *Animal*

Farm owes to its perceived universality as a timeless fable satirizing the course of violent revolutions. Just as we shall see in Chapter 5 in the case of *Nineteen Eighty-Four* as a work of naturalist satire, the satirical referents of *Animal Farm* have been fudged or forgotten. Its allegorical correspondences to the Russian Revolution are largely ignored in favor of a less nuanced interpretation that this "fairy story" represents a warning against revolution in general.[2] In that light, the Aesopian "lesson" of Orwell's little squib about the Bolshevik Revolution—encapsulated by and culminating in the Seventh Commandment of Animalism ("All animals are equal, but some are more equal than others")—stands as a rhetorical feat comparable to Danton's sad remark that "revolutions eat their own children."[3]

The avowedly political magazines of the Left reacted to *Animal Farm* with bewilderment and bluster. They were still committed to the ideal of Soviet-American friendship and thus viewed *Animal Farm* as a lethal threat to that cause. The winds of the Cold War had not yet begun to buffet the American literary scene. Isaac Rosenfeld in the *Nation* offered contrived, ideologically motivated reasons for disliking Orwell's tale that were more obviously concerned with political than literary factors. He disavowed, for example, that Orwell's interpretation had any validity when applied to the USSR. At one time such a view had some relation to reality, Rosenfeld argued, but in the aftermath of the Allies' war effort and the heroic Soviet antifascist campaign, such an interpretation made *Animal Farm* a reactionary work. There was little that Rosenfeld liked about *Animal Farm*. He believed that it not only failed to explain why the revolution had been betrayed, but, what was worse in his eyes, told readers things about the Soviet Union they already knew. This was a strange view from a journal that had sought to justify every jerk and switch of the Communist line during the 1930s.

If Rosenfeld found *Animal Farm* insignificant, George Soule in the *New Republic* recoiled from it with a combination of naïveté and hostility. Soule managed the difficult task of confusing the identities of both Snowball and Napoleon. He thought Napoleon was supposed to represent Lenin, failing to recognize the likeness to Stalin in the diabolical pig leader who betrays the Revolution. According to Soule, *Animal Farm* was "dull" and the allegory was "a creaky machine for saying in a clumsy way things that have been better said directly." He neglected to say how and where these things had been said better. Certainly not in the pages of the *New Republic*, which had been one of the most shameful, blatant apologists for every Soviet atrocity and iniquity for more than a decade.

Soule took strong exception to Orwell's description of the young dogs being trained as secret police, asking if one was supposed to take that seriously as a commentary on Soviet education. He disclaimed any relationship between the slaughter of the loyal old workhorse, Boxer, and any event in Soviet history. That denial further attests to his (perhaps deliberate) obtuseness regarding the lionization of the Stakhanovite worker-hero of the USSR in the 1930s, as well as the millions victimized by the collectivization of agriculture during Stalin's Five Year Plans, and even more so his willful blindness regarding Stalin's mass purge of the faithful Old Bolsheviks who had led the revolution. Yet such unfavorable reviews in the progressive journals could not offset the impact of the endorsement of the mainstream critics and popular magazines.

Quite the contrary. From the moment of its American launch in August 1946, *Animal Farm* was a literary and publishing triumph. Literary gatekeepers, authoritative intellectuals, and mass circulation organs saluted *Animal Farm* as a contemporary classic. In the *New Yorker*, Edmund Wilson, the doyen of American literary critics, compared Orwell as a satirist to Jonathan Swift and Voltaire. The rising star among American political historians, Arthur Schlesinger, Jr., in the lead notice in the *New York Times Book Review*, described it as "a story of deadly simplicity" written "with such gravity and charm that *Animal Farm* becomes an independent creation, standing apart from the object" of criticizing the Soviet Union. Meanwhile, *Time*'s anonymous reviewer devoted three columns to *Animal Farm*, hailing Orwell as "the most brilliant political satirist since Swift."

The American public was enchanted by Orwell's "Fairy Story," which sold more than 10 million copies in the United States alone during the next decade. Three reasons accounted for its popularity. First, the story itself was simple enough to be understood by anyone who wanted to understand it. Second, like all artful fables, it could be appreciated on at least two levels: as a children's tale of how "power corrupts" and as a sophisticated indictment of the Russians' betrayal of their own revolution. Third, *Animal Farm* appeared just as the Cold War began to obsess the American public. People abruptly realized that the USSR had geopolitical aims quite contrary to those of the U.S., that the wartime alliance had been largely a marriage of convenience, and that the USSR was no longer willing to cooperate with the Western Allies—Stalin was no benign Uncle Joe. Orwell's tale of the betrayed revolution thus found a far more responsive audience in America than in Great Britain, not only because the American audience read the fable more than a year after the war's close, when signs of an emergent "cold" war were unmistakable, but also because the United States carried vastly greater global responsibilities as a world power and leader of the West, which brought America into direct conflict with the Soviet Union.

Even before midcentury, *Animal Farm* had become a minor classic in the United States. Celebrated as a short, accessible tale of Bolshevik history precisely when the anti-Communist "Red Scare" years were reaching their crescendo, the fable's vogue was aided by the Cold War success of nonfiction counterparts such as the memoirs of Louis Budenz (*Men Without Faces: The Communist Conspiracy in America*, 1950) and Bella Dodd (*School of Darkness: The Record of a Life of Conflicts Between Two Faiths*, 1954). Scarcely a high school or college student anywhere in America in the 1950s did not encounter *Animal Farm* as an assigned reading. Orwell's cleverness with words and his recognition of the significance of slogans created catchphrases that were soon bandied and bleated everywhere to impugn the grand wartime image of a Mother Russia guided by Uncle Joe. "All animals are equal, but some are more equal than others" captured in an arresting sentence the nightmare regime of hypocrisy and bureaucracy into which the still-heralded Bolshevik Revolution had devolved.

Not only did Orwell's success with *Animal Farm* make him financially secure, but also, according to his good friend, the British anarchist George Woodcock, it mellowed him. He no longer had any problems getting his work published and in fact found himself in demand for writing articles and reviews. In America he contributed to the *Atlantic* and even the *New Republic*, which had finally become suspicious of the Soviet Union, and in his last years wrote as frequently for American publications as for English ones.

Books as Bombshells

I have dwelt at length on *Animal Farm*'s éclat in the United States (soon followed on the wider international scene) because the book is often patronized as "a classroom assignment for junior high pupils." Nor are the circumstances of its extraordinary publishing success, which was much indebted to the changing postwar political climate in the United States, nearly so well known as the reception history of his acknowledged *chef d'oeuvre* published fewer than three years later, *Nineteen Eighty-Four*. Indeed Orwell's ingenious "little squib" stands in the dark, encompassing, ever-lengthening shadow of its towering, flawed successor—an unfortunate case of a *magnum opus* upstaging an *opuscule magnifique*. And quite unjustly so. But Clio is not always concerned with dispensing literary "justice."

Be that as it may, *Animal Farm*'s sensational reception in America paved the way for the stunning impact of *Nineteen Eighty-Four* on the reading public as well as the literary intelligentsia. Orwell's American publisher, Harcourt Brace, retitled the novel *1984*—a diabolically ironic case of what could be termed numerical Newspeak. (Nonetheless, since I refer here to the American edition, I will accede to its *doubleplusungood* abridged title.)

If anything, *1984* occasioned even greater praise than *Animal Farm* and came to exert a far greater worldwide impact. In hindsight, it is as if the atom bomb of *Animal Farm* exploded on the cultural front in 1945–1946, followed by the hydrogen bomb of *1984* three years later. With these two bombshells, Orwell gave Western intellectuals an exclusive ideological atomic option, as it were, a first-strike capability against ex-Comrade Napoleon, his pig tyranny, and all their cultural co-conspirators. As if to confirm the genius of these twin masterpieces and Orwell's status as the Dr. Frankenstein (or Robert Oppenheimer?) of the age,[4] the Trotskyist (and sometime Stalin apologist) Isaac Deutscher could bemoan that *1984* had become by 1955 "an ideological superweapon" in the Cold War of words.

Irving Howe has noted in his essay on *1984*, "History as Nightmare," that readers have a reluctance to reread some books, no matter how impressive they are. Orwell's *1984* is such a work. Its gloomy forecast of the future is almost too vivid and too horrifying to contemplate. That was not the case with *Animal Farm*, which "cushioned" the cruelties of the Russian Revolution within the satirical allegory of an animal story. (Yet less discerning readers— such as the editors of Dial Press—failed to grasp the satire because of the aesthetic "padding" of the beast fable.[5]) The world of *1984* was Orwell's gray vision of what a totalitarian society would look like after decades of protracted war between the West and the communist sphere, a war of rationing, shortages, distortions of the truth, and the killing of innocent people. Indeed the "nightmare" of *1984* has obsessed and petrified millions of people who have never even actually read the book. As Harold Rosenberg states: "The tone of the post-war imagination was set by Orwell's *1984*: since the appearance of that work, [the theme of] the 'dehumanized collective' haunts our thoughts."[6]

Like *Animal Farm*, *Nineteen Eighty-Four* derived from Orwell's personal experience. Always sensitive to linguistic subterfuge and manipulation of history, Orwell had seen how the events of the Spanish Civil War and Russia's role in World War II had been distorted, or "rectified," for ideological purposes. In *1984*, Orwell showed insight into the future superior to that of most of his contemporaries. Hitler had burned books, but henceforth totalitarian regimes would simply rewrite them, Orwell predicted—a process already underway in Russia.

The texture of lived experience in *1984* also revealed the extent to which Orwell possessed a bourgeois sensibility, as his bleak depictions of the regimentation and impersonalization of life in Oceania and the destruction of the individual under totalitarianism portray. Both the nostalgia that imbues the novel and its lament for forgotten traditions generate a mood that resonated with a conservative political interpretation. Moreover, the anti-Communist cultural climate made it inevitable that the book's conservative strain would be narrowly politicized, so that *1984* would be taken less as a vision of the bureaucratic modern state of the near future and more as an antisocialist broadside. Its conservatism appealed to right-wing opponents of progressivism generally and enemies of Soviet communism in particular.

When it was published in June 1949, *1984* was another Book-of-the-Month Club selection (and a *London Evening News* Choice in the U.K. as well). Eventually it rose to No. 3 on the *New York Times* best seller list during 1949. It sold 190,000 copies as a Book-of-the-Month Club choice during 1949–1952 and became an American best seller in 1951 when it appeared as a Signet paperback. *Reader's Digest* also condensed it—a sure sign that Orwell had gained wide popular acceptance in America. The reviews there were uniformly favorable. Unlike *Animal Farm*, *1984* was well received even in the leftist journals of opinion. After the Berlin blockade, the Communist *coup d'état* in Czechoslovakia, and the first signs of Russian espionage, Orwell's projection of the future no longer seemed so unreal to the American Left.

Orwell was disturbed by the way both *Animal Farm* and *1984* were used by conservatives as indictments of British socialism and often protested this interpretation of his writings. Yet even after the practice had begun to occur with *Animal Farm*, he did not remotely fathom how ruthlessly the concepts and catchwords of *1984* would be appropriated and stockpiled by those with diametrically opposed views to become an arsenal of antisocialist "superweapons."[7] What made the (selective) quotation of Orwell's lines so effective was the fact that they came from a man whose own leftist credentials were beyond dispute. His early death at the dawn of the Red Scare facilitated right-wing misrepresentations of his urgent warnings about socialism's dangers. Though censuring socialism for its failures in the modern world was never Orwell's main aim, this crude verdict—"socialist turncoat"—has long been leveled at him, especially by the Marxist Left.

The Unified Vision of a Somber Visionary

The Cold War formed the environment that enabled Orwell to seize the imagination of the American public.[8] Unfortunately, Orwell's major impact on Americans came essentially through his final pair of fictions. As a result, his other work was read through the prism of his somber twin visions. His critical essays—which include pioneering examinations of topics as varied as English postcards, Rudyard Kipling, and the art of the murder mystery— have often been read in the United States as eccentric appendages to his fearsome fantasies. This is regrettable. In fact, I would contend that his forte was the essay, which was supremely well suited to the crisp, clear prose style that he had mastered. He liked championing unpopular causes, and he could make a case with incisive force in the form of a short, concentrated fusillade of prose.

Orwell conceived *Animal Farm* and *1984* as complementary works that would pack a devastating one-two punch against totalitarianism in general and Stalinism in particular—indeed against the betrayal of revolutionary dreams generally and against the Russian Revolution in particular. It often goes unnoticed even by discerning readers that *Animal Farm* and *1984* form a unified whole, not only thematically but also in terms of structure and plot development. Orwell's satiric dystopia represents an unorthodox sequel to his fable. For *1984* opens where *Animal Farm* ends: the pigs are in control. They have become fully humanized. They are now the Inner Party and Outer Party members (with occasional gadfly exceptions, such as rebellious Winston and Julia).

Napoleon has morphed into Big Brother, Snowball has become Emmanuel Goldstein, and the Seven Commandments of Animalism have been transformed into the catchphrases of Hate Week and the famous slogans in Newspeak. The pigs' tyrannical fiefdom of *Animal Farm* is now Airstrip One, the metropolitan capital of the Party's empire of Oceania. Any reader may easily elaborate on these analogues.

The larger point is obvious. It is all one vision. Orwell's fable and dystopia succeed as carefully crafted works that interweave the artistic and the political, the literary and the polemical. They are the masterpieces of a great writer and political adept, and they are also unforgettable mindscapes of the ultimate horrors to which dictatorial power may lead. Orwell could with complete justice joke not long after the publication of *Animal Farm*, as he enjoyed the laudatory reviews and the congratulations voiced by colleagues, that readers had not appreciated his achievement sufficiently. He groused in mock disappointment: "Nobody said it was a beautiful book."

Indeed it *is* a beautiful book. Its successor *1984* is not. Rather, it is a bleak, horrifying, oppressive book. It brilliantly projects a social vision, but—as Irving Howe granted—it is certainly not a book that one looks forward to rereading.

All that notwithstanding, these final two works assure Orwell's place in literature. Like all great writers he understood human nature profoundly. His honesty and his hatred of all cant—what we today would dub "political correctness"—attract new readers as each generation comes to maturity. If he was originally welcomed in the United States for dubious reasons, time has shown the enduring validity and vitality of his artistic and political mission, as he declared about *Animal Farm*, "to fuse political and artistic purpose into one whole."

Yes, time has shown how well Orwell fulfilled this grand mission. Not just his twin masterpieces but his full *oeuvre*—the life as well as the letters—represent "all one vision." *Le style, c'est l'homme.* Or rather, as Proust expressed it in *Le temps retrouvé*: "For the writer just as much as for the painter, style is a matter not of technique but of vision."

A SIGNET CLASSIC • CQ552 • 95c

GEORGE
1984
ORWELL

A SIGNET CLASSIC • CQ552 • 95c

Chapter 5

A "Utopian" Edition of a Dystopian Classic

Nineteen Eighty-Four at 70

Nineteen Eighty-Four is one the best-selling novels of all time, with a sales total of 30 million copies in at least five dozen languages. Just as *anno* 1984 was 35 years from 1949, we today stand 35 years beyond 1984. The relevance of Orwell's novel, with its protean associations, has proven enduring, transcending its Cold War context and acquiring ever-expanding, far-reaching applications as the drone-cum-digital age proceeds. Likewise the afterlife of the author of *Nineteen Eighty-Four*, who died in January 1950, just seven months after his intellectual H-bomb detonated on both sides of the Atlantic, shows all signs of moving robustly through literary history well beyond the biblical three score and ten. Not only has Orwell's dystopia permanently blackened a segment of time, but its vision—and its scarifying catchwords—certainly seem evergreen (or ever-ebony).

So it is hardly surprising that several English-language editions of *Nineteen Eighty-Four* have been published since the 1950s and are currently on the market. The vast majority of them, ever

FIGURE 8. The Signet *1984* commemorative edition, printed on January 1, 1983, the unofficial start date of the ballyhooed countdown to 1984. The new edition featured a foreword by newscaster Walter Cronkite and an afterword by Erich Fromm, psychoanalyst and author of *The Art of Loving*.

since the novel's initial publication in June 1949, have been issued without a preface or introduction, apparently with the assumption that the novel is easily understandable and requires no guidance for the reader. That blithe assumption was questionable from the beginning, and it is completely misconceived as we approach the third decade of the twenty-first century. On its seventieth anniversary, might we interrogate that premise?

First, however, we should examine how this casual assumption has manifested itself in a few well-known editions of the novel that do include some form of commentary. Beginning in the 1950s, Orwell's publishers recruited psychologists and well-known authors to write briefly about the novel for what we may think of as "celebrity" editions. The Russian émigré psychoanalyst Gregory Zilboorg wrote an afterword for the Signet edition in the late 1950s. A few years later another Signet edition included an afterword by Erich Fromm, a German émigré, psychologist, and author of widely selling books such as *The Art of Loving*. The Orwell centennial in 2003 witnessed a new edition of *Nineteen Eighty-Four* that featured a foreword by Thomas Pynchon and an afterword by Fromm. Celebrities with no literary background or scholarly pedigree also have been enlisted to write introductions. The popular television newsman Walter Cronkite introduced Harcourt, Brace and Jovanovitch's 1983 edition of *Nineteen Eighty-Four*. At the opposite extreme is the massive scholarly apparatus attached to the facsimile edition by Peter Davison. It contains Orwell's corrections to the text in detail in a large quarto version, thus showing the reader the painstaking way in which Orwell revised his manuscript.

I regret to say that the common feature among all these otherwise welcome editions of *Nineteen Eighty-Four* is that they provide little or no assistance to the reader as he or she struggles to understand and appreciate the book. But wait! Is such assistance really necessary? Isn't George Orwell the famed master of the "plain" style? Isn't he "England's Prose Laureate," as I title the next chapter of this study? Isn't he the writer prized as the greatest English-language essayist of the twentieth century, the equal of Johnson, Edmund Burke, and Hazlitt? After all, he is the author who, in one of his most widely read essays ("Why I Write"), exalted a literary standard that countless writers have honored: "Good prose is like a windowpane." Right?

Indeed he is. Yet let us not forget another simple fact, the nonpecuniary implications of which are blithely ignored by publishers: George Orwell is also the author of *Nineteen Eighty-Four*. By that I mean that his achievements as a writer represent a paradox that is not so "plain" and "simple" to understand. The paradox is both endlessly fascinating and fraught with potential for confusion. Let me elaborate on the causes of this paradox and its accompanying confusions—which should be thematized in any introduction to the novel.

The Orwell "Paradox"

The vision in *Nineteen Eighty-Four* of a nightmare state of social uniformity in which official policy systematically aims to destroy language was written by an author who insisted (in his most famous essay, "Politics and the English Language") that political reform start by ensuring that language ("the verbal end") draw precise distinctions and communicate truths. The writer who loved the richness and nuances of so-called Oldspeak was also the one who advocated simplicity to the point of offering six easy writing "rules" that "will cover most cases." The writer whose inventions of thoughtcrime, Newspeak, and diabolical doublespeak were encapsulated in the charged slogans of *Nineteen Eighty-Four* is the same one who denounced bureaucratese and deceptive euphemism in essays such as "Politics and the English Language."

Readers unfamiliar with Orwell's work apart from *Nineteen Eighty-Four* need to understand that the novel represented everything that he as a man—and, above all, as a writer—abhorred. For he was not only the author of a nightmarish, tyrannical dystopia, but also the author of the famously plainspoken essays, documentaries, and journalism. His relation to language—a prime source of the "paradox" of Orwell—must be seen in light of both achievements. Orwell sought fresh, powerful figures of speech and precise expression ("to write less picturesquely and more exactly"). He wanted, as it were, the simplicity and economy of Newspeak without its distortions and semantic impoverishment. He was both an engaged pamphleteer and an immaculate stylist. And both the great essayist and the architect of Newspeak knew well— and voiced with indelible power—Maupassant's sacred dictum: "Words have a soul."[1]

In light of this profound tension in Orwell's work between what are sometimes called "art" and "propaganda"—that is, between the transparent, plain stylist and the ingenious polemicist—we ought now to reconsider the misfortune that all available editions of *Nineteen Eighty-Four* omit an introduction or include only a superficial one. That was regrettable even in the 1950s, as the complicated cultural politics of the Cold War rendered the novel less and less accessible to its audience, which expanded far beyond intellectual circles to millions of school-age readers and the broader public. Even the (apparently harmless) practice of telescoping Orwell's 18-letter title down to four fearsome digits—the intimidating 1-9-8-4 bannered on the covers of all American and non-British editions—reflects an ironic form of Newspeak that Orwell would surely have derided. (And even he would have failed to prophesy that the John Birch Society would hijack 1-9-8-4 to use in its Washington office telephone number.)

How (Not) to (Re)Publish a Classic?

And what about us today? I regard the absence of a substantive introduction to the novel as a major opportunity to issue a new edition that would attract and enlighten the current generation of readers as well as future audiences. The need for a substantive, historically informed introduction is even more urgent and important in our time than it was during the early Cold War era. Because the world of the first quarter of the twenty-first century differs so dramatically from the 1940s, with the reference points and standard nomenclature of the postwar West having gone down the cultural memory hole, the absence of substantial auxiliary material to guide readers represents a notable shortcoming. The lack of firm guidance about the history and politics of Orwell's era is based on the unwarranted assumption that contemporary student readers can readily access the novel, which is unrealistic—if not laughable—today. Readers are left with short commentaries that either are ornamental, merely adorning the work, or glide through one or two pet themes of the celebrity, psychologist, or political scientist. Or, if the commentator is a truly famous celebrity (like Cronkite), a series of loosely described comparisons between Orwell's world and our own are delivered, never failing to characterize Orwell as a dark or bitter or prescient "prophet."

The only substantive edition conceived at a level easily accessible to the general reader is *Nineteen Eighty-Four: Text, Sources, Criticism*, edited by Irving Howe. Published in 1963, it has been out of print for decades. It numbers 400 pages in a large paperback format, and its targeted audience is advanced college/university students. The volume consists largely of essays and criticism on the *au courant* Cold War topic of totalitarianism by scholars such as Carl Friedrich and Zbigniew Brzezinski, with excerpts from Hannah Arendt's landmark study, *The Origins of Totalitarianism*

(1951), also featured. With the exception of reprinted material by Howe himself, little direct attention is given to Orwell and *Nineteen Eighty-Four*. Needless to say, such an approach is hopelessly out of date in today's geopolitical and cultural climate. Apart from all that, Howe's edition provides no textual annotations or introduction to the novel.

An expensive scholarly edition of the novel published by Clarendon Press in the United Kingdom in 1984 and edited by Orwell's first biographer, Bernard Crick, has also long been out of print. Clarendon, an imprint of Oxford University Press, is noted for its scholarly editions of fiction classics, but Oxford never published this edition in the United States. (It was, however, distributed in the American market.) Expensively priced at £35 (equivalent to £133 or $123 in 2020 currencies), it was primarily purchased by libraries and professors, not students or the wider public. Heavily annotated and boasting a 136-page introduction, the edition is exhaustive—and exhausting!—in its pursuit of thoroughness. Richly informative, it unfortunately suffers from numerous misspellings, typographical errors, and small factual mistakes. Moreover, while Crick, a political scientist, is strong on the novel's historical background, ideological critique, and social satire, he is weak on literary and stylistic matters.

A Modest Proposal

No authoritative and accessible edition of the novel has ever been available to the public. Instead the vacuum has been filled by punditry and polemics about its meaning—and by loose cannoneering that fires off its catchphrases in all ideological directions. As a result, it is no wonder that *Nineteen Eighty-Four* is usually honored (or dishonored) in the breach. In our 15-nanosecondsof-fame, evanescent, sound-bite culture, Orwell's coinages are endlessly in the headlines, on the airwaves, and on the lips of pundits and polemicists—and his serious political and social themes are ignored or misconceived. Any new edition of *Nineteen Eighty-Four* must take these unfortunate realities as its starting point and feature a judicious reading of the novel that is fully cognizant of both Orwell's literary accomplishment and the work's controversial, confused reception history.

Having taught *Nineteen Eighty-Four* to hundreds of undergraduate and graduate students, as well as lectured about it to hundreds of high school students, I have noticed how young people struggle to grasp its crucial elements of parody and numerous satiric referents. Moreover, having published several books about Orwell's life and legacy—an extraordinary, unprecedented "afterlife" of enormous influence largely attributable to the lasting significance of *Nineteen Eighty-Four*—I also have a few other ideas about how a new edition should be conceived.

So let me speak quite personally about this prospect. First, however, we must grapple with a practical obstacle: publishing rights. The major stumbling block—unless Orwell's current publishers decide to proceed with a new special edition (as Harcourt did with the Howe edition)—is cost.[2] As the Clarendon Press edition exemplifies, such a volume, undertaken by an outside publisher forced to pay for permission rights, would inevitably be priced beyond the means of most readers.[3]

One strategy would be to publish a new edition in those countries where the novel is already in the public domain. The problem with that approach, however, is that these literary markets are small: Canada, South Africa, and Australia are the only English-language markets available.[4] Yet a ray of hope does exist. According to the U.K. copyright laws revised in 2013, a published work enters the public domain 70 years after its author's death. If an enterprising publisher commissions an edition and plans a launch date for 2020 or thereafter (70 years after Orwell's death in 1950), a sufficiently sizable international market that now includes the U.K. would make a profitable new edition plausible. (The novel does not enter the public domain in the United States until 2044. American copyright law for works published between 1923 and 1963 guarantees them copyright protection, with renewal notice, for 95 years after the original U.S. publication date [i.e., June 1949 in the case of Orwell's dystopia].)

Let us assume that a public domain edition excluding the American market might prove enticing to some such enterprising publisher. How could that edition best serve student and general readers today?

Here is a modest proposal. Ever since the presidential inauguration in January 2017, *Nineteen Eighty-Four*, a book originally published in 1949, has stood atop (or near the top) of the fiction best seller lists—truly an unrivaled event in publishing history. Even more astonishing, this is not the first occasion of its postpublication best seller status in either Britain or America, or in both, but rather the mind-boggling fourth—after the 1954 BBC-TV adaptation, the "countdown to 1984" in 1983–1984, and the 2003 centenary of Orwell's birth.[5]

The continued best seller status of *Nineteen Eighty-Four* serves as a reminder that any reissued "utopian" edition should be—to use a popular present-day locution that Orwell's keenly attuned ear would have found jarring—"reader-friendly." (Orwell had a healthy form of what I might term literary hyperacusis.) Above all, such a new edition should be accessible to students and other interested readers. The language of the novel is not difficult, but it is impossible to appreciate or even understand its richness and depth without grasping in detail its context, both historical and political. One easily forgets that the book is a satire on the early postwar world, focused on the geopolitical conflict that was already becoming known as the Cold War. All of Orwell's famous coinages—Big Brother, 2 + 2 = 5, Newspeak, and so on—are satirical references linked to the 1930s and 1940s that the original British audience in 1949 would likely have recognized and valued. So an edition should first and foremost attempt to recover this historical and political context, which is indispensable for grasping the main themes of the novel and the controversies that erupted after its publication and Orwell's death.

I believe that such an edition of Orwell's brilliant dystopia, equipped with a full and detailed explication of its rich historical context, would serve the reading public well, especially younger readers. I have discovered over the years that young people harbor, at best, only a vague idea of what transpired in the 1930s and 1940s, the key periods on which Orwell drew in imagining the world of his novel. Today's readers lack historical knowledge of World War II and the wider political events that serve as its background. A basic grasp of that history is an essential prerequisite for appreciating the novel.

This is not a small point. It is, however, such a simple one that ignoring or casually downplaying it represents a terrible error. Like *Animal Farm*, *Nineteen Eighty-Four* is a satire—and even modest comprehension of its imaginative world entails knowing what the satire is satirizing. To understand Orwell's referents, however, does not mean to focus on the historical context of *Nineteen Eighty-Four* alone. Rather, as *Nineteen Eighty-Four* turns 70 and enters its eighth decade of influence on and salience to contemporary culture, a worthwhile new edition should also address its biographical, psychological, and other pertinent contexts, both in an introduction and probably also in a series of appendices—all of which I believe are crucial for comprehending the novel fully. Among the priorities should be a detailed overview of Orwell's

FIGURE 9. The equation 2 + 2 = 5 symbolizes O'Brien's torture and brainwashing of Winston in Room 101 of the Ministry of Love. Why did Orwell choose that symbol?

One answer has to do with the message of this official Soviet government poster of 1931. The poster was part of a propaganda drive aiming to accelerate the national campaign to fulfill the prescribed norms of the USSR's centralized planned economy, codified in the first Five-Year Plan, which Stalin had launched with much fanfare in 1928. Literally translated, the two captions read: "The arithmetic of the Five-Year Plan" (top right) and "Add the enthusiasm of the workers" (bottom left).

The message? Exceed your work norm, Soviet "heroes of labor"! Fulfill Stalin's grand prediction that the USSR will meet its production goals ahead of schedule! Let "2 + 2 = 5"! (Notice also that the enlarged "5" contains images of an industrial steelworks, evoking the association with Joseph Stalin, whose adopted surname in Russian means "man of steel.")

Bannered on billboards throughout the USSR, this poster was designed by graphic artist Yakov Guminer, who starved to death in 1942 when the invading German armies blockaded Leningrad.

life and times, a nuanced presentation of the ideological issues that shaped his career, and a full discussion of the controversy surrounding *Nineteen Eighty-Four*, which began within days of its publication. An estimable commentary should also devote attention to the politics of Orwell's reputation, especially the political claims to his legacy staked by both the Left and the Right.[6]

What are a few examples of the kinds of satirical allusions and literary references that are invariably lost to present-day readers, even literate ones? Jeffrey Meyers and Bernard Crick have assiduously catalogued a wide variety of such citations in the novel. Consider, for instance:

- Big Brother's mustachioed visage is a composite of Stalin and Field Marshal Lord Kitchener.
- The caption "Big Brother Is Watching You" recalls the famous recruiting poster of 1914 in which a finger-pointing Kitchener glares: "Your Country Needs YOU."
- Victory Square is an analogue to Trafalgar Square, and Big Brother replaces Nelson atop its column.
- Newspeak, which aims to diminish the range of thought by reducing its linguistic resources, is a riff on C. K. Ogden's Basic English.
- The Ministry of Truth resembles the BBC's Broadcast House during the war, where Orwell worked as the producer for the Indian section of the BBC's Eastern Service on the first floor (down the hall from Room 101).
- The Floating Fortress in Oceania refers both to the Flying Fortress of the American air forces during World War II and also to the Floating Island in *Gulliver's Travels* that breaks the will of recalcitrant individuals.
- The division of the world into three rival superstates— Oceania, Eurasia, and Eastasia—is based on James Burnham's *The Managerial Revolution* (1941), a sociologist's

vision of the near-future, post–World War II era in which a technocratic elite of totalitarian ideologues rules the globe.

- The brainwashed Winston's defeatist admission that "2 + 2 = 5" alludes to the billboards erected in major Soviet cities during the 1930s that urged the citizenry to work harder and fulfill the prescribed norms of the first Five-Year Plan ahead of time (i.e., in four years, not five).

- Winston's despairing line, "We are the dead," which both the telescreen and Julia repeat when the couple is arrested by the Thought Police, echoes the recrimination voiced by a corpse in a poem popular during World War I, "In Flanders Fields."[7]

- Like Communist Party members in the Soviet Union and elsewhere, Inner and Outer Party members in Oceania are called "comrade."

- Sexual intercourse in Oceania is for procreation only ("Our Duty to the Party"), which nods to the puritanical, state-controlled doctrines about sexuality propagandized in Stalin's USSR.

- As O'Brien tortures Winston in Room 101, he expresses with exhilaration his sadistic power hunger: "Imagine a boot stamping on a human face—forever." That famous line evokes Jack London's *The Iron Heel*, especially its protagonist's doomsday prophecy that "the Iron Heel will walk upon our faces."[8]

Certain examples of Orwell's satirical allusions have biographical relevance, rather than historical and political significance, and even sometimes are, as it were, private jokes or "insider gossip"— yet are no less important to the fictional satire. For instance, the BBC was a division of the Ministry of Information (MOI), known as "Miniform" in telex jargon (recalling, of course, *Minitru* and *Miniluv* in *Nineteen Eighty-Four*). The MOI's director was Brendan Bracken, whom BBC insiders and *au courant* Londoners dubbed "B.B." Orwell would joke with fellow BBC staffers and his wife Eileen, who worked in the MOI Censorship Department until 1944, that he had never seen "B.B." and was skeptical of his existence (just as his readers are meant to doubt the reality of Big Brother).

As I mentioned, my suggestions throughout this chapter are based on my experience of having taught Orwell's novel to a wide range of student readers. I am well aware of the gaps in cultural literacy among not only freshmen and sophomore college students, but also even Ph.D. students (who are often sophisticated readers of good literature yet lack basic historical knowledge of the recent past). This kind of help is also needed today not only by students, but also by mature, ostensibly well-informed adult readers of *Nineteen Eighty-Four*. If any republication of Orwell's dystopian classic is to effectively assist its audience of millions of classroom student and adult readers, its editorial design must draw on educators with such experience. I would even suggest the formation of an interdisciplinary advisory editorial board. Composed of secondary school and university educators who represent the broad range of fields that the novel addresses (literature, history, sociology, political thought, cultural studies, etc.) and who possess some background as teachers of and/or writers to the proposed target audiences, this board could serve as a useful "sounding board" for the designated editor. It should be not an editorial collective (on the socialist state model) that operates by committee consensus (and thus all too often reduces its work to a lowest-common-denominator hodgepodge), but rather simply a group of scholar-teachers to whom the editor and publisher can reach out for counsel and criticism.

Fundamentally, I am deeply committed to providing "context," not just "text." I believe that good literature teachers need to be good historians—and, frankly, vice versa. That is especially the case when dealing with a writer such as Orwell, who was almost the polar opposite of an "art for art's sake" writer, his concern for good prose style notwithstanding.

Reputation, Legacy, Historiography

Present-day readers should therefore also be guided to look very closely at the reception of *Nineteen Eighty-Four* by Orwell's contemporaries. This emphasis, which should form a central part of a pedagogically sensitive approach to writers such as Orwell, illuminates his work in numerous valuable ways. We can only understand Orwell in the present by seeing how earlier generations of readers—above all, his contemporaries—understood him.

I also believe that student readers especially benefit when they encounter a classic that is presented not just as a dry "school assignment," but as a work of art relevant to their lives. How does one do that with a book written long before they were born—and by an author now dead for seven decades?

Answer: One looks at the "afterlife" of each of them: the author and the book. In the case of George Orwell and *Nineteen Eighty-Four*, that means readers should be told in the editorial apparatus about the emergence of Orwell's checkered, "paradoxical" reputation and posthumous fame and provided a brief history of Orwell's "afterlife" through the new millennium. They should be informed about how Orwell's vision and catchwords have shaped their social and cultural lives—and promise to influence the shape of things to come.

Regardless of whether or not readers possess the literary skills necessary to enjoy Orwell's dystopia, they will require guidance to understand the complexity of *Nineteen Eighty-Four*. By situating it in the context of the times in which it was written and carefully annotating the text with brief and concise footnotes, the extraordinary impact of *Nineteen Eighty-Four* when it appeared and Orwell's unique "afterlife" can make "*Nineteen Eighty-Four* at 70" freshly available to audiences in the twenty-first century.

CHAPTER 6

England's Prose Laureate

Novel or Nothing?

And what about Orwell the sharp-eyed reporter, the virtuoso essayist, the still-unrivaled dean of nonfiction "prose like a windowpane" and scourge of jargon, the Defender of the King's English? After all, Orwell wrote not just fiction, but also reportage, critical and personal essays, film commentary, and BBC radio broadcast scripts, along with hundreds of book reviews, newspaper columns, and other pieces of occasional journalism. Although his active literary career spanned only 18 years, his *Complete Works* runs to 21 volumes, a remarkable output for such a relatively brief period as a published writer, especially given the fact that Orwell's health was poor for much of the time.

As we mentioned in earlier chapters during our discussion of Eric Blair's youth and literary development, after serving five years with the Indian Imperial Police as a junior officer in Burma (1921–1926), Blair determined that he would become a writer. He struggled for years to learn his craft before his first publishing success, a nonfiction work interlaced with memoir and imaginative fiction entitled *Down and Out in Paris and London* (1933). It was a fine debut for "George Orwell," but, like most ambitious writers of his generation, he believed that "writing" really meant writing novels. As Cynthia Ozick once phrased it in a memoir of her erstwhile teacher Lionel Trilling, who published a lone novel and felt ashamed that he had "settled" for becoming a "critic": "For Trilling, it was 'novel or nothing.'" Likewise for Eric Blair.

We noted in Chapter 3 that Blair/Orwell never regarded the literary achievement of his essay "A Hanging," published 18 months before *Down and Out*, as an artistic breakthrough or significant landmark in his maturation. It was "merely" a short piece of nonfiction that made use of fictional elements and devices. Rather, as Orwell stated years later in "Why I Write," he had in his youth always "wanted to write enormous naturalistic novels with unhappy endings."

Between 1933 and 1939 Orwell completed four realistic, rather traditional novels: *Burmese Days* (1933), *A Clergyman's Daughter* (1934), *Keep the Aspidistra Flying* (1936), and *Coming Up for Air* (1939). All four have autobiographical elements; Orwell lacked the imaginative talent in his early fiction to reach beyond his own experiences for inspiration. The novels are conventional in format, with Orwell occasionally attempting to use modernistic, quasi-Joycean narrative techniques. A section of dialogue in *A Clergyman's Daughter*, for example, borrows directly from the "Nighttown" scene in *Ulysses*. All four novels also treat issues of class. Orwell was obsessed by the class problem in England, seeing in it the root of most of the country's problems. Virtually everything he wrote in the 1930s, whether in the form of fiction or nonfiction, addresses the problem of class.

Orwell's traditional novels have been largely neglected, if not denigrated. Because of its bitter critique of British imperialism, *Burmese Days* occasionally finds its way into courses dealing with imperialism in literature. *Keep the Aspidistra Flying*, the most autobiographical of the novels, served in the 1950s as inspiration for the Angry Young Men of that decade (John Osborne, Kingsley Amis, John Wain, Allan Sillitoe, John Braine). Orwell's fiction of the 1930s is also the subject of Loraine Saunders's *The Unsung Artistry of George Orwell: The Novels from* Burmese Days *to* Nineteen Eighty-Four (2008), which argues that Orwell's fictional accomplishments were considerable even before his international triumph with *Animal Farm*.

From England to Spain: Documenting Injustice

What really established Orwell as a recognized author were his documentary writings of the late 1930s, what he called his "semisociological" prose: *The Road to Wigan Pier* (1937) and *Homage to Catalonia* (1938). Unlike his fiction, in which Orwell struggled to find his métier, his documentary writings reveal a pared-down, deceptively simple prose style shorn of literary flourish or ornamentation, a style he further refined in his first-rate essays of the 1940s. Each was groundbreaking in a different way.

Wigan Pier pioneered a style of investigative journalism that had become commonplace by the 1960s and 1970s yet was highly original in the 1930s. Reviewing the first American edition in 1958, Dwight Macdonald called Orwell's investigation of poverty in the midst of the Depression "the best sociological reporting I know." The book is divided into two sections. Part One is a powerful portrait of the ravages of the Depression in a hard-hit section of northern England. It exhibits Orwell's gift for descriptive prose, which he first demonstrated in several scenes in *Down and Out in Paris and London*. His portrait of a young woman attempting to clear a blocked pipe has become a classic: She was "poking a stick up the leaden waste-pipe.... I had time to see everything about her—her sacking apron, her clumsy clogs, her arm reddened by the cold.... She has a round pale face, the usual exhausted face of the slum girl who is twenty-five and looks forty, thanks to miscarriages and drudgery." The second section contains Orwell's analysis of socialism's failure to capture a major following among the English public. He argues that Labour Party activists are elitist and castigates British socialists for failing to understand the working classes.

Even though it was a financial failure, Orwell was proud of *Homage to Catalonia*, which describes how the Communists betrayed the revolution by following Joseph Stalin's orders to prolong the war in order to weaken the capitalist nations of Europe. Orwell had gone to Spain to fight against fascism, only to discover when he returned to England that the portrayal of events in Spain had been distorted by Communists and their fellow-travelers on the Left. Seeing how the war was reported in the left-wing English press, Orwell wrote in his essay "Looking Back on the Spanish War" that "the very concept of objective truth is fading out of the world." Here again is evidence that the seeds of *Animal Farm* and *Nineteen Eighty-Four* lie in Orwell's Spanish testament.

The British Left's derision of his writings about Spain, along with what he saw as the English intelligentsia's slavish adherence to the Communist Party line, set in motion the process of turning Orwell into an obdurate anti-Stalinist and anti-Communist. If Spain thus completed Orwell's mature political education, however, it did so not only in a negative but also in a positive sense, for it transformed him into a "democratic Socialist." Orwell told his friend, the critic Cyril Connolly, that he saw "wonderful things" in Spain and "at last really believe in Socialism, which I never did before."

Orwell's socialism was highly idiosyncratic. He was clearly a man of the Left but was suspicious of those fellow leftists whom he saw increasingly as apologists for Communism. His Spanish experiences also deepened his tendency, first apparent in *The Road to Wigan Pier*, of attacking his fellow leftists as hypocrites for not practicing what they preached. Orwell emerged from Spain an unrelenting critic of his fellow socialists.

By the late 1930s, Orwell had established a reputation as a coming intellectual and junior man of letters, a writer skilled in several subgenres of prose. His talents shone most radiantly by the early 1940s in the essay form, whether critical or personal. It was in the essay that Orwell first perfected the direct, clear prose style that distinguishes his best writing.

Combining elements of the personal essay and the fictional sketch, Orwell could draw directly on his own experiences even more than he did in his fiction. Just as in "A Hanging," where Orwell crafts an unforgettable dramatic narrative while at the same time drawing a universal message, "Shooting An Elephant" (1936) encapsulates the evils of imperialism. The narrator yearns to spare the elephant, but he must kill it or lose face with the Burmese, something a white man in the East couldn't afford to do. As the ashamed narrator confesses, for the first time, he

> grasped the hollowness, the futility of the white man's dominion in the East.... I was only an absurd puppet ... the conventional figure of a sahib. For it is the condition of his rule that he shall spend his life trying to impress "the natives," and so in every crisis he has to do what "the natives" expect of him.... My whole life, every white man's life in the East, is one long struggle not to be laughed at.

During the decade that followed this second *tour de force* blending personal essay with fictional narrative, Orwell wrote a series of fine literary essays on figures who interested him: Charles Dickens, Rudyard Kipling, Henry Miller, George Gissing, and William Butler Yeats, among others. In each case he took strong, if unconventional, stances. He defended Kipling from left-wing charges of being a jingoist and a fascist, noting that Kipling never romanticized war. In "Inside the Whale," which addressed literature between the wars, he praised Miller, who had been labeled a "pornographer" by many critics for his "obscene" novels *Tropic of Cancer* and *Black Monday*, for writing about real people and real situations. Orwell regarded him as "the only imaginative prose writer ... who has appeared among the English-speaking races for some years."

Above all, however, Orwell strongly identified with the writer who could be called England's nineteenth-century laureate of prose (fiction), Charles Dickens. Orwell's outstanding essay "Charles Dickens" (1939) is one of his finest prose achievements. It is frequently quoted, not only for its opener that Dickens is "well worth stealing" (which has become truer of Orwell since his death in 1950), but also for its closer about "smelly little orthodoxies" and statements about Dickens such as "He is always preaching and his sermons are excellent." Orwell admired Dickens's literary skill and found his sense of moral outrage appealing.[1]

One of Orwell's most quoted postwar essays, "Politics and the English Language" (1946), reflects his growing concern about the corruption of language, a preoccupation that would later surface in *Nineteen Eighty-Four*. In this essay he offers six rules for clear writing, such as "Never use a long word when a short one will suffice" and "Use the active rather than the passive voice." These rules were widely quoted and found their way into the curricula of English courses in the United States. The antinomian sixth rule was typical of the schoolboy gadfly Blair and the heterodox radical Orwell—"Break any of these rules sooner than say anything outright barbarous."

Orwell was far from the first writer to worry about how civic society, as a corporate body of living language, suffers when language is abused. Just as Thucydides implicated the crisis of public language in the fall of Athens into anarchy, so too did Cato the Younger during the Catiline Conspiracy and, a millennium later, Hobbes during England's Civil War. Today, whether it manifests in the form of buzzwords or pseudo-profundity, or arcane evasions of legalese and bureaucratese, or the crudities of twittering tweets, fraudulent political language obstructs serious thought, fatally degrading political discourse into Orwellian doublespeak.[2]

From "A Hanging" and "Charles Dickens" to "Politics and the English Language" and beyond, Orwell's essays of the 1930s and 1940s express his liberal ethos in the sense of fostering what could be called the "Republic of Letters," an expression of solidarity that aims to rise above the parochial preoccupations of nation, gender, class, and race. For example, reading a novel entails a willingness to read not for information or self-confirmation, but for edification and self-transformation. You "adopt" the author as a "big brother" (or sister) by attending not only to the work's subject matter, but also to the personality or ethos of the writer, who speaks to some intimate part of yourself. This is reading not for escape, for "keeping up" with breaking news, or for some form of titillation, but rather for self-realization and self-actualization, balancing strong identification with heightened awareness. Such reading becomes an act of discernment, an odyssey of adventure into the deeper recesses of the self. And however unsettling such a journey may be, it exemplifies what literature is fundamentally about.

Orwell's major literary essays fully demonstrate that, even as a schoolboy, he had such encounters with distinguished, inspiring lettered citizens of the Republic. His tributes to Swift, Dickens, Gissing, Wells, and Miller, among others, demonstrate this beyond doubt.

Le style, c'est le laureat

Earlier in this book I contended that Orwell is the most important writer since Shakespeare and the most influential writer who ever lived. I specified that this large claim has mainly to do with his cultural and social impact, that is, with the omnipresence of his coinages[3] in the contemporary political lexicon and his dystopian vision in the political imagination. He possessed a superlative rhetorical ability to coin catchwords, such as those in *Animal Farm* and *Nineteen Eighty-Four*. His talent for composing arresting, memorable lines in both his essays and his fiction, especially openers and closers, is equally unforgettable. For example, here are seven of his best-known lines:

- "Down here it was still the England I had known in my childhood ... the men in bowler hats, the pigeons in Trafalgar Square, the red buses, the blue policemen—all sleeping the deep, deep sleep of England, from which I sometimes fear that we shall never wake till we are jerked out of it by the roar of bombs." (*Homage to Catalonia*, 1938)
- "Dickens is one of those writers who are well worth stealing." ("Charles Dickens," 1939)
- "It is the face of a man who is always fighting against something, but who fights in the open and is not frightened, the face of a man who is generously angry ... a type hated with equal hatred by all the smelly little orthodoxies which are now contending for our souls." ("Charles Dickens," 1939)
- "As I write, highly civilized human beings are flying overhead, trying to kill me." (*The Lion and the Unicorn*, 1941)

- "One has to belong to the intelligentsia to believe things like that: no ordinary man could be such a fool." ("Notes on Nationalism," 1945)
- "Saints should always be judged guilty until they are proved innocent." ("Reflections on Gandhi," 1949)
- "It was a bright cold day in April and the clocks were striking thirteen." (*Nineteen Eighty-Four*, 1949)

And so I would also maintain that Orwell's importance not only is due to his "impact" as a polemicist or rhetorician, but is also explainable on the grounds of literary style, that is, in literary terms too. He is among the most important *literary* figures of recent generations. His direct literary influence in Britain and America on the generations directly following his own—the Movement Writers and the Angry Young Men of the 1950s, the New Journalists such as Tom Wolfe and Gay Talese of the 1960s—rivals that of virtually any other twentieth-century writer. Even more notable, however, is the authority his "clear, plain" prose style has had in shaping nonfiction writing since midcentury. Along with Hemingway, Orwell is the literary stylist whose work has contributed most significantly to shifting the reigning prose style from the orotund, Ciceronian periodic sentence of Dr. Johnson, Gibbon, and the Augustan Age toward the limpid, fast-moving, direct, and hard-hitting sentence of present-day journalism. It is in these respects that Orwell's *literary* influence is sizable indeed and bolsters his claim to the title "England's Prose Laureate."

Until recently, this was not at all the consensus, especially among British and American professors of English. It is easy to forget that until some time after the attention paid to him in academic conferences during 1983–1984—that is, until the late 1980s and early 1990s—Orwell was typically relegated by literary academe to the ranks of a middlebrow author. He was not an eligible author, for instance, for my Ph.D. examinations at the University of Virginia in the spring of 1983—unlike "modernist masters" ranging from Pound, Woolf, and Lawrence to Fitzgerald, O'Neill, and William Carlos Williams. Literary academe was still beholden to the values and sensibility of modernism, from which vantage point Orwell seemed a rather simple "juvenile" author whose books "failed" to engage in the kinds of formal experimentation typical of modernism. Orwell was, at best, a canon-worthy "high school author" (*Animal Farm* and *Nineteen Eighty-Four*) or "college rhetoric model" ("Shooting an Elephant" and "Politics and the English Language"). Ironically, at that time he was in the same position 40 years later as Dickens had been in in the 1940s, when the latter was also not regarded as a suitable author for classroom study for those reading English at university in the United Kingdom. One former Oxbridge undergraduate recalls that Dickens was treated not as "a novelist" but rather as "an entertainer." He adds: "The option was reversed as critics developed broader interests and better tools; but although critical interest has stretched to include Dickens, it has not for the most part stretched to include Tolkien, and is still uneasy about the whole area of fantasy and the fantastic."[4]

Perhaps this reader would find it hopeful that "critical interest has stretched to include" Orwell since the 1990s, which represents a titanic sea change since my years as an undergraduate, when "serious" opinion disparaged the literary value of "allegories with animals or fairies" (as expressed by Anthony Burgess). When I graduated in 1978, Anglo-American departments of English still concurred that the only twentieth-century authors appropriate for university study were those in the tradition of the "modernist masters," because they fulfilled "higher literary aspirations," in

Burgess's approving phrase that year. Given that *Animal Farm* is an "animallegory" and subtitled "A Fairy Story," Burgess's disdain for Orwell's fantasy seems both unmistakable and quite specific.[5]

Leaving aside the issue of curricular adoptions, the disdain is unjust. To the contrary, Orwell accomplished the rare feat of writing easily readable, seemingly straightforward prose fictions, especially the satirical beast fable of *Animal Farm* and the didactic anti-utopia of *Nineteen Eighty-Four*, that are in fact richly textured and densely layered. That is to say, like his realistic novels of the 1930s, his late work disavows narrative or stylistic experimentation and is highly accessible—yet not on that account superficial. For literary scholars with allegiances to formalistic methodologies ranging from the New Criticism to poststructuralism, such absorbingly readable prose is tempting to devalue. Literary academics tend to prize most highly what our "sophisticated" methodologies elaborately decipher or "unpack," for such performances of critical virtuosity purportedly attest to the brilliance of our hermeneutical tools and intellectual acumen. An author working broadly in the realist tradition of prose fiction who is largely uninterested in formal experimentation and whose writings thereby require no grand hermeneutical theories (or "textual strategies") for readers to comprehend them is quite likely to be dismissed as "unserious" or middlebrow.

Culture Critic and Object

So although Orwell's international reputation as an author with a mass readership does indeed largely rest on his two prose fiction satires of the later 1940s, *Animal Farm* and *Nineteen Eighty-Four*, the claim that George Orwell is the most influential writer who ever lived is based not only on the worldwide significance of his last two works of fiction, but also on the tremendous impact of some of his essays. Several book-length studies have been devoted each to *Animal Farm* and *Nineteen Eighty-Four*, which in itself is exceptional. But how often are entire books by leading scholars devoted to exhaustive analysis and far-ranging application of a single essay? "Politics and the English Language" may be the most widely discussed modern essay ever written,[6] as exemplified by *What Orwell Did Not Know: Propaganda and the New Face of American Politics* (2007).

Sponsored by the Open Society Institute, which is funded by the politically progressive financier George Soros, this volume attacks what its contributors deem the far-right-wing political agenda of the George W. Bush administration and the Christian Right by drawing on the prestige and intellectual pedigree of Orwell and his celebrated essay. The collection consists of proceedings from a 2007 conference organized by "the deans of five prominent journalism schools [who] were worried about what was happening to political language." Its 18 chapters feature contributions from prominent political philosophers, cognitive scientists, anthropologists, psychologists, and journalists, including an epilogue by Soros himself. Although the thrust of the book is rather presumptuous and even contradictory—the title dismisses Orwell even as the contents acknowledge him as a visionary—the overt gesture of tribute to his essay is obvious: What other essay could possibly attract this range of thinkers, none of whom are English professors or men and women of letters? In an implicit acknowledgment of the imaginative power and inventive genius of Orwell as a political prophet, *What Orwell Did Not Know* addresses topics ranging from nuclear proliferation, global warming, and the American invasion of Iraq in 2003 to the "carnivalesque" infotainment industry, the role of metaphor in cognitive linguistics, research in neuroscience and the psychology of emotion, and even the "Orwellian" Postal Reorganization Act of 1970 (which hiked mailing rates for journals of opinion and "little magazines"). Several contributors argue that the United States has adopted a permanent "war" footing like that of the three superstates in *Nineteen Eighty-Four*, attesting to the propagandistic success of the allegedly endless, fraudulent War on Terror, which functions (as in Oceania) to keep the masses (i.e., us "proles") in a fixed state of fear and passivity.[7]

"Politics and the English Language" is not the only Orwell essay to have exerted spectacular influence across several decades. Generations of British leftists have regarded "Inside the Whale" (1940) as a forerunner to *Nineteen Eighty-Four*, with the two fatalistic tracts of political pessimism together delivering one-two knockout blows to the radical, activist spirit of the 1930s. These readers charge "Inside the Whale," which addresses the climate of ennui in Henry Miller's *Tropic of Cancer* (1939) and its endorsement of political resignation and private hedonism, with undermining the radical spirit of the 1940s and 1950s. Because of this essay, which expressed a qualified admiration for Miller's "honest" embrace of a politics of withdrawal, contends E. P. Thompson, Britain's leading historian of the early postwar era, "the aspirations of a generation were buried; not only was a political movement, which embodied much that was honorable, buried, but also the notion of disinterested dedication to a cause." What other essay of the twentieth century could possibly occasion such an observation—fully twenty years after its original publication?

I regard this breathtaking claim as utterly outlandish. But that is beside the point. That such a sophisticated historical methodologist as Thompson, the author of *The Making of the English Working Classes*, attributes such catastrophic political effect to a single literary work (a "mere" essay at that) is remarkable. Equally remarkable is that Britain's premier novelist of the next generation, Salman Rushdie, could follow up Thompson's argument a quarter century later in his own essay (also titled "Outside the Whale") to condemn Orwell in similar terms for his "quietest passivity" and its damaging consequences for generations of leftists since the war years.[8]

My larger point is, however, that the reception of these two essays, "Inside the Whale" and "Politics and the English Language"—completely apart from the impact of *Animal Farm* and *Nineteen Eighty-Four* on the course of the cultural Cold War—represents interesting evidence from Orwell's *non*fiction that buttresses further my claim to the unique influence of Orwell—or, rather, "Orwell." Astoundingly, the case can be made by reference to both the prose fiction *and* the nonfiction of England's Prose Laureate. Let us note, however, that Thompson assails the authoritative, august St. George "Orwell" of 1960, not the inglorious Orwell of 1940.

The notoriety of the title essay of *Inside the Whale* (1940), along with the broad recognition and high regard for Orwell's other pieces in both this collection and *Critical Essays* (1946), should remind us that his influence as a cultural critic—especially his pathbreaking role as an evangelist of cultural studies—warrants prominence in any final assessment of his career. (Orwell's chief impact has been in cultural studies and cultural criticism, far more so than in literary analysis, aesthetics, or cultural theory.) His signal achievement as a critic was to craft "semi-sociological" essays on artifacts of popular culture never before taken seriously, such as comic postcards, British and American murder mysteries, English cooking, the habits of toads, the names of English flowers, brewing recipes for good tea, and numerous other "popcult" topics. Orwell thereby introduced a new subgenre of literature—the serious essay about seemingly ephemeral matters of popular or mass culture—marking him as a forefather of the academic field of cultural studies.

It is uncanny that the closer we examine Orwell's influence on "culture," including popular and mass culture, the more we notice here too the distinctive presence of both Orwell and "Orwell." Forming a striking diptych combining deference and dishonor, these twin tableaux alternately profile him not only as a pioneering critic but also as a commercial object of popular culture. No other writer's work has both so decisively contributed to the development of popular culture studies as a formal domain of academic inquiry and so widely penetrated the international imagination (especially his coinages from *Nineteen Eighty-Four*) that it qualifies as a substantial body of material for popular culture analysis. Different works have accounted for his dual status as culture "critic" and culture "object." Whereas his essay collections (especially *Inside the Whale* and *Critical Essays*) and some of his journalism have exerted influence on postwar culture critics, *Animal Farm* and *Nineteen Eighty-Four* have been mined in diverse ways by the mass media and commercial interest groups ranging from the popular, long-running reality TV show *Big Brother*[9] to internationally famous British musical performers such as Sting and the Police (see, e.g., "Every Breath You Take") and the Clash, to name just a few.

Will Orwell ultimately be remembered more for his popular culture criticism than for *Animal Farm* and *Nineteen Eighty-Four*? That prospect seems unlikely. And yet, as one admirer remarks, among those readers "who have really fallen under Orwell's spell, his essays and reviews, assembled in various collections, usually become the most-loved of his writings."[10] He is ever more widely recognized, especially in the literary academy,[11] as one of the greatest essayists in the English language, a figure equal in stature to Johnson, Burke, and Hazlitt. Orwell's popcult criticism represents one of the noteworthy differences between his *oeuvre* and the works of that literary triumvirate, and it is doubtless one of the tallest pillars of his reputation. For a fuller estimate of that outsized reputation and its future prospects, we now turn to Part 2.

PART 2

Legend and Legacy

CHAPTER 7

French Connection, Part 1

Jean Malaquais, a "French Orwell"?

> Posterity is for the philosopher what the next
> world is for the man of religion.
> —Denis Diderot

Jean Who?

An *engagé* leftist, Jean Malaquais was an *intellectuel et littérateur* of the middle years of the twentieth century, an *enfant terrible* often caustically critical of his fellow leftists. Far more unusual, he was also a Polish-Jewish émigré whose fiction and nonfiction earned him not only prizes from the French cultural elite, but also plaudits from admirers ranging from André Gide to Leon Trotsky.

Jean who? That is the response today of virtually everyone, even in Parisian literary circles. The appearance in the twenty-first century of a biography and two collections of his letters (in French, still untranslated) has changed nothing. To a reader from the anglophone world, however, the literary career of this obscure, long-forgotten author bears an uncanny resemblance—irony of ironies—to none other than that of the most famous and influential writer of the twentieth century: George Orwell.

Indeed the parallels between the two men are surprising—almost as if Malaquais, born just five years after Orwell, had paced in the Englishman's footsteps, playing Horatio to his Hamlet, each man unaware of the other's activities, into the 1950s, when, in strangely different ways, both their literary careers abruptly ended. Unlike Orwell, who died at 46 in 1950, Malaquais (1908–1998) lived on yet wrote very little, virtually nothing of literary significance after 1953. That year, when he himself turned 46, witnessed the appearance of *Le Gaffeur* (*The Joker*), his last novel. Thereafter, literary death.

Yet half a lifetime still remained. In the exactly 46 years that followed, he limited his literary activity to penning a handful of reviews and articles, all of them slight and forgettable. His major writing effort was not literary but scholarly—or, rather, academic—a doctoral dissertation published in the early 1970s on the Danish philosopher Søren Kierkegaard. How this specialized monograph on Kierkegaard—famous herald of existentialism, Christian lay theologian, refined bourgeois university graduate, self-professed enemy of Hegelianism, and proud "individualist"—squares with Malaquais's own agnosticism, decades of hard manual labor, ideological fundamentalism, and Marxist-collectivist convictions remains a mystery. Not long before the author's death at the age of 90, a sympathetic French publisher reprinted a few of his early works and helped him gather together some unpublished materials. They occasioned no notice.

Jean Malaquais, Writer; *c'est ça*. The rest is silence.

Literary Immortality Versus the Memory Hole of History

And yet ... and yet. If that were the entire story, Malaquais would not be worth reading, let alone reading about. And yet: he was a celebrated writer during the years of World War II and the early postwar era, fêted in France as a promising young man of letters, translated into English, and positively reviewed in the Anglo-American press. His utter erasure from literary history is not easy to explain.

Before speculating on this vanishing act, let us establish a frame of reference that may startle anglophone readers—namely the French connection, as it were, with George Orwell. This comparison both illuminates why Malaquais should engage our attention and presents his quixotic career in terms compelling to an Anglo-American audience.

The affinities between Malaquais and Orwell are notable. It is nevertheless understandable that no scholar or biographer has ever linked the two men: a cursory glance—which is all that Malaquais typically receives from not just Anglo-American but also French scholars—suggests only glaring incongruities. Why would anyone think to compare this passionate, ultra-leftist Polish émigré in Paris who has been utterly forgotten and Blair/Orwell, the rather undemonstrative Old Etonian and most famous literary Cold Warrior of the century? Unfortunately, such (admittedly conspicuous) divergences between the two men have obscured their noteworthy similarities.

As we shall see, their respective careers unfolded in five overlapping phases. In the first stage, they are gravely concerned about the condition of the working class and the poor, especially miners and the downtrodden. The second stage reflects much more directly their ideological and political commitments, specifically as Trotskyists or independent leftists. A third phase emerges during the years of World War II, when both Orwell and Malaquais write war diaries and grapple with similar political concerns, albeit in the vastly different circumstances of wartime England and Vichy France (and Mexico after 1942, for Malaquais). The fourth stage, which closes their active writing careers, finds each man turning to a different genre altogether and writing works that are much darker than their earlier outputs: anti-utopias set in the near future.

Their subsequent literary reputations undergo a radical bifurcation around midcentury. The synchronicities governing their parallel orbits cease; Clio abruptly consigns their fates to opposite extremes. Orwell's posthumous fame—unprecedented for any modern literary figure—contrasts with Malaquais's near-total disappearance from the cultural scene, even in France. He has vanished "down the memory hole" of history, as if all his writings had been tossed into the *speakwrite* by Winston Smith at the Ministry of Truth.

A closer look at the parallels, paradoxes, and puzzles of their lives and legacies furnishes a revealing glimpse into the surgical ruthlessness of the zeitgeist, whose Darwinian spirit elevates and eliminates "candidates" for the pantheon. The careers and afterlives of our intellectual odd couple suggest much—about both the age and the ages—and represent a fascinating commentary on the movement of ideas and reputations in the modern world.

"Underclass-men" Without Degrees

The story opens at the turn of the last century. Orwell and Malaquais were born within a few years of each other: Orwell in 1903, Malaquais in 1908. Their active literary years were roughly the same: the mid-1930s to the early 1950s for Malaquais, and the early 1930s until his death in 1950 for Orwell. Both adopted new names to signify a new beginning in their lives. Malaquais was born Wladimir Jan Pavel Israël Pinkus Malacki. His father was a secular Jewish schoolteacher from a Russian-speaking area in Poland; his mother belonged to the Jewish Bund. Young Jan left Poland in his teens, eventually reaching France.

Although this chapter will focus on Jean Malaquais, we will review several biographical facts and literary landmarks in Orwell's career in order to highlight the resemblances and disparities between this unlikely pair. As we have discussed, Eric Blair was taken to England as a child, grew up in relatively comfortable circumstances, attended private school, and won a scholarship to Eton. Recall further that he then decided not to attend university like most of his Oxbridge-bound classmates, but rather entered the British civil service as a policeman in Burma. Returning to England in December 1926 after five years abroad, he was determined to write and struggled for years thereafter to eke out a living chiefly from his pen. With his semi-autobiographical first book, *Down and Out in Paris and London* (1933), he gained a modicum of literary success. He wanted to avoid embarrassing his respectable family, however, who would have been ashamed at the prospect of their only son (an Etonian as well!) begging for handouts as a "down and out." So Blair published his book under a pseudonym, "George Orwell," conjoining the name of the patron saint of England (and of a writer he admired, George Gissing) with the name of a small river near his parents' home.

Single-mindedly motivated "to be a writer," as he told a childhood friend, Jacintha Buddicom, during his Eton days—"a FAMOUS WRITER" no less, "whose *Collected Works* would be enshrined in a neat row of blue leather volumes"—Blair went in search of literary subjects. The economic depression in Europe provided him a powerful and poignant topic: "Lady Poverty" (the original working title for *Down and Out*). This interest in the condition of the underclass led Blair to Paris in the late 1920s, where he labored as a dishwasher and took other odd jobs. Returning home to England, he periodically spent several weeks tramping, all the while pondering the condition of the homeless and impoverished. The outcome was the aforementioned *Down and Out*, published in January 1933 as he was approaching 30, an unusual memoir that was quickly translated into French in 1935 and favorably reviewed in Paris and elsewhere. So, as the Depression deepened, Blair launched his first book-length work, which was essentially nonfiction (though, as he put it, "rearranged" as to details and episodic flow). The advice to adopt a pen name came from his publisher, Victor Gollancz.

Meanwhile, a young Polish Jew named Wladimir Malacki had left his native town of Varsovie at the age of 17, eventually arriving in Paris via Marseilles in June 1926. Thereafter he worked for a dozen years as a manual laborer in a series of jobs, including as a miner. He also read voraciously and wrote painstakingly—not in his mother tongue of Polish, but in his beloved French. For more than a decade, he devoted his precious few spare hours to a novel based largely on his brutish working-class experience. Malacki also began sending out short stories for publication in French journals, with mixed results. Finally, with war underway in December 1939, his first work, *Les Javanais* (translated as *Men from Nowhere*), appeared.

Les Javanais caused a minor sensation, catapulting the unknown "French" writer to highbrow fame. Like Blair, Malacki also was 30 at the time of the publication of his first book. Likewise, he too heeded the urging of his editor and adopted a *nom de plume*, publishing his novel under the name Jean Malaquais, which was probably just a francophone version of "Jan Malacki." (One wonders, however, if he was also thinking of the Quai Malaquais, a wharf along the left bank of the Seine in Paris.)

Les Javanais has no central character and no real plot. It is a gritty, prismatic *roman social* portraying the plight of underclass émigrés in a throng of voices, which resound episodically through a series of crisscrossing dialogues and brief narratives. The novel is written in the pungent, foul language of the émigrés from across Europe with whom Malaquais had worked in the mines. *Les Javanais* drew lavish praise from French reviewers and won the coveted Prix Renaudot, edging out Jean-Paul Sartre's *La Nausée*, quite a feat in literary Paris for a self-taught immigrant Polish Jew. Malaquais received another boost when Leon Trotsky gave the book a rave review. Trotsky pronounced the *trotskisant* Malaquais "a new great writer," one whose name "we must remember." A gifted *engagé* novelist whose arresting presentation of the miners' suffering avoided both agitprop and bathos, Malaquais was no propagandist or lowbrow romantic, proclaimed Trotsky; he was an *artiste* of the highest order whose novel brilliantly captured the social reality of revolutionary upheaval in the language of a poet. "[The] combination of personal, defiant lyricism and violent epic poetry," Trotsky wrote, "which is that of its time, perhaps makes the charm of the novel."[1]

The parallels warrant attention. Both Malaquais and Blair arrived in Paris in search of a literary career at approximately the same time: Malaquais in 1926, Blair two years later. Neither had much success at first, and both battled to make ends meet, Malaquais more than Orwell (who had an aunt and uncle living in Paris while he was there). Both men ultimately established themselves as writers of commitment drawing on personal experiences of poverty as they turned 30 years old. Both established contact with the lowest levels of society, with Malaquais working (like Blair) as a dishwasher and *plongeur*. ("Morally and intellectually I was a tramp," he once wrote, "a companion of the dispossessed.") Orwell visited miners' homes and actually crept down a coal mine (despite his six-foot-three frame), quite exceeding his publishers' commission to "report" on the economic conditions of the miners. Going far further, Malaquais recast in thinly veiled fiction his personal experience of backbreaking, soul-deadening drudgery in the lead and silver mines of Provence. *Les Javanais* depicted the dreadful existence endured by immigrant miners from throughout Europe toiling in the south of France; Orwell's work of documentary nonfiction on a similar topic, *The Road to Wigan Pier* (1937), combined straight autobiography with an analysis of mining conditions and miners' families in the industrial Midlands of England. The book also reflected the contrarian streak in Orwell, as he scolded the left-wing intelligentsia for failing to understand the working classes. *Wigan Pier*, published just 18 months before *Les Javanais*, likewise represented Orwell's first breakthrough to national attention, selling 37,500 copies as a featured selection of the Left Book Club (a Popular Front initiative sponsored by Orwell's publisher, Victor Gollancz).

These similarities derived from their shared anti-Stalinism and anticapitalism notwithstanding, large differences between the two men during this first phase in the 1930s are also evident, both in their ideological outlooks and in their career arcs. Malaquais was a political zealot and ultra-leftist (and remained such), whereas Orwell was radical yet more flexibly pragmatic (and closer to a left-wing Social Democrat in later years). Moreover, Orwell was by 1939 already a modestly successful, frequently published author: he wrote seven full-length books during the decade (one per year), had two of his novels also published in the United States, and composed a pair of essays ("A Hanging," 1931; and "Shooting an Elephant," 1936) that foreshadowed his mastery of that literary form in the 1940s.[2] Still, like Malaquais, he was not yet able to support himself by writing and had to find "day jobs" (successively as a schoolteacher, bookshop assistant, and storekeeper).

By any measure, however, Malaquais's years in the literary wilderness were much harder. He started out with three strikes against him. He was a *métèque* ("dirty foreigner," a term akin to "wop," "dago," etc.). He lacked a "proper" French accent (unlike the refined English of Etonian Blair/Orwell). He was an immigrant Jew. Understandably, for years Malaquais's own half-ashamed, half-defiant self-image was that of a prole first and an intellectual second. Until the war years, he endured exhausting, arduous working-class jobs (ranging from dishwasher and journeyman mechanic to laborer in the abattoirs of Les Halles). Ironically, his literary deliverance came when a distinguished man of French letters recognized his talent. Malaquais had written an indignant letter in December 1935 to André Gide, rebuking him scornfully for an article lamenting the disadvantages of never doing hard manual work, a fantasy that merely reflected Gide's naïvely romantic view of the working class and his privileged life as a wealthy bourgeois author.[3] Surprisingly, Gide responded positively and generously to Malaquais's reproach. The two became friends, and Gide's support proved vital both to the publisher's acceptance and to the intelligentsia's enthusiastic reception of *Les Javanais*.

"True" Rebels

The second stage in the literary and political evolution of Orwell and Malaquais during the mid- to late 1930s, characterized by further resemblances, finds both men speaking out as iconoclastic left-wing radicals fervently opposed to Stalinism and alarmed by the rise of totalitarianism—in fact, more outraged by the Stalinist nightmare on the Left than by fascism and Nazism on the Right. It is this antinomian stance of both Orwell and Malaquais—as dissidents, as men of the Left always "against" something—that marks them most recognizably as Janus-faced twins. Eric Blair was known, even in his schooldays, as his friend and fellow writer

Cyril Connolly recalled in a memoir, as a gadfly: "I was a stage rebel, Orwell a true one." And iconoclasm colors the profile of Malaquais that biographer Geneviève Nakach sketches, a portrait titled *Malaquais rebelle* (2012). Temperamentally, Orwell and Malaquais were keen skeptics. Politically, both men were fierce anti-Stalinists. They were also deeply interested in the fate of Spain, which had witnessed in 1936 a revolution under the aegis of the left-wing Republicans, opponents of both the Church and the armed forces under General Francisco Franco.

A biographical parallel that demands attention—yet has also gone without mention by any biographer or critic—concerns how Orwell and Malaquais each decided to oppose Franco. First, unlike so many successful European left-wing writers, they did not go to Spain to "cover the war" as journalists and rub shoulders in "solidarity" with their peers in comfortable hotels. No, they went to "snipe at the Fascists," as Orwell put it.[4] Second, and quite remarkably, both men enlisted in the POUM militia, not the International Brigade, which most foreigners joined (and both Stalin and the Spanish Communist Party supported). Formed by factions of the Spanish Trotskyists (the so-called Left Opposition to Stalin) and Bukharinists (the Right Opposition), the POUM was a contingent mainly composed of anti-Stalinist leftists united in their shared hostility toward Stalinism, their ideological purity, and their deeply held idealism. Trotsky opposed this fusion and broke with the POUM, which then joined a loose international federation consisting of other radical, unaffiliated European parties (including the Independent Labor Party, to which Orwell belonged).

Still, although both Orwell and Malaquais signed up with the inadequately equipped POUM militia rather than enter the Loyalists' main army, the well-financed International Brigades, which had the official backing of the Popular Front both in London and in Paris, it appears that the two men's paths never actually crossed in Spain. Malaquais ventured there soon after the war broke out in July 1936 and stayed until October, leaving before Orwell arrived in late December. Orwell himself stayed seven months, largely in Catalonia, until he was wounded. He narrowly managed to escape the dragnet of Stalin's secret police, which suspected all Trotskyists and received its orders directly from Moscow. The Spanish conflict became a powerful cause for both Orwell and Malaquais, vindicating their unorthodox (indeed heretical) convictions among radicals that communism and Nazism were fraternal if not identical twins, two faces of totalitarianism.

Here again, however, emerge significant differences in the two men's ultimate response to the Spanish war, in both political and literary terms. For Orwell, the Spanish revolution was a noble failure. Despite his anger and growing hatred of the Soviet regime as an unconscionable traitor to the Republican cause in Spain, he felt imbued by hope. "I have seen wonderful things in Spain," he wrote to Cyril Connolly, "and at last, I really believe in socialism." Energized, Orwell wrote vehemently about the significance of the war, the Stalinists' "betrayal of the Left," and the tragic counter-revolutionary triumph of fascism. Returning home, he quickly composed his fine memoir *Homage to Catalonia* (1938), along with reviews, essays, and even a poem about Spain.

By contrast, Malaquais ultimately became disillusioned with the POUM. He had followed the lead of his friend and lifelong political associate, Marc Chirik, and affiliated with the Bordiga column, a militia led by Amadeo Bordiga, a former leader of the Italian Communist Party (PCI) and an outspoken renegade who had been expelled from the PCI for defending Trotskyists. Like Chirik, Malaquais opposed Stalin's Popular Front strategy to ally Communist and other non-Trotskyist left-wing parties, fearing (accurately) that this coalition would co-opt and overwhelm non-Stalinist leftist groups through the ruse of an antifascist "united front." The two comrades suspected correctly that this tactic would lead not only to the castration of the POUM, but also to the subversion of the Spanish revolution. As a result, they regarded the POUM as insufficiently aggressive in its resistance to the calls for "unity." Like Trotsky and the (sectarian) Spanish Trotskyists supporting him, both Chirik and Malaquais deplored the fact that the POUM participated in the Frente Popular of Manuel Azaña, who headed Acción Republicana. (As part of the Popular Front government, POUM introduced some radical proposals, largely without success, since the centrist factions objected to them.) Disenchanted with the POUM, which he judged guilty of appeasement, Malaquais left Spain after little more than two months there. Unlike Orwell, on returning to his adopted homeland of France, he wrote nothing about it. Instead he struggled to finish *Les Javanais*.

La guerre: Of Diaries and Despair

The outbreak of World War II shaped a third phase of literary-political convergence between Orwell and Malaquais that lasted from 1939 to 1945. Orwell would have preferred an active military role. But he was rejected for military service on the grounds of poor health, namely the disease of tuberculosis that would ultimately kill him. Too much of a health risk to gain admission into the military, Orwell served instead in the Home Guard. Living in London, he nonetheless kept a war diary (first published in the mid-1990s) and followed events closely as the war unfolded, first privately, then at the BBC as Talks Assistant Producer, then Talks Producer, for the Indian section of the BBC's Eastern Service (1941–1943), and later as literary editor of the left-wing *Tri-*

bune (1943–1945). He wrote his breakthrough fable, *Animal Farm*, during his tenure at *Tribune*. Orwell initially thought that the war could transform Britain's class-bound social order, ushering in a peaceful revolution as a result of the social cataclysm. When that failed to happen, he nonetheless loyally supported the war.

Malaquais's fate was harsher. Just weeks before receiving a chorus of *laudatios* for his first novel, he was drafted into the French army. He spent nine months as a soldier, an experience that appalled him. It also apparently failed to arouse his literary imagination, no more than had his war experience in Spain. He did keep a journal, however, which was printed by a small publisher based in New York associated with the Free French. Considering what Orwell did with his pen after just six months in the Spanish Civil War, Malaquais's silence may seem disappointing, but it indicates how different they were emotionally, despite their skeptical casts of mind. When Malaquais's causes were betrayed, he became discouraged and morose, and fell into silence. When Orwell suffered betrayals, he fought by other means, raising his literary voice to elegize the loss or failure. Indeed, if Orwell had experienced what Malaquais went through, he might have written a great war novel, or at least reportage of the stature of *Homage to Catalonia*. But his health had disqualified him from enlisting.

While *Les Javanais* was still receiving accolades, Malaquais was cut off and miserable in the trenches, experiencing no fighting but much discomfort and depression. He had been called up in September 1939, serving first in the 620th Pioneer Regiment, where he was engaged in exhausting manual labor during *le drole de guerre*, then transferred to other units posted along the Maginot Line in Alsace-Lorraine. When he heard about his literary success, he requested and was granted leave. He enjoyed his 15 minutes of literary fame, but it was an isolated moment during what was, according to Nakach, "the worst" period of his long life. His army service represented a turning point that would scar him permanently.

Malaquais himself was deeply shocked by his own intense disgust toward his fellow servicemen: he reviled the crassness of their talk, their nauseating smell, their seeming delight in all things base. "I envy those with the ability not to think about tomorrow, not to think about the cement and the dirt, about life itself. Not thinking. Whatever happens, those who can avoid thinking have already won the first round," he wrote in *Journal de guerre*, which appeared in English in 1943. His revulsion was always colored with shame, for his comrades were largely working-class men, not pampered intellectuals like Gide. "The men with whom I am forced to live!" he wailed. "God, how I despise them! And how, through them, I despise myself!" He added: "The majority of the unfavorable judgments which I form about people have to do almost exclusively with their intellect, rarely with their heart."

Yet no amount of guilty thinking could alter Malaquais's visceral feelings of abhorrence and nausea. However much he may have yearned to proffer an *hommage* to his comrades—a work in the spirit of Orwell's soaring threnody to Catalonia—his months as a soldier left him with a view of men as beasts.

All the same, *Journal de guerre* captured attention both in the French-language press abroad and in New York. Unlike Orwell, whose war diary consisted of notes (about the home front) that went unpublished until long after his death, Malaquais published his testimony about the fall of France as the war was still raging. It was favorably reviewed and won kudos from the French intelligentsia, including a ringing endorsement from André Malraux, who called it "an extraordinary document." In New York literary circles, its English translation (as *War Diary*) occasioned a prominent review from Isaac Rosenfeld in 1943. (By coincidence, *Les Javanais* also appeared in English that spring under the title *Men from Nowhere* and also received respectful notices in New York, including one from Lionel Trilling.)[5]

At the same time, Malaquais also published a collection of six short stories, *Coups de barre*. Written mostly in the mid- and late 1930s, these stories, modernist and experimental in nature, remind one of those sections in Orwell's *A Clergyman's Daughter* (1935) that draw on Joycean stylistic techniques such as stream of consciousness. *Coups de barre* made little impact and, unlike the war diary, was not translated into English.

Demobilized by the Vichy regime under German occupation, Malaquais fled to the unoccupied zone in the south of France until 1942. He found temporary refuge in the haven set up by the valiant American journalist Varian Fry under the auspices of a private group (similar to what we today call an NGO) named the Emergency Rescue Committee, which assisted hundreds of activists and intellectuals to escape Nazi-occupied Europe. (Gide also came to the rescue and secured a Mexican visa for Malaquais and his second wife, Galy.) Along with other left-wing intellectuals such as Victor Serge, Malaquais spent time in Mexico with his fellow radicals bemoaning the fate of the West (and clashed with Serge, a fellow POUM veteran whose political convictions after the Spanish Civil War had moved rightward, away from a sternly principled, far-left anti-Stalinist position—congruent with Malaquais's own politics—toward a less puritanical, more pragmatic stance that included features of social democracy).[6]

In Mexico Malaquias largely wrote his second novel, *Planète sans visa*, which finally appeared in 1947. It is not a war novel, but rather a combination of resistance novel and *roman social*, with a curious mixture of autobiography and political analysis. Set in 1942, it features a group of dissident intellectuals awaiting a crackdown by Marshal Petain's Vichy government in France (or, as Malaquais sardonically puns on the collaborationist general's name, *putainiste* France [*putain* = whore]). Malaquais argues in the novel that the war effort is corrupt, given that the Soviet Union fights on the side of the bourgeois democracies.

Here again, as the war unfolded in 1940–1941, Orwell was pondering similar themes: the war effort, the home front, democracy and revolution, and both the fate of the common man and the role of intellectuals and the Left in the war. Yet Britain under Churchill, however embattled, never succumbed to tyranny, thus rendering it a totally different place from Vichy France. So Orwell's major publication during the war was, unsurprisingly, utterly different in spirit from *Planète sans visa*. Orwell's *The Lion and the Unicorn* (1941) is an ebullient manifesto that trumpets the potential for a progressive democratic revolution. Subtitled *Socialism and the English Genius*, it envisions how the war and the "genius" of the English liberal tradition might transform British society and lead to a viable left-wing alternative to Stalinist collectivism: democratic socialism. Orwell soon realized that he was mistaken, but he never lost faith in the "genius" of the English common people. Nor did he abandon his allegiance to "democratic socialism." Above all, he never stopped sounding his warnings about the evils of Stalinist totalitarianism. (And he was not wholly mistaken about the transformative potential of the war, given that a Labour government gained power in the July 1945 elections, when the electorate overwhelmingly rejected the Conservatives despite Churchill's inspiring role in the Allies' victory.)

By contrast, Malaquias had no such hopes for France, the Allies, or the Left. Admittedly, *Planète sans visa* is a work of fiction, not a political tract that can be read as a straightforward statement of his views. Nonetheless, the novel's tone of disillusionment is transparent. As he remarks on *la France* in his war diaries: "*Adieu Marianne, mon amour, ma catin* [whore]."[7] Unlike Orwell's profound sense of patriotism, voiced in *The Lion and the Unicorn*

and other wartime writings, Malaquias harbored feelings of in-
difference, if not cynicism, toward *la France*.

That point deserves emphasis. The single most significant area
of commitment and sensibility that separates the two men has
to do with the concept of patriotism. Whatever else he was, Orwell was an English patriot, someone who cherished his country's
customs and eccentricities without overlooking its foibles and
flaws. Orwell always drew a careful distinction between patriotism and nationalism. Whereas the former was a cultural matter
that found expression in folkways and social traditions, the latter
was an aggressive, even invasive and predatory, ideology that reflected a sense of political superiority or vainglory. Orwell's patriotism imbues his writings, especially essays such as "My Country, Right or Left" and "England Your England." He desperately
wanted to see England prevail in the war, albeit an England that
had gone through a true social revolution that fully dismantled
the class system.

Malaquais could hardly have been more different. Patriotism
was an empty word for him. His soldiering in Spain and World
War II had indeed scarred him, and he would have readily agreed
with Hemingway's protagonist Frederic Henry in *A Farewell to
Arms* that there "were many words that you could not stand to
hear.... Abstract words such as glory, honor, courage, or hallow
were obscene." Malaquais retained no love for the Poland he dis-
owned, a homeland discredited by visceral anti-Semitism, nor anything approaching *élan patriotique* for a France that never deigned
to grant French citizenship to this *métèque*. Although he mastered
the French language, he remained always the rootless cosmopolitan, the proverbial "alienated" émigré intellectual disgorged by
the political convulsions and mass displacements of the twentieth century. Malaquais spent long periods of time away from
France and took no part in her liberation in 1944–1945. In his

last years he resided in Geneva, the home of many cosmopolitan exiles throughout history—though in fact he had acquired American citizenship decades earlier. The author of the once-celebrated *Men from Nowhere* became, by the 1960s, a real "Nowhere Man." In fact, the Beatles' hit single could have been modeled on him.

We must not leave the topic of patriotism without one further observation. The subject not only suggests the yawning gulf between the two men in their attitudes toward love of country as "homeland" (the German *Heimat*) but also raises a much larger issue that is a recurrent leitmotif of this book: *l'influence d'Orwell—et d' "Orwell."* In this instance, our attention is drawn to his notable shaping influence on the modern-day conception of English national identity, shifting it beyond the late Victorian, Kiplingesque self-images (John Bull, the White Man's Burden, "the sun never sets," and "Britannia rules the waves")—that is, toward his notion of patriotism as a matter of cultural sensibility rather than political (or ideological and nationalistic) outreach—and overreach. His legendary plain-speaking "common man" persona and reputation as "quintessentially English"—the storied "English Quixote"—have made him not only an architect but also an archetype of "Englishness." As a result, Orwell is the British writer of the twentieth century who may be said to have contributed most to the post-Empire idea of "England" and the "English" national character.

In these respects he joins a literary tradition stretching back to Shakespeare, Spenser, and Milton, so that he stands alone in recent history with Dickens, both of whom bear comparison with symbolic national figures among the latter's nineteenth-century contemporaries such as Balzac and Hugo in France, Goethe and Schiller in Germany, Pushkin and Tolstoy in Russia, and Emerson and Twain in America. Among twentieth-century British icons, Orwell is often paired not with fellow writers, but rather with Winston Churchill, certainly England's greatest public figure of the century, who defined "Englishness" (albeit from the conservative side of the spectrum) in his speeches as well as in his style and sensibility.

Orwell's famous essays ("Politics and the English Language," "England Your England," "A Good Cup of Tea," etc.), as well as works such as *The Lion and the Unicorn: Socialism and the English Genius* established him as his generation's literary voice of Englishness, his eccentric left-wing attitudes notwithstanding, and no prominent successors have yet emerged. The images of "Orwell" as the incarnation of Englishness are diverse. He is the whimsical devotee of boys' weeklies and penny postcards. He is the solitary knight (errant) of English cuisine ("In Defense of English Cooking"). He is the relentless (albeit tender) scourge of Colonel Blimp. He is the self-appointed champion of "the common man" (*The English People*). He is both the celebrant of "English genius" and the (half-affectionate) carper about his hapless "England" ("a family with the wrong members in control"). And on and on, all of it expressed in language that projects a critical yet endearing populist vision of an already disappearing "England," this "sceptred isle." This imagery—based on the writer's prose and the man's conduct—helped downshift the English imaginary from the imperial "great" Briton of *Punch*'s John Bull to the simple working-class Lancashire family, the gritty Wigan miner, the unshrinking Londoner of the Blitz, and the countless ordinary folk dotting the Yorkshire byways and strolling the Surrey countryside, "all sleeping the deep deep sleep of England," per the closing sentence of *Homage to Catalonia*.[8]

Doomsday Dystopians?

The defeat of the Axis powers, especially in the wake of Hiroshima and the USSR's rapidly growing domination of Eastern Europe, did nothing to allay the anxieties troubling both Orwell and

Malaquais about the postwar world and the spectre of a totalitarian future. The war's aftermath opens a fourth stage of broadly parallel development linking Orwell and Malaquais.

During this period, Malaquais toted his second major work—another *roman social*—into print and trudged with steady, if glacial, speed through his third (and last) novel. As we have noted, although Malaquais's major literary project of the war years, *Planète sans visa* (translated as *World Without Visa*), is set in wartime France, it did not see print until mid-1947, when addressing the Nazi occupation and Vichy collaborationists had already given way to grappling with the breakup of the victorious Allies, the confrontation between Stalin's USSR and the capitalist U.S., and the emerging Cold War. Malaquais's novel addresses none of these developing issues. Rather, it recasts his personal experience with miners and other workers, including aspiring young intellectuals, in the late 1930s and early 1940s.

Nonetheless, it received positive, sometimes glowing, reviews both in Paris and in New York. The 500-page novel appeared in American publication from the respected publisher Doubleday. It was a *succès d'estime* and momentarily brought Malaquais to wide public attention in the United States for the first and only time, thanks to a substantial review in *Time* magazine, which included a photograph of the author and swooned over his "huge and exciting novel about 'shamed and sunken France,' a novel on the grand scale, packed with enough action to fill a dozen less ambitious books, burning with dramatic and melodramatic energy, written and overwritten from a gnawing sense of social urgency." *Time* was impressed by Malaquais's ability to produce "a desperate, ear-splitting wail of grief at what human life has become in the twentieth century, a book that communicates as no other has yet—the feeling of what it meant to be a European in Hitler's heyday." Addressing the novel's histrionic touches, the *Time* reviewer concluded that "all such objections are ultimately swept aside by the power with which Malaquais has raised a verbal monument to the martyrdom of Europe." The rave review is surprising and especially impressive in light of publisher Henry Luce's conservative politics, which the book review section of the magazine often mirrored. Such an enthusiastic notice for an avowed Trotskyist ran counter to the magazine's political philosophy. Still, despite this and other positive reviews, Malaquais failed to gain a following in the United States.

World Without Visa spotlights the brutal Vichy regime in Marseilles, which, searching for its "load of Jewish meat," proceeds to round up the city's Jews and deliver them to internment camps. Featuring a cast of more than two dozen characters—resembling *Les Javanais* in that respect—*World Without Visa* expresses the complexity of war and its confusions, rendered in diverse voices in ways that remind the reader of the panoptic aspirations of John Dos Passos in *Manhattan Transfer* and his *U.S.A.* trilogy.

Three protagonists of the French Resistance are, however, the focus of Malaquais's kaleidoscopic novel, which is also a veiled *roman à clef* featuring a trio of characters loosely based on close colleagues of Malaquais. Two of them in fact represent plausible projections of different sides of Malaquais himself. The first character, Marc Laverne, is a version of Malaquais's friend Marc Chirik. Laverne is an anti-Stalinist leftist who is a failed Lenin, a pure revolutionary being and Marxist ideologue who in the face of Nazi dominance collapses into existential despair. The second figure, Stepanoff, is drawn from the Russian Victor Serge. Stepanoff is an Old Bolshevik who has miraculously escaped from Stalin's gulag but falls into the hands of the Gestapo, receives a seductive offer to become a Soviet Lord Hee-Haw, spurns his captors, and—in a confusing mix of defeatism and heroism—starves himself and slits his wrists. The third character is a valiant American who works underground to assist antifascists seeking to escape German-occupied Europe—obviously based on Varian Fry.

Orwell's major literary preoccupation during the postwar years was another political fantasy, this time in the form of a dystopia, *Nineteen Eighty-Four*. Unlike his whimsical, understated "Fairy Story," it is a piercing *cri de coeur*, a booming siren of alarm to the West about the menace of totalitarianism in general and the USSR in particular. Widely lauded in both Britain and America except by orthodox Marxist reviewers, it became Orwell's final testament. As they had with *Animal Farm* (1945) and *Critical Essays* (1945; American title: *Dickens, Dali, and Others*, 1946), critics and intellectuals hailed Orwell variously as a dying voice in the wilderness and a visionary prophet (or, in the view of hostile leftist detractors, a "doomsday" prophet and enemy of socialism who projected his tubercular suffering on the entire world). As we shall see, under completely different conditions, Malaquais too was at work on a dystopian novel located in the indefinite near future.

Like many other European refugees after the war, Malaquais pursued residence in the United States. After leaving Mexico, he briefly returned to France in 1947 for the publication of *Planète sans visa*. Then he settled in New York, having garnered an appointment, like many of his fellow European refugees, at the New School for Social Research, where he taught for several semesters. Unlike many of his fellow European émigrés, however, Malaquais made little lasting impact on the school or its students. The standard histories of the New School do not even mention his name.[9]

More significant for Malaquais in the early postwar years was his friendship with the rising star of American letters, Norman Mailer. While in France in 1947, he had become acquainted with the 25-year-old Mailer, then residing in Paris on the GI Bill, who had just completed a war novel, *The Naked and the Dead*. With each of them residing in New York in 1948, they became closer friends. Mailer introduced Malaquais to numerous other writers in the city, among them friends and colleagues such as James Baldwin and Irving Howe, along with various other writers associated with the journals *Partisan Review* and Dwight Macdonald's *politics*.

Malaquais's tutelage of Mailer in Marxist history and theory, which had begun in Paris, intensified in New York. Alfred Kazin went so far as to label Mailer at this time a "disciple" of Malaquais.[10] Irving Howe mentions in his autobiography, *A Margin of Hope*, that he and other members of the *Partisan Review* circle took note that Mailer's speech at the Soviet-sponsored Waldorf Conference held in New York in March 1949, in which he unexpectedly denounced Stalinist cultural policy in unequivocal terms and provoked much agitation, bore distinct echoes of Malaquais's influence. So too did Mailer's second novel, *Barbary Shore* (1951). Dedicated to Malaquais, it is a political novel heavily laden with ideological pronouncements about "state capitalism" and leftist rhetoric about the Cold War, which most critics have savaged as a turgid tract.

Mailer often publicly acknowledged Malaquais's role as his guide through the intellectual and ideological landscape of Marxism. According to Mailer, during those early postwar years Malaquais was "not only my best friend, he was my mentor." Mailer later declared to Steven Marcus that Malaquais was the only man he knew who combined "a powerful dogmatic mind with the keenest sense of nuance." When Mailer was interviewed toward the end of his life by Christopher Hitchens, he told Hitchens that Malaquais was not just a "mentor," but "my most enduring intellectual friendship ... we were like a party of two."[11] The pair also engaged in a number of literary adventures, including an effort to convince Goldwyn Mayer in Hollywood to produce their left-slanted screenplay of Nathaniel West's *Day of the Locust*—a mistimed, hopeless endeavor as the Red Scare and McCarthyism swept the movie industry.

The Naked and the Dead (1948) became an overnight literary sensation in America, selling more than 200,000 copies in its first three months and remaining on the *New York Times* best seller list for 62 weeks. It was published in France by Albin Michel in 1950 under the title *Les Nus et les Morts*. Malaquais did the translation. Regarding the $2,000 payment from the publisher as an insult, Mailer added an extra $1,000 of his own money. Malaquais appreciated Mailer's generosity, but that did not stop him from faulting the book publicly—a shocking, if not unprecedented, act by a handpicked translator. Once again, such "honesty" owed to the unsparing, at times brutal, candor of "*Malaquais rebelle*," his inveterate antinomian streak. "It was so badly written," he noted, "I am often forced to incredible gymnastics to extricate myself from it."[12] The intimacy and tensions in the two men's friendship are apparent in *Norman Mailer–Jean Malaquais: Correspondence, 1949–1986* (2008), edited by Elisabeth Malaquais (Malaquais's widow) and Geneviève Nakach. The correspondence has never appeared in English, and this French edition received almost no notice and has gone totally unacknowledged in the English-speaking world.

Apart from its linkage to André Gide, the name "Jean Malaquais" seldom surfaces in French literary history. (And even here, it arises seldom—not a single major biography of Gide, in French or English, mentions Malaquais.) Likewise, reference to him is virtually absent in all anglophone sources, except in connection with Norman Mailer. Unlike the stable, mutually respectful Gide–Malaquais friendship, however—in which Malaquais never fully outgrew his awe of Gide and his self-image as a (very) junior man of letters—the Malaquais-Mailer relationship was volatile, probably in no small part because, though the senior–junior roles were reversed, the comparative literary statuses were not.

Malaquais's relationship with Mailer constitutes his sole claim to notice in the second half of his life, after Gide's death in 1951.

But Malaquais certainly never treated the friendship as valuable or fragile cultural capital. Rather, he patronized his young protégé as a political naïf, describing him as "eager, touching, romantic and even uncouth."[13]

As his precocious young American protégé was—like the post-humous George Orwell—scaling the heights of literary fame (and notoriety) in the early 1950s, Malaquais himself was laboring quietly to complete what would prove to be his last work of fiction. It is a daringly original novel titled *Le Gaffeur* (1953; English title: *The Joker*). The style of the novel bears affinities with the fiction of Raymond Queneau, combining the baroque and the slangy and including colloquialisms that sometimes strike with a (purposeful) awkwardness. To an English-language reader, *The Joker* evokes an eighteenth-century picaresque novel that reminds one of the first-person narratives of a hapless *picaro*'s adventures, illustrated by chapter titles such as the following: "Wherein, Losing My Job, I Find My Key"; "Wherein I Resemble Myself Less and Less"; "Wherein the More I Run the Less I Overtake Myself"; and "Wherein It Is Confirmed That Bad Things Come in Threes."

The Joker is partly a satirical fantasy with echoes of E.T.A. Hoffmann and partly a dystopian fiction crossing Kafka with Zamyatin and Orwell that portrays a totalitarian society with a doomed protagonist much like Winston Smith. As such, it possesses a resemblance to aspects of *Nineteen Eighty-Four*. Like Orwell's dystopia, *The Joker* is set in a bleak postwar urban world known as "The City," which strongly resembles the decrepit Airstrip One. The City is a bureaucratic nightmare, and it combines—as does Oceania—the worst aspects of Soviet bureaucratic collectivism and American advanced capitalism, presenting a Weberian rather than a standard Marxist critique of bureaucracy.

The protagonist, Pierre Javelin, comes home one day to discover that he has lost his identity and begins to question his very existence. Like Winston Smith, who is unable to escape the watchful eye of Big Brother and the Thought Police, Javelin is watched by secret police called "the Inspectors." Javelin discovers that the individual exists for the sake of "being one with the City," that is, with the powers that rule—just as Winston Smith must learn to "love Big Brother." Moreover, just as Winston keeps a secret diary in which he denounces Big Brother but that he fails (deliberately?) to stash in a secure hiding place, so too does Pierre slander the City's officialdom in brash poems that he impetuously leaves scattered in public places for potential fellow freethinkers to read.

Similarities also prevail between O'Brien in *Nineteen Eighty-Four* and Javelin's interrogator, Dr. Babitch, both of whom "re-educate" their victims for the new world order. Dr. Babitch tells Pierre, in a confrontation analogous to that of O'Brien and Winston in Room 101: "Say any word at all and I will have you hanged." This scene also recalls the Freudian/Orwellian "slip" that lands Winston's Outer Party colleague Syme in Room 101. Syme mumbles a seditious word about Big Brother in his sleep, which his little daughter dutifully reports to the authorities. So too does Winston find himself, as he is tortured by O'Brien, suddenly screaming in desperation: "Do it to Julia!" His love for Julia curdles into hatred, and he wishes her to be tortured rather than him. It is a short step from Dr. Babitch's threat to Oceania's thoughtcrime. Significantly, the original title of *The Joker* was *One Against the City*, which resembles Orwell's initial choice of *The Last Man in Europe* for *Nineteen Eighty-Four*. In both cases the title evokes a single individual battling in vain to retain his identity in a totalitarian world.

The Joker received respectable reviews on its American publication in 1954. Yet it too failed commercially, doubtless because it was too symbolic and too alarmist to suit the American public in the comfortable 1950s of Eisenhower's America. Unlike the dystopias of Kurt Vonnegut, Ray Bradbury, and others, Malaquais's work introduces no sci-fi gadgetry. Unlike *Nineteen Eighty-Four*, it also lacks memorable catchphrases like "Big Brother Is Watching You," "2 + 2 = 5," doublethink, thoughtcrime, memory hole and Newspeak. In 1974, in an attempted revival 20 years after its first appearance, a new edition with a glowing foreword by Mailer appeared. Echoing Trotsky's review of *Les Javanais* 35 years earlier—surely unintentionally—Mailer applauded *The Joker* as an artwork free from formulas, propaganda, and clichés.[14] Despite this sincere attempt to stimulate interest in the novel, however, this second edition exited the scene even more quietly than the first.[15]

Clio Favors, Clio Forgets

So much for the congruences in subject matter, sensibility, genre, and career shape between these two (ostensibly so different) writers—Malaquais, the displaced Polish-born Jew in Paris, and Orwell, Old Etonian and left-wing patriot. The fortunes of Orwell and Malaquais after 1953 diverge completely. We have noted that the "afterlives" of Orwell and Malaquais moved in opposite directions, ultimately coming to rest at polar extremes: worldwide fame versus literary neglect. It is indeed astonishing to observe how utterly the receptions of Orwell and Malaquais contrast in literary history.

Consider this: Few people outside London are aware that the "Orwell" is a small river in Suffolk. Untold millions, however, recognize "Orwell" as the name of a famous writer (unaware that it is a pen name), and millions more cringe at the adjective "Orwellian" (without knowing its derivation). By contrast, "Malaquais" is a well-known Parisian embankment along the Seine in the Saint-Germain-des-Près quarter. The name signifies nothing literary—even in Parisian cultural circles. Malaquais was infrequently reviewed in France and—despite praise from Trilling, Rosenfeld, Mailer, and others on the Left—never promoted by the critical establishment in Britain or America. After becoming an American citizen in 1952, Malaquais visited France irregularly. In 1970, he earned a doctoral dissertation from the Sorbonne with a thesis on the philosopher Kierkegaard[16]; he had begun the dissertation in 1954 under the direction of the philosopher Jean Wahl. But Malaquais wrote no more fiction and little nonfiction.[17] Increasingly, he suffered from a writer's block similar to that experienced by fellow leftist contrarian Dwight Macdonald. Like Macdonald, Malaquais began to pursue visiting lectureships as a substitute for his energies and to distract himself from the block. After publishing three novels during the period 1939–1953, he wrote virtually nothing in his last 40 years.[18]

Despite a long life, therefore, Malaquais's career as a man of letters was rather brief, shorter even than that of Orwell. Malaquais did, however, retain an interest in politics to the end, remaining true to the revolutionary Marxism of his past, whether in the form of fervent anti-Bolshevism or a version of anarcho-syndicalism. Occasionally, as in the case of the student uprisings in France in 1968, he was drawn back to an active role. He returned to France and wholeheartedly supported the *bien-pensant* student radicals of 1968 and their attack on the corrupt capitalist world, seeing in them the rebel whom he himself had once been. Shortly before his death at the age of 90 in 1998, the Paris publishing firm Phebus reprinted his *pièce de résistance*, the long-forgotten *Les Javanais*, along with some of his other early writings. They aroused scant interest. Despite the biographical study by Geneviève Nakach, which finally gave him the recognition he deserved, followed by a long review-essay of Nakach's biography by the Parisian journalist Emilie Bickerton in *New Left Review*, no sign of a Malaquais revival, either in the francophone or anglo-phone world, has been discernible.

For the literary historian, the comparison with Orwell never-theless raises a number of intriguing questions: Why have no scholars or biographers noticed the connections between the two men, beginning with the obvious fact that they were both in the POUM? Why did Orwell go on to win recognition in his own lifetime and far greater fame in his literary afterlife? And why did Malaquais, after launching his career in a flash of literary radi-ance, vanish like a shooting star from literary history? Appar-ently, the last half of his life—the 45 years after the publication of *Le Gaffeur* in 1953—doesn't even interest his biographer, Gen-eviève Nakach, whose 381-page biography skates over them in a brisk 36 pages.

Perhaps the most intriguing question is: Why didn't Orwell and Malaquais themselves show any awareness of each other's work? We know that Malaquais was aware of Orwell: he penned a single-paragraph preface to an extract from *The Road to Wigan Pier* when it appeared in French in 1981.[19] But nowhere is there any indication that he ever read *Homage to Catalonia* or even knew of Orwell's membership in the POUM. Nor did Orwell ever refer to Malaquais, whose writings about the sordid side of life in France were precisely the kind of books that he often read and reviewed.

The omission is puzzling when one considers that both Orwell and Malaquais stayed in touch with Victor Serge and admired the murdered Catalonian POUM leader Andrés Nin. Moreover, when one reads the voluminous correspondence between Gide and Malaquais, one wonders why neither Malaquais nor Gide ever mentioned Orwell to the other.[20] All three men—Orwell, Gide, and Malaquais—shared similar views on the Soviet Union. Gide had returned from a visit to Stalin's "paradise" and penned a bitter indictment of the failures of Communism, *Retour de l'URSS* (1937). Malaquais, after a brief flirtation with communism, became a lifelong enemy of Soviet communism, which he regarded as a totalitarian system no better than Nazism. Orwell's denunciation of communism in general and Stalin's cult of personality in particular, thematized in *Animal Farm* and *Nineteen Eighty-Four*, were well-known in literary Paris at midcentury. In June 1945, Orwell visited Paris and sent an advance copy of *Animal Farm* to Gide, as well as to other French intellectuals (such as Albert Camus and André Malraux) who were likely to be sympathetic to the fable's anti-Stalinist critique.

To top off the mystery—which given the omission of any mention of such a connection by critics and biographers almost represents an absurdist conspiracy of silence—Orwell's translator, Yvonne Davet, became Gide's secretary in 1938. She had already begun translating *Homage to Catalonia* into French that year, completing it in 1939 with advice from Orwell. Publication of the work in France, however, was rendered impossible as the war neared. (Her translation did not appear in France until 1955.) Still serving as Gide's secretary in 1945, Davet also translated *Animal Farm*. Her translation was obviously the one that Gide received from Orwell's publisher in Paris. She also translated other works of Orwell before and after Gide's death in 1951. The Gide–Malaquais correspondence includes numerous references to Davet, to whom Gide dictated his letters to Malaquais and others. Moreover, the Gide–Malaquais correspondence makes it clear that Malaquais was very friendly with her. Both belonged to Gide's inner circle, having met him in the mid-1930s. (Gide not only encouraged Malaquais's literary ambitions but also became his patron.) Surely the trio must have been quite aware of Orwell's reportage on the Wigan miners, his POUM affiliation, and all the rest? And yet the only trace in print that Malaquais ever knew even Orwell's name is his nondescript, factually based, one-paragraph introduction to a short extract from *The Road to Wigan Pier*, excerpted in *Le Debat* in November 1981 to promote the first French edition. Malaquais makes no mention of anything personal or autobiographical in this paragraph.

Fame and Its Vicissitudes

The whirligig of fame is a whirling dervish, whose Dionysian dance sweeps up a handful of artists, vaults them into the "starry" heavens—whether for 15 seconds or 50 centuries—and leaves countless others by the wayside to gather dust. That is the *modus operandi* of History. Reputations are made, not born. Orwell received little public notice until the last four years of his life—and ubiquitous international recognition soon thereafter. And Malaquais? Even informed readers in France respond, "Malaquais who?" They assume you are talking about the Quai Malaquais in Paris—which, needless to say, is emphatically *not* named after him.

The cultural world has come to know a great deal about George Orwell. Thousands of articles and books have been written about Orwell the man, the writer, and the political icon. And Malaquais? Until 2011, with Nakach's publication of *Malaquais rebelle*, virtually nothing was known about his life. His literary achievements had tumbled down the memory hole—and still remain there, all Nakach's efforts to arouse interest (even including the creation of a Société Jean Malaquais in Paris) notwithstanding.

Malaquais lived an extraordinarily dramatic life that warrants the attention of not only biographers and critics, but also screenwriters. After being persecuted in Poland as a young Jew and emigrating to his fantasized "land of liberté," *la France*, he found himself little more than a decade later suddenly a literary celebrity.

Weeks thereafter, and equally abruptly, the fall of France in June 1940 landed him in a German P.O.W. camp. Before being discovered to be a Jew, he escaped from the Germans and then without a passport slipped out of occupied France into the unoccupied zone in the south, only to go into hiding from the Nazis as a Jew again. There he made the acquaintance of a left-wing intellectual fraternity that included Serge, Heinrich and Golo Mann, André Breton, Max Ernst, Franz Werfel, and Walter Benjamin. Eventually, with the assistance of Varian Fry, he was shepherded across the Pyrenees into Spain, where he was able to ship out from Cadiz to Venezuela. From there he traveled to Mexico, where—thanks to a visa arranged by Gide—he survived as a penniless émigré for the rest of the war.

All that—and not yet 35 years old.

Is it any wonder that by the 1950s, burned out—perhaps shell-shocked—from decades of physical and emotional upheaval, he was hopelessly blocked as a writer, even though he was only in his early 40s? This wandering revolutionary Jew had already lived the equivalent of several lifetimes. By the postwar years, sheer exhaustion—or what we today might term "posttraumatic stress disorder"—had snuffed out whatever few sparks of idealism and *joie de vivre* remained, transforming the once unthinkable prospect of an academic retreat and literary quietism into a welcome respite.

If only Malaquais had been able to write fiction or reportage simply and directly, rather than obliquely or impersonally! If only he had gotten the drama of his life into his work! Perhaps rather like the thinly veiled fiction of fellow émigré Pole Jerzy Kosinski. Or Mailer's "nonfiction novels"—or, for that matter, Orwell's *Wigan Pier* and *Catalonia*. Then Jean Malaquais would have been an international best seller. Instead Malaquais exemplified the lonely, purist outsider, the odd man out, adamantly and eternally ensconced on the far-left fringe of the political world. He was never at home in any movement for long and warred not just with his enemies but with his comrades (such as Serge)—surely another reason that he failed to make a lasting impact.

By contrast, Orwell's declared aim to turn "political writing into an art," voiced eloquently in "Why I Write" (1946), was magnificently fulfilled in that manifesto and several other nonfiction pieces, and above all in *Animal Farm* and *Nineteen Eighty-Four*. In that essay he also confessed that any author's first great motive for writing is "sheer egoism," including the ambition "to be remembered after death."

By any measure, he certainly has been. Since his death at mid-century, he has witnessed a level of posthumous fame unprecedented for any serious modern writer. In fact, his boffo second act—starring "Orwell"—has far outshone (and partly eclipsed) the first. It is a stunning and still-unfolding sequel that epitomizes the (secret) dream of so many secular intellectuals that "death is not the end, but rather the supreme morning."[21]

And "Malaquais"? The name is known as an embankment, not an *écrivain*. Jean Malaquais is a forgotten writer, a man without not just a country, but a legacy—unmourned, unsung, unread, unknown. Yes, "Nowhere Man." Such are the vicissitudes of literary history and cultural celebrity as Clio delivers her verdicts and divides her spoils.

FIGURE 10. The uber-cool, debonair Albert Camus, hero of the Resistance for his service as editor of the underground newspaper *Combat*, 1947. With his collar turned up like a gorget and a cigarette dangling from his mouth, Camus, then 34, was nicknamed the "Humphrey Bogart of French letters." Immortalized by photographer Henri Cartier-Bresson in this casual pose, Camus became associated forever after in the minds of literary-minded people with the élan of Bogie and the wartime heroics of *Casablanca* (1942).

CHAPTER 8

French Connection, Part 2

Camus and Orwell, *Rebelles avec une cause*

Speaking Truth to Power

You could hardly pick a Parisian literary contemporary of Jean Malaquais more different from him. We turn now to a writer universally known, lavishly honored, and passionately cherished: the Nobel laureate Albert Camus, virtually a French "Everywhere Man." Moreover, unlike the long-lived Malaquais, who survived another 46 years, virtually an entire lifetime, after his pen fell silent in the mid-1950s, Camus died a tragic early death—ironically, at the age of 46, like George Orwell. January 2020 marks the anniversaries of the deaths of these two famous men of letters: the seventieth for the Englishman Orwell and the sixtieth for the *pied noir* French Algerian Camus. That occasion warrants acknowledgment, if only in order to reaffirm the heritage that Orwell and Camus represent, a legacy of intellectual integrity, moral courage, and literary excellence.

Both of these men exemplified the rare temerity to speak truth to power, to voice a cry against oppression and injustice. They did so not only against the malfeasance of government officials and the cowardice of the so-called Establishment, but even against their own immediate reference group, their fellow intellectuals on the Left, what the New York intellectual and social critic Harold

Rosenberg called "the herd of independent minds" stampeding together in the same direction. Rosenberg was referring to his own group of New York intellectuals, but he was in fact merely echoing what Orwell had repeatedly said three decades earlier in London and Camus shortly thereafter in Paris. Yet in order to appreciate fully the heritage that Orwell and Camus represent, a short history lesson is in order.

The Intellectual as Critic and Conscience

The very word "intellectual" was not even part of the Western lexicon until the late nineteenth century. Yes, there were men of letters, essayists, journalists, and gentleman scholars. But there was not an identifiable class—"the intellectuals"—as we have come to understand the term. This locution arose after the conviction in 1894 of Alfred Dreyfus, a captain in the French army who had been unjustly convicted of treason on trumped-up charges. The truth—that Dreyfus, a Jew, was the victim of vicious anti-Semitic prejudices during his trial—was suppressed by both the French military and the French government. However, some writers, especially Emile Zola in *J'Accuse!*, could not and would not remain silent once they had discovered the truth. In his explosive manifesto, Zola wrote, "I accuse the government, I accuse the military, I accuse the powers that be of lying and corruption and deception of those whom they would proclaim to serve, the public." Published in 1898, *J'Accuse!* caused a firestorm of controversy in Paris. Plenty of Parisian writers and men of letters wanted to suppress the truth. "Let this French Jew take the blame," they muttered. There were others, however, who agreed with Zola. And thus "the intellectual" was born, that is, the thinker who insists that the truth must be expressed in language clear and direct and simple and concrete—and, wherever possible, fluid and euphonious.

And so the role of *l'intellectuel* became, first in France and then throughout the continent and elsewhere, to speak out as a critic of power. Yet what happened when, soon thereafter in the twentieth century, the intellectuals themselves began to demonstrate that they were corrupt and deceptive, when they began fully collaborating with power, such as during the French occupation? Or for a much longer period shortly thereafter with Soviet Russia? The Western intellectuals' betrayal of their calling continued even after the USSR occupied all of Eastern Europe—partly because "Uncle Joe Stalin" had been the West's ally against the Nazis, "our Russian comrades," even if only between June 1941 and the end of World War II.

It is much more difficult, and it requires much greater intellectual integrity and moral courage, to be a critic *of your own side*, of your fellow intellectuals. Yes, it's easier to speak truth to power if the powerful are in faraway places like the White House or Number 10 Downing Street or the Palais Élysée, where they ignore you like an elephant does a fly as you declaim and breast-beat in your academic publications and your ephemeral newspaper columns.

But what happens when intellectual integrity obligates you to become the unwelcome truth-teller to colleagues and friends and even family members whose shoulders you brush day after day? Or who are the writers and editors of the journals and magazines to which you (would like to?) contribute? Then it's not so easy to criticize, because then you pass from merely being a critic of power to a "conscience."

A conscience is a critic *from within*. Yet a conscience criticizes not in order to weaken, but to strengthen his or her own side, to hold it to the highest possible standard, even higher than that of the opposing party. A critic who is also a conscience insists that truth comes before beauty, power, or any other value or attribute. That scale of commitment is not so easy to maintain faithfully, which is why we seldom find writers of the caliber of George Orwell and Albert Camus.

Foes of Fascism

As in the previous chapter, we are engaging here in comparative biography, aiming to rivet attention on the arresting similarities and important, if sometimes subtle, differences between two writers. Because Camus, unlike Malaquais, is a household name in contemporary literary history, we will sketch his *annales* in broad strokes, forgoing an overview of his dramatic journey and instead concentrating our attention more narrowly on the congruities and contrasts with Orwell. And once again, as in our diptych of Orwell and Malaquais, closely tracking these resemblances and disparities will occasionally entail covering a few already mentioned aspects of Orwell's life and work.

On the three great political issues that faced them in the mid-twentieth century—fascism and Nazism, colonialism and imperialism, and Communism and Stalinism—Orwell and Camus took unorthodox, indeed heterodox, stances toward their representative intelligentsias, both of which were left-dominated. Both men suffered greatly as a result. Nevertheless, they have been vindicated by history.

The first issue is best exemplified in Orwell's case by his response to the outbreak of the Spanish Civil War. Orwell was not content like most of his fellow writers and intellectuals to stay home safely in England or even to venture to Spain as a journalist to report on events. Instead he decided to enlist in a predominantly Spanish militia. That decision separated him from almost all other foreign writers and intellectuals (and nonintellectuals) who came to Spain to defend the Left and repulse Franco. They joined the USSR-backed and Communist-dominated International Brigade, financed by Moscow, which was in the process of trying to suppress the POUM, the quasi-anarchist/Trotskyist militia that Orwell had entered. Orwell's allegiance was neither to the fascist Right nor to the Stalinist Left. His service in the POUM was abruptly cut short when he got a bullet through his windpipe, almost died as a result, and, as he attempted to flee from Spain, was nearly arrested and murdered by the Stalinists, managing to escape simply by good fortune. He lost his voice for almost two years but later was able to speak, if softly. But he did not write softly. His indignant pen was louder and clearer than ever.

His memoir, *Homage to Catalonia* (1938), describes what happened. Orwell insisted on intellectual integrity, and so the book was "ruined," he later wrote, by the necessity of introducing several long passages from various British newspaper reports on the war. He felt he had to document chapter and verse the lies of the British press that had supported Stalin's version of what was happening in Spain and how the International Brigades collaborated with it. Of course, Franco won the Spanish Civil War. The fascists dominated Spain for decades thereafter, and *Homage to Catalonia* thus represents an elegy for a socialism that Orwell believed he momentarily saw from his sickbed in Barcelona but was never fully realized. Although the book sold a grand total of fewer than 900 copies before Orwell's death and was soon remaindered, it stands today as the most widely read nonfiction book on the Spanish Civil War in any language.

Camus faced an even more direct and difficult challenge: the Nazi occupation of France. He became the editor-in-chief of *Combat*, the French Resistance newspaper that as an underground publication reached a circulation of more than a quarter million. Camus thereby exerted an enormous, if clandestine, intellectual and moral influence within the Resistance. Meanwhile, of course, many intellectuals made their peace with the Vichy government and the occupation and became collaborators. Others on the Left, while firmly opposed to the Vichy government, such as Jean-Paul Sartre and Simone de Beauvoir, largely limited themselves to literary activities. Sartre spent much of the occupation completing his dense 900-page philosophical treatise, *Being and Nothingness* (1943), which was his reply to Heidegger's *Being and Time*, published 16 years earlier. Needless to say, *Being and Nothingness* was not read by many people in the French underground who were trying to get rid of the Nazis. So here too, like Orwell, Camus did not take the easy ideological stance, whether fascist or Stalinist, collaborator or inner émigré.

Enemies of Empire

And what about the second issue, imperialism and colonialism? Both men had the experience of living in exile, one could say. As we discussed in Chapter 1, Eric Blair was born in Bengal and brought as an infant to Edwardian England, where he was reared. But in his 20s, after graduating from Eton, he ventured back to the East and spent five years as a member of the Indian Imperial Police in various stations in Burma, where he began to hate his role as an oppressor of the Burmese natives, doing what he later referred to as "the dirty work of imperialism." Coming home to England in 1927 with a resolve to become a novelist, he struggled as a writer for several years. His first novel was *Burmese Days* (1934), which represents a worthy successor to E. M. Forster's *Passage to India* (1927). Orwell's rebel hero, John Flory, is in some respects remarkably like Orwell himself. Throughout the last quarter century of his life, despite an abiding affection for Rudyard Kipling's verse and prose, Orwell consistently opposed British imperialism, including the paternalistic vanities of Empire and the idea of the White Man's Burden. He supported Indian independence and expressed equivocal support for Mahatma Gandhi—despite his own outspoken atheism and opposition to what he saw as Gandhi's political naïveté and anachronistic spirituality.

Here again, Camus faced perhaps an even more vexed and harrowing dilemma. Born of French parentage in 1913 in Algeria, he suffered the loss of his father in World War I. While he later traveled to France, his mother, his brother, and the rest of his family remained in Algeria their entire lives. When the call for Algerian independence arose in the mid-1950s, Camus was torn. Both a European and an Algerian, he understood that to support Algerian independence and the concomitant anti-Americanism of the Algerian revolution meant that his own family would be at risk. As he put it in his Nobel Prize acceptance speech in 1957, "If revolutionaries are planting bombs in the subway and calling that justice, well, my mother travels on that subway every day. If that is justice, I choose my mother." For that statement, he was widely condemned not only by the Algerian revolutionaries, but also by the entire Left, from Marxists and Communists to the so-called fellow-travelers led by Jean-Paul Sartre and Maurice Merleau-Ponty. As Sartre later wrote in his preface to Frantz Fanon's famous treatise of the 1960s, *The Wretched of the Earth*: "To kill a European is to kill two birds with one stone. In the end, one is left with the oppressor dead and the oppressed [man] liberated. And so a dead man and a free man."

Because Camus was both a European and an Algerian, the choice was not so easy for him. For him to support Algerian independence meant that one day his mother might be blown to smithereens. No, it is not an easy decision to criticize your own side, your fellow intellectuals. For the herd of independent minds stampeding in the same direction may set their sights on *you*. Still, in historical hindsight, it is a modest consolation to know that during the brutal civil war in Algeria, which began in the early 1990s and lasted more than a decade, it became quite common in Paris to state that Camus had been vindicated by history, for Algeria would have been much better off if it had evolved into a multiethnic state with limited self-government, closely linked to France. If Orwell had been a prophet about the geopolitics of the late twentieth century and the seductions of leader worship, Camus was a prophet about the future of Algeria.

Scourges of Stalinism

And what about the last and thorniest of the three issues— Stalinism and Communism? We have already mentioned Orwell's outraged memoir addressing the Stalinist betrayal of socialism in Spain, *Homage to Catalonia*. A pertinent Orwell anecdote concerns a lunch he had with a friend, during which Orwell spotted the editor of the *New Statesman*, Kingsley Martin, at a table across the room. Orwell told his friend that he had to move and asked if they could change places. The friend asked him why. Orwell replied, "I can't bear throughout the lunch to look at Kingsley's corrupt face." Martin had commissioned articles from Orwell about the Spanish Civil War and rejected them because they would "give ammunition to the enemy." Truth-telling would hurt "our own side." Thereafter, Orwell rarely wrote for the newspaper, which was the leading left-wing publication of the day in Britain.

As the 1940s progressed, Orwell instead increasingly turned his attention to the spectre of totalitarianism, which he feared might prevail worldwide. He realized presciently that it represented a new, vastly expanded, and more powerful form of dictatorial despotism, and that its manifestations on the Right (fascism and Nazism) and on the Left (Stalinist communism)—whatever their superficial differences—were actually mirror images. In *Animal Farm* and *Nineteen Eighty-Four* above all, Orwell spoke truth to power, voicing his premonitions of a totalitarian future with uncompromising fierceness and frightening clarity. *Nineteen Eighty-Four* is justly read as a fictional blueprint of totalitarian tyranny covering both its right- and left-wing versions—and thereby contributed significantly to the birth of the academic subfield of totalitarian studies. In fact, when I think of the landmarks in scholarship addressing totalitarianism during the 1950s and 1960s—celebrated books widely read in comparative government classes such as Hannah Arendt's *The Origins of Totalitarianism*, Richard Löwenthal's *World Communism*, and Carl Friedrich and Zbigniew Brzezinski's *Totalitarian Dictatorship and Autocracy*—I am reminded of Alfred North Whitehead's famous if hyperbolic remark in *Process and Reality* that "the safest general characterization of the European philosophical tradition is that it consists of a series of footnotes to Plato." One could make the same claim about the debt of the early post–World War II literature of totalitarianism to *Nineteen Eighty-Four*—and with far less exaggeration.

Nonetheless, it needs emphasis that Orwell devoted no more than intermittent attention to fascist Spain and Nazi Germany. His pen was typically pointed in the direction of Stalinist communism, particularly the twisted rationalizations and hypocrisies of his fellow intellectuals on the British Left. He became the "conscience" of the Left because he invariably directed his main energies against the moral and political vices of "our own side," insisting that the Left hold itself to the highest standard of intellectual integrity. The prime target in *Animal Farm* and *Nineteen Eighty-Four* is Stalinism and its "duckspeaking" intellectual defenders in the Anglo-American world.

Orwell was especially outraged by the Left's mindless sloganeering and "quacking" of the ever-shifting Soviet party line, and he satirized these habits with gusto. Part of our Western literary heritage today consists of satirical catchphrases introduced into the political lexicon not only from *Nineteen Eighty-Four* but also from *Animal Farm* (e.g., Sugarcandy Mountain, "four legs good, two legs bad," "All animals are equal, but some are more equal than others").

Unsurprisingly, these books firmly solidified Orwell's already well-established status as *persona non grata* on the Left—a distinction that Camus would soon also share. It warrants mention here that the publication of *Animal Farm* in France furnished the occasion for Orwell and Camus to have some slight contact, even though events conspired so that they never personally met. During his weeks as a war reporter for the *Observer* in liberated Paris in April 1945, Orwell arranged to have lunch with Camus after sending him an advance copy of the French translation of *Animal Farm*. Unfortunately, Camus had to cancel the scheduled meeting at the Deux Magots because of illness. (Orwell did meet with André Malraux and a few other French writers.)

Orwell was castigated by the British Left for branding the Soviet leaders "pigs" and for lampooning "Uncle Joe" Stalin as Big Brother. He paid a high price among British radicals for his audacity. Yet Camus, here again, confronted an arguably even more painful challenge in opposing the French Left of the 1950s on the issue of Stalinism. The French Communists, along with the fellow-travelers led by Jean-Paul Sartre, acknowledged the existence of the Soviet gulag, but they subscribed not only to *tiers mondisme* ("third world-ism"), but also to its corollary, anti-Americanism. Those dogmas forbade public criticism of Stalin's genocidal labor camps. Whenever criticism of the gulag was brought up, leftist French intellectuals immediately referred to McCarthyism in the United States and proclaimed them equivalent. And so the Soviet gulag and mass starvation policies, a campaign of mass murder exceeding 20 million people under both Stalin and his successors, was compared to a truly awful, though comparatively modest, witch hunt against American Communists by Senator Joseph McCarthy during the early 1950s.

Camus was unwilling to accept that easy equivalence. He refused to indulge in the cynical illusions and double standards of Stalinism, the Marxist-dominated French intelligentsia's ideological drug of choice throughout most of the postwar era, which the conservative French intellectual Raymond Aron famously referred to as "the opiate of the intellectuals" in his book of that title, published in 1955.

Yet Camus had already voiced a similar warning to the Left—and been ostracized by his onetime friends and political comrades, such as Sartre and Simone de Beauvoir. He had been vilified when he wrote *The Rebel* (1951), in which he analyzed the history of Marxism, concluding that even revered French figures on the Left such as Robespierre were guilty of a schematic and simplistic politics whereby they succumbed to romantic abstractions and rationalized the legitimacy of genocidal murder for the revolutionary idea of Utopia.

Camus would have agreed with Orwell that history had already shown that "one revolution after another—although usually producing a temporary relief, such as a sick man gets by turning over in bed—has simply led to a change of masters." Orwell's views of revolution anticipate and even echo those of Camus in

L'homme revolté, which declares, "In the minds of active revolutionaries … the longing for a just society has always been fatally mixed up with the intention to secure power for themselves."

Although both Camus and Orwell remained "men of the Left" to the end of their days, they were always most critical of their own side. They had good reason to be so: socialists of the Left (in Stalin's Union of Soviet *Socialist* Republics) as well as of the Right (in Hitler's National *Socialist* Germany) had proven time and again to be ruthless exploiters of the common man once they rose to power. One cannot help but think of Orwell's quip to his friend Richard Rees about the mentality of socialist ideologues: "I notice people always say 'under socialism.' They look forward to being on top—with all the others underneath, being told what is good for them."

The self-satisfied revolutionary, the political "virtucrat," always carries a whiff of the sanctimonious, a sense of moral smugness or superiority—all of which is not infrequently betrayed by glaring hypocrisy. As Camus wrote in *The Rebel* about such leaders of the French Revolution as Saint-Just: "Pure and unadulterated virtue is homicidal." From the French to the Russian to the Chinese Revolutions and beyond, he was sadly right, failing only to specify that the consequence in the latter cases was often *mass* homicide.

Religious Fellow-Travelers?

A final important yet seldom-acknowledged similarity between these two iconic twentieth-century men of letters concerns an ever-burning issue transcending the immediate, topical events in the headlines of their eras. It has to do with another aspect of their moral profiles: their stances toward—and, formally speaking, against—religious belief. Both men were avowed and adamant nonbelievers. Orwell, as we have noted, was a hardline atheist and a vociferous critic of Christianity in general and the Catholic Church in particular, which he sometimes compared in its hierarchical structure and doctrinal orthodoxies to totalitarian ideologies such as Nazism and Stalinism (and the forms of leader worship that their party functionaries inculcated in their followers). As such, he has been adopted as a hero by the so-called New Atheists in the U.K. and the U.S., especially the media celebrities known as the "Four Horsemen" (Richard Dawkins, David Dennett, Sam Harris, and the late Christopher Hitchens).

By contrast, Camus was not a militant atheist. "I do not believe in God, but I am not an atheist," he once wrote. Instead his mode of religious unbelief was actually a form of what could be called "minimalist faith," an ethics of belief guided by his concept of "lucidity." According to Camus, lucidity entailed the resolve to keep one's mind "unclouded" by the temptation of or nostalgia for the ultimate answers about the meaning of life that the established religions offered. Camus was thus a secular humanist and rationalist who insisted that one lived only with what could be known from reason and should never base one's existence on the mystical or the ineffable. The universe possesses no transcendent meaning, Camus maintained, though the condition of what he called "the Absurd" consists not in this absence, but rather in our irrational pursuit of the solace of religious faith. Intellectual maturity and moral responsibility thus turn on the refusal of a weakminded surrender to comforting pieties. Instead, we must steel ourselves to a proactive commitment to an ethics of lucidity.

And yet, on closer examination, both Orwell and Camus were, in the phrase of Max Weber, "religiously musical." Although firmly opposed (indeed deliberately tone-deaf) to the sermonics of religious faith, they nonetheless valued its spiritual dimension. They derided chiefly the historical crimes of organized religions, and they worried deeply about how the decline of religious belief had facilitated the rise of totalitarian dogmas and the exaltation of science and technology, which flourished amid the panic to fill the vacuum. For example, addressing the dangers of the atom bomb, both Orwell and Camus perceived that the Gnostic tendency to exalt knowledge was now playing itself out in modern science's destructive reign. Such a doctrine glorified human intelligence while approaching material reality in purely instrumental fashion. If this state of mind reflected the modern world's highest form of knowledge, what was badly needed, Orwell wrote, was "faith." While he explicitly ruled out a return to religious belief as a backward step that would signify a refusal to "grow up"—and would be historically impossible anyway—his implication was that the only corrective to the ersatz religions of the totalitarian ideologies was the real thing.

Camus differed from Orwell in his much more sustained and thoroughgoing engagement with Christianity, and moreover with philosophical and even theological matters more broadly. Much of his master's thesis, submitted to the University of Algeria in 1936, deals with an analysis of Augustinian dogma; its title was: "The Relationship between Greek Philosophy and Christianity in Plotinus to Augustine." Moreover, the Christian ethos of Dostoyevsky and Tolstoy exerted a strong influence on Camus's own work. For instance, his last novel, *The Fall* (1958)—as its title transparently suggests—addresses the theme of Christian redemption and is imbued with religious imagery, including references to Eden and "sin."[1] The name of the narrator and protagonist in *The Fall*, Jean-Baptiste Clemence, is described as a modern Adam and likewise possesses obvious Christian overtones.[2] It is also notable that Camus spent a substantial period during his last years staging productions of William Faulkner's *Requiem for a Nun*, and that he professed to have "a sense of the sacred."

All this is why one might describe Camus, like the agnostic Max Weber, as "religiously musical." Admittedly, however, the evidence cuts both ways. As in the case of Orwell, many readers of Camus have adamantly maintained that he stood against both organized religion and soft-headed mysticism. Camus explicitly stated: "I feel closer to the values of the classical world than to those of Christianity." Like Nietzsche, Camus held that Christianity promoted joylessness in this world, redeemed by bliss in the next one. From this standpoint, like Orwell, he subscribed to a post-Christian liberalism, exemplified best by his ardent commitment to justice and adamant opposition to violence and the death penalty. In spite of Camus's belief in the absurdity and irrationality of existence, he never descended into nihilism, but rather voiced strong stands against terroristic violence, capital punishment, and totalitarian ideology.

And yet again, on the other hand, Camus once called himself an "independent Catholic" (to his friend Paul Raffi), an identity that he seems to have considered similar to his stance as an independent radical, a man of the Left yet also a political freelancer unaffiliated with the French Communist Party or the socialist movement formally. Some critics have even suggested that if Camus had lived longer, he might have become a professed Christian. Camus in fact became an exemplar of moral discernment for some Christian antiwar activists during the Vietnam era. For example, Father Daniel Berrigan, a Catholic priest and leading figure in the protest movement who burned draft records and released government documents such as the Pentagon Papers, posted a statement of Camus in large letters in his office, "I wish I would love my country as much as I love justice."

Religion, then, was central to the outlooks of my two cherished unbelievers, Orwell and Camus, but not in a creedal way. They were what Paul Elie calls "secular postmodern pilgrims." I view them in the spiritual tradition of *homo viator*—man the wayfarer—and call them "religious fellow-travelers." The secularist seeker is, as Elie phrases it, "not a believer himself, but a person who is attracted to belief, prone to it, often covetous of it in others, and is brought to the threshold of belief imaginatively through his reading." Such intellectual fellow-travelers experience no kind of religious conversion. But admiring believers often lionize them as "good agnostics," that is, believers in all but name, perhaps even secular saints. Such secular pilgrims acknowledge the *need* for faith, but they themselves disavow religious convictions.

Both Orwell and Camus acknowledged the tragic and the Absurd in a world that dealt out disappointment and hope in uneven, unexpected ways. Yet they also remained convinced, through hours dark and bright, that trust is never completely extinguished. I believe they would have quickly seconded the agnostic American social critic Christopher Lasch that "if progressive ideologies have dwindled down to a wistful hope against hope that things will somehow work out for the best, we need to discover a more vigorous form of hope."

Lasch himself distinguished between optimism and hope: Hope, he suggested, possesses a "religious quality" and requires a fundamental confidence in "the goodness of life and some kind of underlying justice in the universe, in spite of all the evidence to the contrary." Optimism is far different, especially in its vapid contemporary varieties, and one "mustn't confuse [material, Marxist] 'progress' with the true and only heaven," which is characterized by a state of both world and inner peace.

Orwell and Camus might have phrased it differently, but in the main they would have agreed. Above all, they too inveighed against soft-minded, sunny optimism—though both men remained cautiously hopeful despite the horrors of their time, which ranged from the European Holocaust to the bomb and beyond.

A Heritage of Heroism

Such is the valuable legacy of George Orwell and Albert Camus, both principled critics of their own sides and "consciences" within the intelligentsias of the two leading Western European capitals of their day. These comparisons are illuminating, for the contrasts between the two men are so pronounced—as in the case of Orwell and Malaquais—that they obscure their notable resemblances regarding political stance and moral probity, which have been widely overlooked by historians. (Another seldom-noticed, odd similarity is the prominent motif of rats in their *chefs d'oeuvre*. O'Brien tortures Winston by placing a cage of ravenous rats up against his face in Room 101. In Camus's *The Plague* [1947], which allegorizes how the Nazis overran and occupied France, the fatal "disease" that spreads throughout the population is caused by rats.)

Orwell was sometimes described by his friends as a St. Francis, an ascetic, a "secular saint" who in the end actually came close to killing himself for the sake of truth and art. Even while suffering tuberculosis, going in and out of sanatoria throughout the late 1940s, he insisted on remaining on the remote island of Jura in the Scottish Hebrides and finishing *Nineteen Eighty-Four*. After he concluded the final chapters of the novel in December 1948, he left Jura to enter a Gloucestershire sanatorium a few weeks later, then transferred in September to University College Hospital in London, from which he never reemerged. What he left us was his political testament and urgent jeremiad, *Nineteen Eighty-Four*. He risked, even invited death to complete that book, and in that sense, he died for us readers.

Camus, by contrast, though also tubercular as a young man (he suffered a severe bout of tuberculosis when he was 17, and he never fully recovered from the disease), was an extraordinarily dashing and romantic figure, sometimes called even during his lifetime "the Humphrey Bogart of French letters." Camus looked remarkably like Bogart, especially when he wore his trench coat. After hearing that he had won the Nobel Prize at the age of 43 in 1957, an award that brought him anguish rather than pleasure, he remonstrated, "No, no! It should be Malraux, Malraux!" Then he sent a telegram to André Malraux, the distinguished elder man of letters, saying the same thing. Malraux immediately wrote back, "Camus ... your telegram does you honor." Malraux was not congratulating him, but rather more or less acknowledging, "You're right! I deserve it."

As a result of receiving the Nobel Prize, Camus became an international celebrity and gained worldwide recognition. His charm and his fame brought him another nickname in Paris in the early 1960s: the "Jack Kennedy of letters." The telegenic, witty Kennedy, with the enchanting, à la mode francophone Jacqueline Bouvier at his side, captivated the French public, and the couple acquired the status of political royalty on his November 1960 election as president, also at the age of 43. Yet Camus's nickname was conferred, of course, with somber overtones, for the affectionate sobriquet arose posthumously, given that the comparison occasioned by Kennedy's victory emerged only in the wake of Camus's death months earlier.

The concomitant, if perhaps inevitable tragedy of Camus's "tragic" death was how, just as had happened with Orwell a few years earlier, death transformed a life into a destiny. The automobile accident that befell Camus was memorialized and mythologized as his fatal, perhaps fated, collision with the Absurd, the existential spectre depicted in his macabre early novels, *The Stranger* (1942) and *The Plague* (1947). Traveling with his publisher Michel Gallimard in Provence, Gallimard's speeding car crashed. When Camus was found on the roadside, the manuscript of his unfinished new novel, *The First Man*, lay in his hands. (Next to the manuscript of *The First Man* was also a copy of Nietzsche's *The Joyful Wisdom*.) To add to the absurdity and tragedy, Camus had intended to take a train home to Paris; an unused ticket was found in his pocket. No other passenger was seriously injured.

More comparisons immediately flooded forth, now drawn between the premature death of the youngish Camus and that of matinée idol James Dean, star of the teen hit film *Rebel Without a Cause* (1955), who (alone among the victims) was killed, barely three weeks before the movie's release, when his new Porsche 550 crashed.[3] (Ironically, the opening scenes of *Rebel Without a Cause* also portray a deadly smashup suffered by the teen gang leader, Dean's schoolboy rival in the film.) And so another romantic myth arose: Albert Camus, the "James Dean of French literature," forever "the rebel," per the title (in English translation) of his celebrated nonfiction study of historical radicals, *L'Homme révolté*.

Intellectual integrity, moral courage, and literary excellence: George Orwell and Albert Camus. As we mark the anniversary milestones that link their passing, let us reflect on that heritage. For we are as much if not far more in need of those virtues and their standard-bearers today in the twenty-first century—and doubtless will be long hereafter.

CHAPTER 9

How and Why Orwell Became "A FAMOUS AUTHOR"

Surfing the Tides of Time

The Contingencies of Fame

The last two chapters have meditated at length on the vicissitudes of reputation, the whirligig of fame, and the prerogatives of Clio—and specifically on the utter obscurity of Jean Malaquais in contrast to the spectacular renown of Albert Camus and especially George Orwell.

But how? Why? Comparative biography and history can furnish us with some specific, local clues for this pair of instances. Yet the hows and whys of the macrocosmic processes in a sociological sense remain to be answered. Given the scale and extent of Orwell's phenomenal reputation—which extends (unlike that of Camus) far beyond intellectual circles and cultural opinion expressed in his native language—let us broach the larger hows and whys in his own case. After all, no modern writer has a higher overall literary reputation, that is, a greater aggregate balance of critical esteem and public recognition.

Orwell is not just the most famous British writer of the last half of the twentieth century, but also the highest best seller of serious fiction in any language. Not only is he the English intellectual most revered (and possibly reviled) by several generations of intellectuals since 1950, but his last two works, *Animal Farm*

and *Nineteen Eighty-Four*, are scholastic fixtures, firmly institutionalized in Anglo-American school curricula and even taught
outside the anglophone world, especially in Germany and Austria.
(Berlin even boasts a George Orwell Oberschule in Lichtenberg.)
Not a single book that he wrote is presently out of print in English;
meticulously edited by Peter Davison, the multivolume *Complete
Works of George Orwell* have been published in 22 volumes, presently available both in cloth-bound and in paperback editions.

Yes, it is hardly believable, scarcely even imaginable. Yet it also
needs emphasis: this was not always so. Indeed it is likely that
if Orwell had passed away little more than three years earlier,
before his premature death in early 1950—that is, before the
American edition of *Animal Farm* appeared in an aggressively
promoted *Reader's Digest* edition in August 1946—he would be
utterly unknown today outside academic circles. Perhaps he would
only be familiar to literary scholars who specialize in British studies of the 1930s. In fact, I would argue that if he had died even a
year before his death at midcentury, in autumn 1948—that is, before completing his last book, *Nineteen Eighty-Four*—he would be
regarded as a clever fabulist, a one-book author who had finally
found his métier by abandoning the realistic novel and turning to
satirical fantasy. *Animal Farm* would have been touted not just as
a devastating allegory applicable to the history of Stalinist Russia,
but also as a modern parable that offered salutary lessons for the
probable course of revolutions in general. Yet it would not have
contributed numerous coinages to the political lexicon, for the
circulation of its catchphrases came no earlier than the mid-1950s,
that is, only in the aftermath (and as a consequence) of that very
practice occurring with *Nineteen Eighty-Four* as his dystopia per-
meated Western culture. Nor, of course, would Orwell's fable have
made his name as a proper adjective—"Orwellian"—a synonym
for "sinister," "nightmarish," "oppressive," and even "totalitarian."

And for those reasons, along with some others, it would not have established "George Orwell" as a name to set argument going whenever politically minded readers with a literary bent meet and debate.

I indulge here in counterfactual history—or what could be called "counterfactual biography." My claim is simple: If Orwell had never published *Nineteen Eighty-Four*, he would be largely unknown today, certainly outside literary academe. In fact, my contention is even more extreme. I hold that the fame of Orwell and *Nineteen Eighty-Four* owe mainly not to literary or even publishing events at all; rather, their omniprescence today is attributable almost entirely to the TV adaptations of *Nineteen Eighty-Four* (or *1984*, as the pundits, aka Newspeak wordsmiths, have invariably abridged it) that coincided with the birth of nationwide television and the rise of the age of celebrity.

And therein lies a story.

The "Perfect Storm" on the Night of December 12

In September 1953, NBC's Studio One opened its fall season with a widely praised adaptation (titled *1984*) that emboldened and inspired BBC-TV to follow up with its own broadcast of the novel a year later. It is this period in the mid-1950s that the historian can in hindsight identify as the juncture at which the "myth of Orwell" arose. As I shall argue, the latter broadcast flung Orwell into the "statusphere" of fame, moving him decisively and permanently beyond mere literary circles into the realm of popular and mass culture and the domain of ideological politics. It was during the closing weeks of 1954 that his neologisms and catchphrases were first splashed in screaming headlines and wielded against political foes, when they became, in Isaac Deutscher's panic-stricken pronouncement voiced in January 1955, "ideological superweapons" in the Cold War of words. Yes, it was at this fateful, if little remembered, moment that the late George Orwell —and far more so, the cultural symbol and literary talisman "Orwell"—became caught up in the battles between the West and the Soviet Union and gained his status as the leading Cold Warrior of the postwar West.

Although NBC's *1984* in the fall of 1953 was well received—it reached a viewing audience of 8.7 million homes (a 53 percent share of the market), making it the highest-rated Studio One program for 1953—its moment soon passed. The program left no visible, lasting impact. Or perhaps it represented the calm before the storm. After all, a mere 15 months later, in December 1954, a historic "perfect storm" of cultural politics struck Britain like a social *blitzkrieg* and spread within a decade throughout the world. Let us dwell at greater length, therefore, on the events that unfolded in Britain during this time.

It was the British adaptation of Orwell's last novel—or, more precisely, the debate that ensued after its two telecasts in mid-December—that ignited the disputes that established "St. George" Orwell as the patron saint of Cold War patriots in cultural circles. The NBC adaptation arguably made "George Orwell" temporarily better known to the wider American audience. But it did not raise book sales significantly or establish Orwell as a "doomsday prophet" and totalitarian visionary who had predicted the inevitable course of Stalinism as an anti-utopian nightmare.

Instead it was the BBC-TV adaptation of *Nineteen Eighty-Four*—which used the Secker & Warburg title—that ultimately proved responsible for Orwell's outsized public reputation. I would argue that the latter production was the determining event that moved Orwell from merely bigger circulation (and temporary notoriety) to literary canonization and (apparently) enduring fame.

It is unusual that one can precisely identify a historical event marking the moment when a writer's popular reputation is "launched." As I discussed in *The Politics of Literary Reputation*, however, in Orwell's case the date is clear: Sunday, December 12, 1954.[1] Directed by Nigel Keale, the two-hour evening program appeared during primetime, on what was then Britain's only television channel. It starred Peter Cushing and Yvonne Mitchell, who were among the small screen's most popular actors. By and large, the production was faithful to Orwell's vision and sensibility. Unlike the subsequent film version (by Columbia Pictures in 1956), which featured two different endings, Keale adhered to Orwell's own narrative throughout.

As if to anticipate controversy and, in a defensive maneuver, shift any responsibility for the depiction of violence to Orwell himself, the show opened with a warning to the tune of Holst's "Mars": "This is one man's alarmed view of the future." Viewers were then presented with Cushing as an emaciated Winston Smith—a gaunt version of Britain's 80-year-old prime minister, after whom Orwell had mischievously named his ill-fated hero.[2]

Most critics hailed the teleplay as an intelligent adaptation and praised the BBC's courage in presenting it. Thousands of viewers, however, protested that the show was "sadistic" and "horrific," characterizations that the tabloid press bannered on the morning of Monday, December 13. A debate over the "propriety" of the telecast took shape and soon escalated into a classic confrontation over the proper function of art in the state and, more particularly, the role that the emergent medium of television should assume in British society. Conservatives intent on limiting the presumed "adventurism" of the state-supported BBC and parents outraged by the graphic depiction of violence on an "entertainment" medium ranged themselves against socialists preaching free speech and literary men defending the production's naturalism and fidelity to Orwell's book.

Within the space of a single week, the BBC production became what the *New York Times* called "the subject of the sharpest controversy in the annals of British television." Some observers compared the row to the furor in America over Orson Welles's 1938 radio hoax, *War of the Worlds*. When the teleplay aired again the following Thursday, December 16, more than 7 million Britons tuned in, the largest audience for any BBC-TV production in British history to that date.[3] (This figure was exceeded only by the audience for the special coverage of Queen Elizabeth's coronation a year before.) Within five days, therefore, a total of almost 14 million viewers had watched the BBC *Nineteen Eighty-Four* in British living rooms. At the week's close the *Times* of London editorialized: "The term 'Big Brother,' which the day before yesterday meant nothing to 99 percent of the population, has become a household phrase." That public declaration, delivered by the authoritative journalistic voice of the British Commonwealth, essentially sums up the argument of this chapter. Or as E. M. Forster, with whom Orwell became acquainted during the war, might have phrased it, *Nineteen Eighty-Four* was no longer the work of a "small-public" author. It was now familiar even to Uncle Willie, the broad public at least minimally interested in the world of culture.[4]

As if to corroborate the statement from the *Times* of London that "Big Brother" had overnight become a "household phrase," the best seller list immediately registered the impact of the telecast. Indeed the most tangible outcome of the BBC telecast was its enormous effect on sales of *Nineteen Eighty-Four*. After having sold 22,700 copies by the end of 1949 and almost 50,000 within its first year of publication, sales of the Secker & Warburg hardback edition had slowed to 150 copies per week in mid-1954. A new Penguin paperback edition had just been published. During the week following the first telecast, 1,000 hardback and 18,000 paperback copies were sold. The perfect (fire)storm of controversy catapulted *Nineteen Eighty-Four* into what the book industry has since dubbed "supersellerdom." As John Sutherland (who watched the original broadcasts in December 1954 as a 15-year-old boy) remarked, the novel's "rise to supersellerdom took off like a Guy Fawkes rocket from a milk bottle."[5] Having rocketed into the statusphere, it stayed there: no fewer than three dozen Penguin editions alone have been issued since the BBC telecasts. Equally significant, sales of Orwell's other works were permanently boosted. It should be reemphasized that NBC's 1953 telecast, despite its 8 million viewers and excellent ratings, exerted no such impact; it did not launch the proper adjective "Orwellian" into general circulation or boost sales of *Nineteen Eighty-Four* sharply. We see, then, that it is not audience numbers alone that make a public reputation; the controversy over the BBC telecast was crucial. If not for it, Orwell might well have remained strictly a literary figure and never have entered the political pages and letter columns of the press—and "Orwell" might never have arisen at all. Thus, it is no exaggeration to pinpoint the after-dinner, late evening hours of December 12, 1954, as the instant when the language of Orwell's novel entered the popular imagination and the book became, as Deutscher could glimpse within two weeks of the second telecast, "an ideological superweapon." That December marks the firm establishment of Orwell's status as a "public" writer. In a single week, more than 15 million Britons saw *Nineteen Eighty-Four* on their home telescreens, some of them viewing it not just once but twice. The goggle box had left the nation gaga.

In hindsight, we can appreciate how the night of December 12 represents the little-recognized Big Bang of Orwell's enduring public reputation. In a process especially pertinent for the mak-

FIGURE 11. This cartoon by David Low, Britain's best-known political cartoonist of the postwar era, appeared in the *Daily Mail* on December 17, 1954, the morning following the second BBC-TV broadcast of its adaptation of Orwell's *Nineteen Eighty-Four*. Overnight "Big Brother" had already become, as the *Times* of London editorialized, "a household phrase."

The Thursday evening BBC teleplay of December 16, which followed the telecast of the previous Sunday, attracted more than 7 million viewers, the second-largest audience for a television program in British history to that date (exceeded only by the broadcast of Queen Elizabeth's coronation in June 1953). The combined audience for the two *Nineteen Eighty-Four* telecasts approached 14 million.

ing of literary reputations in the twenty-first century, one big media event transformed Orwell into a public personality in the 1950s, at the moment of nationwide network television's emergence. It is likewise noteworthy that the rise of the "Orwell myth" and the popular success of *Nineteen Eighty-Four* coincided with the dawning of this age.

Ah, yes, for "as the dawn follows the night," it is otherwise doubtful that the rapid international circulation of words such as "Orwellian," "Big Brother," and "doublethink" could have occurred without the TV plays of the 1950s—before, that is, the "telescreen era."

The Dynamics of Reputation-Building

So much for the incredible, long-forgotten "how" of Orwell's posthumous fame—that is, for the single most important historical event that transmogrified the writer Orwell into the spectre "Orwell."

The "why" of Orwell's fame is more complicated and conceptual, having much to do with historical-cultural issues of social structure, including circles and networks of interpersonal relations and literary influence. George Orwell was an outsider within the intelligentsia during the 1930s and 1940s, hated and relentlessly castigated by the Stalinists of his day, who dominated the London intellectual world, yet he also had a claim to knowledge of the inside and so was perfectly positioned to become, as V. S. Pritchett eulogized him, "the wintry conscience of his generation." That is to say, Orwell occupied a position of "optimal marginality" throughout his lifetime (unlike T. S. Eliot, who acquired a position of "optimal centrality" as London's leading Modernist poet and its reigning gatekeeper in his role as editor of the journal *Criterion* and editorial advisor at Faber & Faber). At least until the publication of *Animal Farm* and *Nineteen Eighty-Four* during the last three or four years of his life, Orwell was little known outside London and New York intellectual circles. Within five years of his death, however, he had become the hallowed "St. George" Orwell, and the posthumous figure "Orwell" assumed a place of "optimal centrality" as a world-historical author before the next decade was out.

Orwell's early death turned him in the 1950s into an intellectual Lenin, as it were, a safely encased, sanctified sepulcher, even a romantic icon à la Albert Camus a few years later—an intellectual's James Dean—within the Left intelligentsia. Orwell had similarly died "too young." Yet his premature death, particularly its timing less than one month before the anticommunist hysteria (associated with the rise of Joseph McCarthy and the onset of the Red Scare) surged, proved the ideal prelude for the chorus of hosannas to "St. George" the Cold Warrior soon intoned by liberals and conservatives alike. If he had lived just months longer, he could not possibly have maintained his stature on all fronts across the political spectrum. Inevitably he would have taken positions on McCarthyism, the deepening Cold War, nuclear disarmament, and other contentious issues that would have disillusioned (and outraged) some of his later followers. And if he had even lived a little longer—say, no more than into his mid-50s—his stands on burning controversies ranging from decolonization and East–West *détente* to the Vietnam War and the counterculture would have unavoidably rendered him *persona non grata* for certain segments among his legions of loyalists—as occurred with his contemporaries in the succeeding decades. Orwell's "early" death is the temporal factor associated with his "moment of exit."

The "Right Stuff": The Roles of Timing and Placement

Early death is by no means always a boon to reputation. In fact, the reverse is just as frequently true. More often than not, longevity— the capacity to have followers or disciples (or maybe even a literary widow) promote your work—is far more valuable. Yet reputation is radically contingent. There is no way for the cultural historian or sociologist of art to isolate—and thereby analyze discretely and accurately—any particular factor, or even group of factors, that conditions reputation. The zeitgeist is far too subtle for that. The innumerable complexities involved in the synchrony of repute (being situated in the right place, i.e., a propitious social location) and the diachrony of repute (arriving at the right time, i.e., with historical conditions emerging just at the moment when the achievement is ready to be exploited) defy all strategizing and tactics. I would caution the ambitious wannabe Orwells with their eyes fixed on the statusphere: "Go ahead and employ various image-makers and reputation theorists to promote you, but beware! There is no guarantee that their embroidery will result in fame." For Orwell is the very rare case of someone dying at precisely the "right" historical location and moment. That is to say, his "moment of exit" from literary life—or his "moment of entrance" into his posthumous reputation—was perfectly (if inadvertently) timed to vault his reputation into the statusphere.[6] Like Lenin, his early death allowed a cult to arise more easily because "dead men pose no threats." Lionized and canonized, Orwell and Lenin invited hero worship, especially by the succeeding generation. It became part of a Left intellectual's moral and ideological pedigree to claim a figure such as Orwell or Lenin as a forefather.

Yet not merely at the moments of his entrance and exit from this life was Orwell "in the right place at the right time." His timing was also uncanny, however adventitiously, at four crucial moments in his afterlife: the dawn of network television in the mid-1950s, when televised versions of *Nineteen Eighty-Four* ricocheted him to public international stardom; the "countdown to 1984," when his reputation was revived to the unprecedented extent that his last book topped for months the *New York Times* best seller list 35 years after its original publication date; his centennial year of 2003, when he once again rocked the airwaves as the intellectual icon whom both proponents and opponents of the "War on Terror" and the invasions of Afghanistan and Iraq sought to claim for their own side; and autumn 2016 to spring 2017, when Donald Trump's presidential election victory and early months in office spurred Orwell's novel to leap yet again atop the best seller lists, almost exactly another 35 years after its ascent in the title year.

These (ill-)starred events in Orwell's afterlife have occurred at ever-shortening intervals. Ingeniously timed to keep pace with the accelerating tempo of the zeitgeist and hastening mutability of the past, as it were, each recurring (sun)spot of time has acted as a propulsive booster shot to sustain (or even raise) his position in the statusphere, ensuring that "Orwell" remains securely in orbit before successive new generations of readers and viewers—and digital surfers. Is this the music of the (status)sphere? The historian of reputation beholds this grand spectacle, unfurled across seven decades, aghast and overawed by the stupefying virtuosity of Clio's designs.

Models of Stardom

All that is to say: the "Orwell phenomenon" is without comparison among modern writers, unprecedented (and doubtless unrepeatable) in its scope and scale. His reputation raises the intriguing question: What does it mean to be a literary "phenomenon"? Is it a matter of name recognition, best seller lists, and sales totals? Or is it about informed readers, critical literary esteem, and canonical standing? Size or stature? Breadth or depth? Sales volume or artistic renown? Mass appeal or cult appeal?

To put it in somewhat different terms, Orwell is the last of what could be called the "big-tent authors." This sales model of stardom measures success and fame by the absolute number of book buyers and readers. The big-tent author offers something for everybody. And this Orwell does: he magnificently exemplifies the man of letters of the mid-twentieth century, having excelled in opinion columns, prose essays, documentary reportage, literary reviewing, and of course political fantasia (the beast fable, the anti-utopia).

Yet the size of Orwell's audience accounts only for his fame, that is, the breadth of his reputation (associated with data such as name recognition and citation counts). By contrast, the intensity with which his readers have identified with him explains the honor, sometimes bordering on reverence, countless admirers have bestowed on him. Orwell's readers *care* about him, both as a writer and as a man. His literary personality and personal life have attracted and inspired generations of readers, so much so that many writers not only prize Orwell as a prose stylist, but also want to *become like Orwell*. Given all this, Orwell is also an outstanding example of the "niche author." This model scales success and fame according to the passion of a writer's following. Whereas the big-tent author is the old-school exemplum of a public figure whom we all share—a national figure, even a culture hero in the tradition of Dickens, Hugo, and Tolstoy—the niche author represents a form of stardom based on fandom: it depends on the admirer's sense of personal investment. The niche author is precisely *not* for everyone; the cognoscenti pride themselves on being different. They relish the fact that their allegiance to their author-hero is a special, highly cultivated taste, a refined aesthetic judgment.

Is one kind of reputation better than another? Is it ultimately more advantageous to your reputation to have a smaller group of fans who care intensely about what you write? Or a bigger number of fans who just care enough to purchase (if not always read) your books? Admittedly, more people buy Danielle Steele and Stephen King novels than those of Jonathan Franzen and John Updike. But that doesn't necessarily make Steele and King "greater," let alone "higher," than Franzen and Updike. The analogues are the old worlds of network TV versus digital cable. Orwell possesses a reputation nonpareil, for he has been both renowned and revered throughout the entire post–World War II era. He thus serves as a bridge between the two ages, illuminating the transition from the first to the second.

Surfing the Tides of Time

All this is to say that there is indeed "a tide in the affairs of men," as Shakespeare's Brutus puts it. The conditions must be propitious for a reputation to emerge and flourish.

A forgotten story by Stephen Vincent Benet illustrates this point. In "The Curfew Tolls," Benet portrays a retired military officer in the French army during the early eighteenth century. The aging officer, a rather cantankerous and curmudgeonly figure, is widely regarded by his fellow senior officers, and even many junior colleagues, as something of a crank—even his own family treats him as such. He is constantly talking about battle plans, about political designs, about military campaigns that he would like to conduct—but he is usually treated rather patronizingly or even dismissively by all who are within earshot.

We discover at the end of the story that this "little man" with the grandiose fantasies is none other than a Monsieur Bonaparte— Napoleon Bonaparte. His fantasies about "what he would do" if he were in power remain just that. People are content with the way things are at present: the early eighteenth century in France, after all, was the period immediately before the rise of the French *philosophes*, an era of relative calm rather than revolutionary upheaval—unlike the climate that would prevail a few decades later, in the latter half of the eighteenth century. The Napoleon of Benet's story "came too early": his moment of entrance was premature. If the conditions are unripe, Benet implies, even a Napoleonic force of will cannot shift the tides of history. Under unripe conditions, one is unlikely to go down in history, but rather simply down the memory hole.

So reputation is indeed partly a matter of being in "the right place at the right time." The conditions must be propitious for one to surf the tides of history. That is to say, a revolutionary moment of upheaval was crucial even for a "great man" such as Napoleon Bonaparte to be taken seriously and to emerge as a French general (and ultimately be crowned the French emperor) by the end of the eighteenth century.

Let us reconsider in Orwell's case the idea of moments of exit (from life) and entrance (into afterlife). If Orwell had passed away before the mid-1940s, he probably would have disappeared long ago down the memory hole, unread and even unknown, except perhaps among scholars of British literature specializing in the 1930s and wartime periods. Why? Because he would have died without having written *Animal Farm* and *Nineteen Eighty-Four*. That is, he would have had no climactic, dramatic exit. The controversial masterpieces would not exist. Nor would he have become the "secular saint" of the early post–World War II era— the political "St. George" claimed by liberals and conservatives alike.[7]

Indeed the battles among intellectuals of the Right and Left for Orwell's mantle since 1950 have contributed immensely to his becoming a cultural icon. Literary controversies involving his likely posthumous pronouncements—the lament "If Orwell were alive today …"—largely account for the popular headlines and countless citations of his work, all of which have spread his international fame.

Contexts, Contingencies, and Reputations

As we have argued, if Orwell's life exemplifies what could be referred to as "optimal marginality," his astounding posthumous fame illustrates "optimal centrality." He began as a marginal political writer, a "pre-mature anti-Stalinist," but ended his days as the leading Cold Warrior of his generation and soon became the iconic figure at "the bloody crossroads where literature and politics meet," in the famous phrase of Lionel Trilling. In the 1950s, as Raymond Williams acknowledged, "Down every road that you traveled, Orwell seemed to be waiting."

An unfamiliar comparison is illuminating here. We may note a strong, arresting resemblance between how the reputations of George Orwell and Harriet Beecher Stowe owe to the prevailing conditions of their eras: Stowe to the era of slavery and Orwell to the Cold War. The point of the comparison is that the rise to literary fame is less a matter of "great works" than of the structure of opportunities available and the "fit" of various candidates within the structure formed by the zeitgeist. The "contingencies of repute" are a web of advantages and inheritances that anyone will encounter in the course of forging a life and legacy. Reputation is not based only—and sometimes not even predominantly—on merit (i.e., aesthetic value). One of Orwell's favorite authors, Somerset Maugham, alerts us to this fact in *A Moon and Sixpence*.

In an exchange between an art dealer and a landscape painter, the former goes to the opposite extreme, claiming that merit is really nothing more than reputation (i.e., "success"). "Is merit enough to bring success? Don't believe it," the dealer insists. But the painter remonstrates: "Remember Monet, who could not get anyone to buy his pictures for a hundred francs? What are they worth now?" The dealer is skeptical: "There were a hundred painters as good as Monet who couldn't sell their pictures and are worth nothing still. How can one tell?" Outraged by this "philistine" reply, the painter demands: "How, then, will you recognize merit?" The dealer coolly answers: "There is only one way—by success."

I disagree with the dealer, but his extreme position provokes reflection, for it induces us to question the deeply ingrained, romantic (and Romantic) idea that "genius" or "brilliance" account for reputation or success. My own point is related to yet different from the dealer's. Because reputation is not entirely attributable to merit, it is also not therefore a matter of individual achievement alone, but rather a collective matter. It is often difficult to see how the individual is connected to the collective, but it is always crucial to look at the context—to see what lurks in the shadows around the individual—whether historical, generational, cultural, class-oriented, gendered, racial, and so on. These extrinsic features, which bear so decisively on the formation of reputation, are often lost in the ceaseless tide of passing events. What survives and ascends to a peak visible from a vast distance is textual rather than contextual: the prose style, the narrative skill, the plotting, and the power of characterization.

This is all very useful for the literary critic, but it is misleading and even disadvantageous as a focus for the literary and cultural historian. If we demand immediate evidence for this contention, let me refer the reader to "Exhibit A," which I presented earlier in this chapter: the fateful "Night of December 12," when *Nineteen Eighty-Four*—or rather *1984*—became "a household phrase."

For "reputation" is very different from interpretation or evaluation. The reputation of a work and author are a matter of context, whereas the latter two functions of criticism are a matter of text. The literary historian primarily looks "around" a work, not at it or into it. He recovers the reception "scene," because that scene explains the conditions that gave rise to what seem to be superhuman exploits or feats of "genius."

Let me share here a personal anecdote about the contingencies of reputation and the importance of historical context: in 1982 I lunched with a good friend of Orwell, the crime writer and literary critic Julian Symons, at a Fleet Street pub. Most Americans have never heard of Julian Symons, whereas hundreds of millions of people possess at least passing acquaintance with Orwell's name and work. Unlike Orwell, Symons has clearly gone down the memory hole. After my interview with Symons about his relationship to Orwell and his impressions of fellow contributors to *Tribune*, Symons remonstrated:

> Let me remind you again that George Orwell was no celebrity when I first got to know him in 1941. He was simply a bloke with whom I would walk down the street and have a drink in a pub like this. If he would have boasted to me that, 40-odd years from now, a young Yank would cross the ocean in order to interview me about him, I would have replied, "But George, why isn't that chap coming to interview *you* about *me*?!"

I laughed out loud and so did Symons. For me, the answer to his question could only be: because George Orwell became my (and countless other readers') intellectual "big brother."

Every Intellectual's "big brother"

I am reminded of Tolstoy's remark that all modern Russian writers "came out of Gogol's overcoat." If you consider the roster of prominent Anglo-American intellectuals of the generations since 1950, you can identify an impressive number who came "out of Orwell's overcoat." (Or better: his huge size 12 boots.) One can in fact speak of an extended family of intellectuals so touched by his work that they feel like they are his progeny. I have referred to them in one of my books, *Every Intellectual's big brother*, as Orwell's "literary siblings."

But if Orwell has stood forth as a (usually benevolent) "big brother" for generations of readers, he has also stood askance, quite paradoxically, as "the intellectual who hated intellectuals." He certainly regarded himself as an "intellectual," yet he was not much proud of that fact. He derided those literary intellectuals who believed that intellectuals must inevitably feud bitterly with their rivals, be given artistic license to indulge their narcissistic excesses, and merit public respect for political exhibitionism. He would have concurred with W. H. Auden's ditty: "To the man-in-the-street who I'm sorry to say, / is a keen observer of life / the word Intellectual suggests straight away / a man who's untrue to his wife." Despite his early castigation of Auden for some of the vices just enumerated, Orwell would have fully agreed with the writer of this jocular stanza, the mature poet who later became Orwell's friend. Both men felt that many intellectuals sought to separate themselves from "the masses." Unlike such pretentious figures, snugly ensconced in their literary coteries and writing in abstract jargon exclusively for one another, Orwell himself has often been considered an intellectual's "common man," blessed with a certain common sense precisely because he refused to separate himself in this way and wrote in a language accessible to anyone.

Nowadays all kinds of consultants, image-makers, and spin-doctors have devised tactical and strategic methods for positioning fame seekers to attain renown. Back in Orwell's day—and given the kind of person he was—it was inconceivable that he could or would have planned his meteoric rise to international prominence in the last four years of his life. He wrote *Animal Farm* simply out of a sense of righteous indignation and festered grief. He had never written a book like that before. He had written realistic novels in the 1930s; usually, he was scraping by as a freelance journalist. Never did he expect that *Animal Farm* would have the kind of success it did; after all, it was rejected by several publishers before it was accepted. Of course, its "moment of entrance" on the literary stage proved auspicious. If it had reached print in a timely fashion soon after it had been completed in February 1944, it might have disappeared. Instead its appearance was delayed until August 1945, just as the war was ending and the alliance with the Soviet Union was breaking up.

Orwell could never have planned the circumstances so well. Imagine planning to delay its publication 18 months by sending it around to several different publishing houses that would reject it until the war ended. Such clairvoyance (or promotional *legerdemain*) is impossible to conceive even in today's digital wonderland of technological wizardry. Can the endlessly complex social formations of history be reduced to quantifiable, analyzable data points? Will even the most skilled practitioners of cliodynamics and cliometrics ever be able to calculate the functioning of the innumerable interlocking cogs and transmission gears in the whirligig of fame?[8]

"To Be A FAMOUS AUTHOR"

So how do writers become famous? How did George Orwell achieve his boyhood dream to become "A FAMOUS AUTHOR"? We have seen that literary reputation is inevitably a matter of historical timing and placement. As Germany's chancellor Helmut Kohl once expressed it, he and his generation of Germans had received "the blessing of late birth." By that Kohl meant that Germans of his age had had the accidental good fortune of being born "too late" to have come to maturity during the era of the Third Reich under Hitler. Instead, they had been mere children during that era, either *Pimpfe* (little comrades) or members of the Hitler Youth. As a result, they were not responsible for any of the decision-making or execution of policies under Hitler's Reich, unlike their older brothers and sisters, let alone their fathers and grandfathers. In the case of the fame of George Orwell and many other people, we might think of the "blessing of early death." To reiterate: if Orwell had died just months later, his haloed reputation among some supporters would doubtless have been tarnished.

How, then, does a writer acquire fame? The short answer involves the Greek concept of *kairos*. First, be in the right place in the right time. Position yourself in relation to the zeitgeist so that you will be perceived—once conditions are propitious—as a candidate eligible for elevation. Get out in front of the tides of history so that you can surf the biggest waves when the tsunami hits. And that is just what Orwell fortuitously did. How did he do it? Let us summarize.

Orwell, as the Cold War was dawning, penned a little fable called *Animal Farm*, which was rejected by publishers because it directly attacked Stalinism, and the United States and Britain were allies of "Uncle Joe" Stalin. But then the war ended, and political conditions altered; the Cold War began. Stalin was now our enemy—and *Animal Farm* and *Nineteen Eighty-Four* were already there as ideological weapons, with their catchwords ready to be used.

Then Orwell died in 1950, just as the Cold War freeze was deepening. His death immediately preceded the onset of McCarthyism a few weeks later—that is, the rise of a vulgar pro-Americanism and crude pro-capitalism. Orwell was spared the difficulty of taking a firm position on the ensuing controversies that his coevals not granted "the blessing of early death" had to confront. A dead man is a blank slate on which his successors can write as they please. To be "in the right place" means that the structure of conditions will conform to Clio's designs and support your candidacy for service to the zeitgeist; to be "at the right time" means that you'll be sufficiently malleable to be used or abused for whatever purposes your claimants deem necessary to achieving their ambitions.

And, of course, not only the dead become objects of desire with whom "fans" identify and on whom they project their hopes and dreams. Some political leaders, occasionally even before they attain national office, win a following across the ideological spectrum, especially if they seem to carry the aspirations of an underclass, or to represent a rising social movement, or to plausibly symbolize some historic watershed or coming breakthrough. Barack Obama is a recent example. As he wrote in 2008 in his "candidate book," *The Audacity of Hope*, "I serve as a blank screen on which people of vastly different political stripes project their own views."

Literary Immortality: The Visions and the Vanities

"We are going to slander him, destroy his reputation, and finally ruin him forever," vows U Po Kyin, the local tyrant in Orwell's *Burmese Days*. Soon thereafter, the good Dr. Veraswami describes the rebellion this petty dictator has secretly engineered and then ruthlessly suppressed, resulting in numerous injuries and deaths. "U Po Kyin is now the Hero of the district," the doctor bemoans. "It is the *triumph of the crocodile*" (emphasis in the original).

Given the slanderous lies that some of Orwell's critics—especially those on the Marxist Left—advanced in his day (and still do in ours), one could say that their aim has been likewise to "destroy his reputation and finally ruin him forever." Unlike the unprincipled, malicious U Po Kyin, however, Orwell's enemies have not been successful. History has not witnessed "*the triumph of the crocodile*" or the ultimate victory of "the pigs." Orwell's dark visions of brutal domination in *Burmese Days*, *Animal Farm*, and above all *Nineteen Eighty-Four* have helped raise public consciousness and warn audiences about the dangers of authoritarian leaders and totalitarian dictatorship. Today, although culture wars continue to be fought, one can fairly say that Orwell's positions from the middle decades of the last century have been largely vindicated by events: he has been proven right about imperialism, about fascism, and about Stalinism. His salvoes in his last two fantasias of aggression exploded like atom bombs on the cultural front. And because post–World War II readers listened and were powerfully affected by *Animal Farm* and *Nineteen Eighty-Four*, Orwell has played a cameo role in preventing the triumph of the bestial.

Orwell developed a very tough outer shell when the Stalinist Left of his day castigated his books and derided his character. His attitude toward the dominant literary establishment of intellectual London, the Marxist intelligentsia that ostracized him as an "antisocialist," resembled the sentiments expressed by Keats in a letter written shortly before his death about the harsh reviews of his poetry: "This is a mere matter of the moment—I think I shall be among the English Poets after my death." In the cases of both Keats and Orwell, Posterity has concurred.

But what is literary immortality? According to one of Orwell's favorite boyhood authors, Samuel Butler, "immortality" is a matter of continued existence in the thoughts and lives of others. Butler conceived of heaven as a gift of posterity whereby we bask in the radiant glow of good wishes from those still alive. If this is so, then it can certainly be said that the literary immortality of George Orwell is affirmed by the esteem accorded him by millions of readers decade after decade.

The fascination with and yearning for (posthumous) fame lays bare the impassioned—if often carefully veiled—vanity of human wishes. I do not chiefly mean Orwell's own vanity (though he once remarked that "to be remembered after death" was an element of the "sheer egoism" that represented one of his motivations for writing). Rather, I refer to our own vanity, that of his readers and especially his admiring critics and fellow intellectuals, given the fact that so many writers of his own and succeeding generations have dreamed of attaining the kind of literary immortality gained by Orwell alone among contemporary writers.

In his *Selected Letters*, Sherwood Anderson remarks about literary fame: "Fame is no good, my dear.... Take it from me." He added: "If I could work for the rest of my life unknown, unnoticed by those who make current opinion, I would be happier." Orwell might have echoed those statements—and let us remember that he achieved real fame only posthumously, spared its bittersweet ordeals. By virtue of his "premature" or "early" death and uncannily timed moment of exit just before the Cold War heated up, Orwell "escaped," as it were, the shadowy side of fame that weighed so heavily upon contemporaries such as Thomas Mann. At an age when Eric Blair was still an unknown Burma ex-policeman who only dreamed of becoming a writer, let alone a famous one, Mann became a literary celebrity with the publication of *Buddenbrooks* (1901) and was forced to wrestle ever after with the mixed blessing of tremendous early success. The novel would go on to sell more than 1.5 million copies in German alone during the next three decades, during which time Mann also received the Nobel Prize in 1929. But the world's acclaim oppressed Mann: "One feels as if one were exposed in the beam of a gigantic search-light," he bemoaned, "one's whole body visible in public, burdened with responsibility for disposal of the gifts one was imprudent enough to reveal." Mann perceived himself as suffering the fate of royalty, set on a pedestal and exalted as a living icon who "leads a symbolic, representative life—like a prince!"

A writer identifies with icons such as Mann—and far more so the symbolic "Orwell"—at his own psychological peril.[9] For George Orwell himself could not have imagined "Orwell." In fact, Orwell himself never really sought to be "Orwell"—and how could he have possibly done so? As we have discussed, nothing less than a cascade—or perfect storm—of unique and fateful events miraculously converged and thereby precipitated the fashioning of "Orwell." Whether we call it the handiwork of Fate or Providence or Clio or Posterity or the zeitgeist—or a *Minitru* editorial collective headed directly by B.B. himself—it represents a (still ongoing) project vastly more ambitious and dubious than the successful forgery that Winston Smith's *speakwrite* fabricates in the form of a heroic Comrade Ogilvy.

As the Laurel Grows

A poem with which Eric Blair would certainly have been familiar as he scampered across the playing fields of Eton is A. E. Housman's "To an Athlete Dying Young." (Blair devoured the realistic fiction of nineteenth-century Britain and also the Edwardians, and he harbored a special affection for the poetry of Housman.)

In fact, the star-crossed passing of Orwell himself could even be titled "To an Author Dying Young," for it is as if the mature writer, George Orwell, followed the didactic counsel of Housman:

> Smart lad, to slip betimes away
> From fields where glory does not stay,
> And early though the laurel grows
> It withers quicker than the rose ...

> Now you will not swell the rout
> Of lads that wore their honours out,
> Runners whom renown outran
> And the name died before the man.

The "renown" of George Orwell only began with his death in 1950: Blair the man died, but the name of the writer Orwell lives on. It has been emblazoned in glory—and endless controversy—for seven decades. Orwell slipped away before the Cold War battles that enmeshed his work started to rage, and Posterity has seen to it that his laurels have never withered.

George Woodcock once wrote that Orwell decided to not use his pen name on his tombstone ("Here Lies Eric Blair") because he understood that while Eric Blair would return to dust, George Orwell might survive as one of the literary immortals. Although Woodcock was a close and insightful friend of Orwell, surely this contention, expressed more than a quarter century after Blair's death, represents historical hindsight.[10] Neither Woodcock nor Orwell himself—his boyhood dream "to be A FAMOUS AUTHOR" notwithstanding—could have possessed even the slightest intuition that George Orwell would one day stand as the most widely cited literary figure since Dickens or even Shakespeare, let alone that his neologisms and coinages would become not only part of the contemporary cultural lexicon and political imagination, but also battle-certified ideological superweapons in the Cold War of words.

Orwell said he would never write his autobiography. Yet I wonder if he somehow did intuit on his deathbed, as his extraordinary afterlife was already dawning, the challenge of such a memoir. If so, he might have voiced his reservations in terms that resemble the celebrated claim of Matisse: "If my story were ever to be written down truthfully from start to finish, it would amaze everyone."

CHAPTER 10

"Catholic Exceptionalism"

Why Catholic America Canonized "St. George"

The "*Commonweal* Catholic" Orwell?

Some of the climactic scenes in the amazing story of Blair "becoming George Orwell"—and Orwell "becoming 'Orwell'"—have already been sketched in this book. But a key, little-known passage remains to be narrated. It begins with the arrival of *Animal Farm* on the desks of the American reading public on August 25, 1946, just a year after its initial appearance in England. That date, as we shall see, represented the literary equivalent on American shores of the D-Day landing in Normandy. While *Animal Farm* had been a success in England, selling well and making Orwell known beyond left-wing intellectual circles, where his reputation was that of a talented contrarian, the beachhead established by his "little squib" marked his moment of entrance to Fame, that is, of his breakthrough to cultural prominence, first in America and soon thereafter throughout the world.

A few details of that story found their way into Chapter 4. Yet the crucial (and most surprising) episode is still to be told: the role of the Catholic bimonthly *Commonweal* in introducing Orwell to American Catholics and securing his reputation—not only in American Catholic circles, but also with the wider public. Remarkably enough, this process had already begun in the mid-1930s, fully a decade before *Animal Farm*'s American appearance and the postwar dawn of Orwell's fame in the United States and beyond.

The Cold War Context

Let us limn the immediate postwar scene of the U.S. during 1945–1946, but in much closer detail than the broad brushstrokes of Chapter 4. In America *Animal Farm* won broad support from intellectuals on the Left and Right for its brilliant exposé of tyranny's flaws. To some extent the satire's enormous appeal was literary rather than political. In the tradition of Aesop and Fontaine, it seemed a work not just for the age but for the ages, a timeless tale whose charm, simplicity, and seeming innocence (e.g., its use of common farm animals to show the corrupting effects of power) made it appealing even to the politically unsophisticated. Yet the speed with which this fable became a literary sensation in the United States owed everything to timing. It is important to remember how quickly and dramatically the international political climate altered following *Animal Farm*'s publication in England. The Cold War chill struck within weeks of the defeat of the Axis powers. During the next 12 months, the real face of the Soviet Union was revealed as Stalin took increasingly aggressive actions around the globe involving atomic weapons, the new United Nations, the division of territory in Europe, and the independence of Iran.

On February 9, 1946, Stalin delivered an uncompromising speech in which he declared that communism and capitalism were incompatible, and that communism would prevail. A week later, on February 16, the Canadian government announced the defection the previous fall of Igor Gouzenko, a Soviet code clerk in Canada. Gouzenko disclosed that a sophisticated Soviet spy ring existed throughout the West, including in North America, and that it had been successful in stealing top-secret information to manufacture an atom bomb. Furthermore, he reported that both the U.S. Treasury and State Department harbored top-level Soviet spies. Immediately the FBI began a dragnet.

These matters alerted the new Truman administration and the American public to how dangerous the international scene was. A series of labor strikes, rising inflation, and a housing crisis pushed the nation in an increasingly conservative direction. The mood of angst about the future, both domestically and internationally, would translate in the November elections into a runaway victory for the Republicans, their first since 1930. Truman lost his majority in both houses of Congress and had to battle an aggressive opposition leadership during the next two years. Throughout the summer and fall of 1946, the Republicans had frequently prophesied in cataclysmic terms about the spectre of Communism haunting the West—namely that "it could happen here." (Soon thereafter, Truman famously dubbed the Republican-controlled Eightieth Congress the "good-for-nothing, do-nothing Eightieth Congress.")

During the year between *Animal Farm*'s initial publication and its appearance in the United States, the quickly emerging Cold War transformed attitudes toward "Uncle Joe," the Soviet Union, and the nature of communism in American political circles. The imposition of a Communist government in Poland through a manipulated election in the fall of 1945 first signaled that the Russians would not abide by the Yalta Conference accords. During the next two years, the Sovietization of Eastern Europe continued with mass arrests, Party purges, and installations of satellite regimes in Bulgaria, Hungary, and Romania. The Soviet onslaught culminated in March 1948 with a communist *coup d'état* in Czechoslovakia, where a reign of terror that included a series of show trials of 10 leading Jewish Communists, persecutions of dissidents, and a crackdown on religious groups soon followed.

A galvanizing force in changing American opinion of the Soviet Union was Winston Churchill's "Iron Curtain" speech in Fulton, Missouri, on March 5, 1946, during which he uttered the oft-quoted line: "From Stettin in the Baltic to Trieste in the Adriatic, an iron curtain has descended across the continent. Behind that line lie all the capitals of the ancient states of Central and Eastern Europe." His doomsday language about the perils of Soviet imperialism and the threat of a future war stunned the American public and made his expression "Iron Curtain" famous. (It is little known that Churchill actually floated the phrase in a wartime cable to Truman [on June 4, 1945], warning the new president about the imminent "descent of an iron curtain between us and everything eastward." But Truman at that time still shared the outlook of the recently deceased FDR, who had thought he understood Stalin better than anyone and could "manage" him.)

At approximately the same time, although unknown to the general public, George Kennan sent his famous 8,000-word "Long Telegram" to Washington outlining the sources of the Soviet Union's aggressive political objectives. (A public version would appear a year later in the journal *Foreign Affairs*.) Kennan's warning sent shock waves through Washington's corridors of power. Meanwhile, in the early spring of 1946, civil war broke out between the Chinese Communists under Mao Zedong and Chiang Kai-shek's Nationalists. As debate raged in America over the import of Churchill's warning, the even more alarming news broke of Gouzenko's exposure of a network of Soviet spies in England, Canada, and the United States who were plotting to steal information on the development of the atomic bomb.

Suddenly the Communist sympathizers and fellow-travelers who had cheered on the Soviet Union found themselves and their cause unpopular. The impact of these events on the Soviet Union's image in America can be traced in a series of Gallup polls: In August 1945, after the Allied victory, 54 percent of the American public had a "positive view" of the Soviet Union. By January 1946, that figure had dropped to just 25 percent. In March 1946, following Churchill's speech and Gouzenko's revelations, 71 percent of the American public identified the Soviet Union as a nation seeking world domination.

Weeks later, Victor Krevshenko, a middle-ranking Soviet *apparatchnik* who had defected to the United States two years earlier, published his shocking report on the Stalinist Soviet Union's crimes and the Soviet Gulag. *I Chose Freedom* appalled and outraged the American liberal intelligentsia and, if anything, had an even bigger impact in Europe—even though both European and American progressives tried to discredit and smear him.

The geopolitical global warming stoked by wave after wave of these events generated a torrid cultural climate by the summer of 1946 that soon became a tempest—what may be viewed as the perfect storm of Orwell's lifetime—primed to break as Orwell's Red-hot "animallegory" reached American shores in late August.

"Some Animal Stories Are More Equal ..."

We have noted that Orwell had a difficult time securing a publisher for *Animal Farm* in England—at least four major English presses rejected it, largely because of Orwell's (mis?)timing, since the manuscript was making the rounds of London editorial offices during the closing months of World War II, when publishers were skittish about offending Whitehall with a book about the villainy of a much-needed ally. As the war ended, the Soviet Union still remained popular for its role in defeating Nazism. Although the Cold War did not develop as quickly in England as it would later in the United States—the new Labour government tried at first to accommodate the Russians ("Left speaks to Left" was one of the slogans of the time)—Prime Minister Clement Attlee and Foreign Secretary Ernest Bevin had no illusions by the end of 1945 about the Soviet Union's aggressiveness. Bevin had never been an Uncle Joe fan, having fought bloody battles in the past over the attempts by Communists to seize control of the British trade union movement.

The gathering storm of American public opinion against the USSR made it far easier for Orwell to find a publisher in the United States, though certain liberal circles continued to oppose serious criticism of the Soviet Union, which was often dismissed as "Red baiting." As the Cold War deepened, Peter Viereck, writing in *Confluence*, a publication edited by the young Henry Kissinger, claimed that *Animal Farm* had been rejected by 20 publishers. Certainly this was an exaggeration, but there was still considerable pro-Soviet sympathy in intellectual circles. The prevailing progressive atmosphere in New York publishing offices was still strong enough for the editor of Little, Brown, the prominent fellow-traveler Angus Cameron, to reject the book out of hand. (Some idea of the political naïveté throughout America can be judged from the fact that Dial Press turned down *Animal Farm* on the grounds that "it is impossible to sell animal stories in the USA.") Harcourt Brace, on the recommendation of one of its representatives, took a chance on Orwell's fable and got rich in the process.

Animal Farm was an immediate blockbuster in the United States, as we outlined in Chapter 4, with reviews of Orwell's "fairy story" (as he subtitled it) in the popular press almost uniformly laudatory. Yet as we shall see, it would turn out to be *Commonweal* that presented the most perceptive and well-informed discussion of Orwell's fable—a review that not only dealt with *Animal Farm* but also demonstrated a thorough acquaintance with his *oeuvre*, most of which in 1946 was still unpublished in the United States and unknown even to regular readers of *Partisan Review* and *politics*. (Orwell had contributed a "London Letter" to *Partisan Review* during the war and had also published in *politics*, which featured a blend of radical politics and pacifism.)

Orwell's enthusiastic reception in America—first and foremost among the erstwhile Trotskyists in New York around the *Partisan Review* and Dwight Macdonald's *politics*—was little surprise, given his own independent socialist, quasi-Trotskyist stance. But who would have thought that a Catholic magazine also might champion this belligerent atheist's writings over the next decade? These seemingly contradictory groups, former Trotskyists and liberal Catholics, shared little save for a distrust of the fellow-travelers and progressive "liberals" defending Stalin who had served as apologists for every about-face of Soviet politics since at least the 1930s. What we may term the "*Commonweal* Catholic" Orwell was not at all an easily foreseeable phenomenon.

Orwell and *Commonweal*: Elective Affinities

While we may be tempted to speak of a "Catholic" view of Orwell—and subordinate *Commonweal*'s specific role in his acceptance within American Catholic intellectual circles—that decision would overlook a significant historical fact: *Commonweal* alone among Catholic periodicals—whether in America or in the United Kingdom—devoted extensive space and positive attention to Orwell's work, beginning with his realistic novels of the 1930s, continuing through to *Animal Farm* and *Nineteen Eighty-Four*, and extending throughout the 1950s as his heretofore unpublished work first appeared in the United States. *Commonweal* recognized Orwell's work as early as 1937, when it reviewed his first two novels, *Burmese Days* and *A Clergyman's Daughter* (something that not even the Trotskyist or English Catholic press had done). The magazine was the only Catholic periodical to take note of his work—fully two years before the English journal *Month* (notably also a Catholic magazine) published the first full-length article dealing with Orwell. (The Jesuit-run magazine *America* did not review Orwell during his lifetime or his earlier work, except for a brief anonymous notice of *Animal Farm* and a pedestrian review of his first American essay collection). It was only after his death in 1950 that most American Catholic organs (including *America*) paid much attention to Orwell.

Why the difference in the case of *Commonweal*? One possible answer is: Spain. Why did *Commonweal* wait until 1937 to review *Burmese Days* and *A Clergyman's Daughter*, which had been published in the United States in 1935 and 1934, respectively? It makes no apparent sense whatsoever that a Catholic weekly—or any newspaper or magazine, for that matter—would wait two or three years to review a largely unknown English writer, especially given that his novel about Burma bears little relation to Catholic or Christian topics. Again, the plausible answer is: Spain.

In December 1936, recall, Orwell left England to fight in Catalonia with a motley left-wing militia (consisting of Trotskyists, anarchists, and other radicals) known in Spanish as the POUM. Already he was becoming well known in London intellectual circles for his independent left-wing reviews, gritty realistic novels and reportage, and anti-Empire essays such as "Shooting an

Elephant" and "A Hanging." English Catholics could not abide his writings about the Spanish Civil War, which disregarded the atrocities directed against the Catholic Church, particularly the murder of priests and nuns, while emphasizing the atrocities committed by General Franco's forces. It is to *Commonweal's* credit that it acknowledged this dimension of Orwell's work and dared nonetheless to seek common ground with him on other issues, especially given that the issue of the Spanish Civil War had been one of the most divisive in the magazine's history, precipitating the resignation of one editor, George Shuster, and the forced retirement of its founding editor, Michael Williams. Both men had resisted the Church's pro-Franco stand and condemnation of the Loyalists running the Spanish Republic.

Shuster and Williams urged a more balanced, nuanced view of the war, arguing that neither side was composed of angels of light or darkness. Yes, the Republicans desecrated churches and murdered clergy, the editors emphasized, but Franco was reinforced by modern tanks, fighter planes, and troops from Nazi Germany and Fascist Italy, who were using Spain to test weapons and tactics that soon might devastate other parts of Europe. The Loyalists were drawn to what they considered a utopian society and what they rightly saw as the opening round in a global battle against fascism.

The Republicans' bloodthirsty anticlericalism, manifested from the outset of the conflict, plus the Vatican's crusade against "atheistic Russia" and condemnation of Stalin's aid to the Popular Front, settled the question in favor of Franco for most Catholic Church officials and publications abroad, almost all of which were either under episcopal control or sponsored by religious orders with Spanish confreres who had suffered loss of life or property. Although polls showed that 4 out of 10 Catholics supported the

Popular Front, *Commonweal*'s even-handed, nuanced approach to the war was very unpopular with the Catholic establishment, especially among uncompromising Vatican backers such as Cardinal Francis Spellman in New York, the conservative diocese in which the magazine operated. No other American Catholic publication, with the single exception of the *Catholic Worker*—the pacifist, radical newspaper of Dorothy Day and Peter Maurin, which was also based in New York City—shared the *Commonweal* editors' point of view. The magazine's stance on Spain unleashed an onslaught of criticism stronger than that received at any other time in *Commonweal*'s history.

The issue of the Spanish Civil War also remained problematic for many American Catholics into the 1940s and 1950s. That is probably why *America* did not even review *1984*. The Jesuit editors—not Catholic laymen but priests understandably hesitant to buck Spellman and the Vatican—were uncomfortable dealing with an avowed atheist who expressed nothing but contempt for Catholicism, wrote a moving tribute to the Spanish Loyalists, and even took up arms to fight at their side. In dealing with this emotional topic, Frank Getlein in *Commonweal* recommended that Catholics view the conflict with the same "ruthless honesty" that characterized Orwell's writings on the war, especially *Homage to Catalonia*. Whereas Orwell had fiercely attacked those fellow leftists who downplayed Stalin's betrayal of the revolutionary cause, American Catholics closed their eyes to the failings of Franco's cause.

That the Trotskyists would embrace Orwell is understandable, but it is more difficult to explain his appeal to American Catholics. Besides his well-known contempt for religion in general and Catholicism in particular, Orwell considered Catholicism's political tendency plainly fascist, distinguishing it from Anglicanism, which did not "impose a political 'line' " on its followers. The collaboration of the Spanish clergy with Franco in the Spanish Civil War permanently hardened his attitude, though his bitter anti-Catholicism is evident throughout his work. Orwell mocked notions of heaven and the Catholic (and Anglican) priesthood in *Down and Out in Paris and London* and *A Clergyman's Daughter*, denounced "Romanism" as the ecclesiastical equivalent of Stalinism in *The Road to Wigan Pier*, compared "orthodox" Catholic intellectuals to Communist Party writers throughout his journalism, satirized religious belief via the figures of Moses the Raven and Sugarcandy Mountain in *Animal Farm*, and linked religious with political orthodoxy in O'Brien's power-crazed speech in *Nineteen Eighty-Four*. Guerrilla campaigns against "the enemy" pleased Orwell. After spotting a Bible Society sign noting that the local Protestant shop did not carry the Catholics' Douay Bible, he wrote a friend: "Long may they fight, I say; so long as that spirit is in the land we are safe from the RCs."

Fighting words for sure. Yet Orwell's attitude toward Christianity in general and Catholicism in particular was more nuanced than such vituperations suggest. If Orwell had no time for organized religion, he did express sympathy for the traditions of the Anglican faith—he was buried in an Anglican churchyard, and his biographers note that he seems to have had a phase of regular church attendance during his early 30s. Even his notorious hostility to Catholicism was more complex than most observers recognize. It would be fair to say that he was not so much anti-*Catholic* as anti-*Church*: it was not the faith as such that he found noxious (he briefly attended a private Catholic academy as a small boy)[1], but the illiberal institution behind it. Orwell's focus was always on the evils of the institutional Church, that is, on issues related to secular power rather than religious devotion. He never regarded the Church in spiritual terms or as a body of religious believers, but saw it always as a secular organization dominated by egotistic clerics, smug lay intellectuals, and blinkered Church apologists. That is to say, Orwell always approached ecclesiastical doctrines and faith itself in an ideological context, leading his close friend Sir Richard Rees (a fellow Old Etonian and practicing Anglican) to characterize Orwell's writings as a critique of "political Catholicism."[2] Wherever Orwell looked, it seemed as if Roman Catholic theology and Church dogma represented a cover for consolidating earthly power. Whether he was observing the Spain of the sixteenth-century Inquisition or of the civil war of 1936–1939, the cruelties and corruptions of the Church seemed to be everywhere. Orwell would have readily seconded the indictment of Lord Acton: "If a man accepts the Papacy with confidence, admiration and unconditional obedience, he must have made terms with murder."[3]

Unlike most Marxists, whose rigid historical materialism led them to treat religious ideas as unworthy of consideration, Orwell engaged with such ideas directly. His outspoken atheism and aggressively anti-Catholic rhetoric notwithstanding, *Commonweal*'s editors considered Orwell—as did Christopher Hollis—a religious writer, for he was preoccupied with uncomfortable questions of Christian doubt inevitably linked to matters of religious faith and because much of his journalism and fiction (especially *A Clergyman's Daughter*, *Animal Farm*, and *Nineteen Eighty-Four*) traffic in religious themes and images. Moreover, Orwell essentially agreed with the heart of the social gospel and with Catholic teachings on the just wage and the dignity of all workers, though he lamented that the Church's defense of private property kept it from going far enough. It was the hypocrisy of the Catholic Church— above all the extent to which it betrayed its own teachings and values, thereby turning Catholicism into another mere "ism" like Marxism—that Orwell scorned. Orwell could have borrowed and inverted a Chesterton quip about socialists to sum up his anti-Church attitude. "The worst thing about Catholics is Catholicism," he might have said, with a strong emphasis on the "ism."

Some Catholic thinkers earned strong praise from Orwell. He highly respected the French novelist and essayist Georges Bernanos, who shared his hostility to totalitarianism. He was keenly, though not uncritically, interested in G. K. Chesterton, whose novel *The Napoleon of Notting Hill* exerted some influence on the conception of *Nineteen Eighty-Four*. In a review of Frank Sheed's *Communism and Man*, Orwell observed that Sheed's analysis of Marxism was honest, intelligent, and free of the complacent sense of moral superiority he detected in many Catholic intellectuals. Orwell also respected those Catholic writers such as Georges Bernanos who showed a deep social conscience. By contrast, he was severe in his judgment of Graham Greene's work precisely because he thought that Greene did not take his faith seriously enough. In a negative review of *The Heart of the Matter*, Orwell pointed out that Greene repeatedly suggests that a Catholic sinner is superior to a good pagan, a suggestion Orwell considered snobbish, glib, and flippant. No serious Catholic would take the eternal damnation of hellfire so casually. He lamented that Greene "appears to share the idea, which has been floating around ever since Baudelaire, that there is something rather *distingué* in being damned." He suspected that this idea was a symptom of Christianity's decline: "This cult of the sanctified sinner seems to me to be frivolous, and underneath it there probably lies a weakening of belief, for when people really believed in Hell, they were not so fond of striking graceful attitudes on its brink."

Besides being morally frivolous, the "cult of the sanctified sinner" also made Greene's novel psychologically implausible in Orwell's judgment. Its Catholic protagonist, a commissioner of police in a West African British colony, traps himself in an adulterous affair. He commits sacrilege and, finally, suicide to avoid hurting either his wife or his mistress. Orwell wasn't buying it:

> If he really felt that adultery is mortal sin, he would stop committing it; if he persisted in it, his sense of sin would weaken. If he believed in Hell, he would not risk going there merely to spare the feelings of a couple of neurotic women. And one might add that if he were the kind of man we are told he is—that is, a man whose chief characteristic is a horror of causing pain—he would not be an officer in a colonial police force.

The reviews of Sheed and Greene alone demonstrate a surprising theological sophistication on Orwell's part—and an unusual degree of interest in Catholic teaching for a British socialist. So too does his two-part essay in *Time and Tide*, "Notes on the Way" (1940), show evidence of a religious sensibility and how seriously he regarded the modern world's denial of the soul's reality. He opens this brief article by recalling "a rather cruel trick I once played on a wasp." In a brilliant feat of understatement, he makes this little anecdote speak volumes about the fate of the modern world and the consequences of the decline of religion:

> [The wasp] was sucking jam on my plate, and I cut him in half. He paid no attention, merely went on with his meal, while a tiny stream of jam trickled out of his severed esophagus. Only when he tried to fly away did he grasp the dreadful thing that had happened to him. It is the same with modern man. The thing that has been cut away is his soul, and there was a period ... during which he did not notice it.

Two paragraphs later, Orwell switches metaphors and observes that European intellectual history from Gibbon and Voltaire to

Shaw and Joyce was imprinted by freethinking rebels who had converted "nearly every thinking man [into] a rebel." The consequence was that "for two hundred years we sawed and sawed at the branch [of religious faith] we were sitting on," oblivious to the fact that our humanitarian ethics had its roots in religious morality—and that if we cut away the soul, felled the Tree of Good and Evil, and razed the Judeo-Christian tradition, "a world ... founded on ... machine guns" spiraling "downwards into abysses ... too horrible to contemplate" would ensue. "In the end, much more suddenly than anyone had foreseen, our efforts were rewarded and down we came. But there had been a little mistake. The thing at the bottom was not a bed of roses after all, it was a cesspool of barbed wire." The prophesied socialist utopia turned out instead to be "the nightmare" of anti-utopia, an inferno "of endless war ... [and] slave populations toiling behind barbed wire.... We are living in a nightmare precisely *because* we have tried to set up an earthly paradise." We modern sophisticates have "sawed and sawed," blithely unaware that we dwell in a social sphere created and conditioned by Judeo-Christian civilization, the moral values of which have been deeply internalized by and (at least partially) inoculated the West against leader worship and cults of personality. Yet now, worried Orwell, with the bough broken and totalitarians on the march, could secular humanism sustain these inherited values without the religious topsoil and tillers that had cultivated them? We are like the heirs to a great fortune, he implied, but one that ceased accumulating long ago: we live on the principal of that fortune, which dwindles with each generation. Inevitably, at some point, bankruptcy looms.

As we noted in Chapter 8, Orwell (like Albert Camus) was, to use the poetic phrase that Max Weber applied to himself, "religiously musical." But he also had a nose for hypocrisy and posturing. His criticism of Catholics sometimes focused on these vices.

Orwell was appalled by the fact that Catholics often behaved no better—and indeed frequently much worse—than non-Catholics (and even nonbelievers).[4] He was suspicious of the fashionable upper-class vogue for "swimming the Tiber" during the 1920s and 1930s and thought the conversions of Evelyn Waugh and Christopher Hollis were motivated at least in part by class snobbery and nostalgia for aristocratic pretensions. (It did not help that both Waugh and Hollis were politically conservative.) By contrast, although Orwell disliked Irish nationalist writers such as Sean O'Casey, he felt affection for the 3 million working-class Irish laborers in Britain, almost all of whom were Catholic. His argument was with Rome, not with the Irish Catholic worker in the pews of London's East End.

Overall, Orwell regarded the Church as fundamentally and irremediably illiberal. The *raison d'être* of *Commonweal* was, then as now, to prove that this need not be the case. If the magazine embraced Orwell, it was not only because of his political courage, but also because of his moral seriousness—what one might call his heroic decency. Whereas Orwell's critique of Catholicism seemed ineffectual to orthodox believers and loyal churchmen such as Christopher Hollis because it was largely confined to the realm of rational discourse and secular affairs rather than the domains of scriptural authority and spiritual experience, *Commonweal's* editors could not so easily separate the spiritual and the secular, Church and state. To the lay intellectuals at *Commonweal*, Orwell's anti-Catholic polemics raised nagging questions that people of "decency" (a favorite Orwell word) could not avoid.

Whatever their differences, then, what we might term their "elective affinities" mattered more to *Commonweal's* editors—and were not negligible. Despite their disagreement with Orwell, therefore, these American lay Catholic intellectuals embraced him.

Commonweal's pioneering role in establishing Orwell's appeal for this important segment of the Catholic community warrants closer examination, for it also reflects much larger issues pertinent to both Catholic intellectual history and the magazine's own.

The American Catholic Context

In July 1946, just a month before the publication of *Animal Farm* in the United States, Charles Brady reviewed Orwell's collected essays, *Dickens, Dali and Others,* for *America.* The review was headlined "Virtuous Skeptic" and described Orwell as "that tonic thing among left-wingers, a man who applies his healthy skepticism to his own collectivist theories ... and has the mother wit to see that 'most revolutionaries are potential Tories.'" The relatively unknown Orwell was "a man we Catholics ought to get on reading terms with for he is very definitely on our side," Brady advised, casting him as a kind of Catholic fellow-traveler.

That is precisely how *Commonweal* had approached Orwell in the mid-1930s. Accenting the Orwell whom Catholics could admire and emulate, in its review of *A Clergyman's Daughter* in 1937 *Commonweal* highlighted the fact that the grim portrait of the protagonist, Dorothy Hare, had been written by someone who knew the harsh face of poverty in Depression England. Despite Orwell's sneers at what he often called "the racket of religion," noted the magazine, he showed sympathy for Dorothy's condition.[5] The review represents a ringing assent to Michael Williams's summons, proclaimed in the inaugural issue in 1924, to avoid the partisanship he saw in most Catholic publications. *Commonweal* practiced what it preached, for the magazine regularly exhibited toward the Church's dogmas and orthodoxies what Brady hailed as Orwell's "healthy skepticism."

The magazine's bridge-building aspirations and open-minded, conciliatory response to Orwell reflected also the distinctive origins and history of American Catholicism as a largely immigrant church. During Orwell's lifetime, English and American Catholics were—and still are—very different. American Catholics consisted mainly of European émigré and first-generation working-class families who were poorly educated and even illiterate—and in many respects not at all unlike the mining families with whom he stayed during his trip to the industrial Midlands in 1936 to gather material for what became *The Road to Wigan Pier*. Orwell's distrust of English Catholicism was rooted in his old-fashioned radical view of it as the religion of upper-class recusants and fashionable Oxbridge intellectual converts (such as Chesterton, Ronald Knox, Evelyn Waugh, Arnold Lunn, and Christopher Hollis). The latter group included talented, often aggressive Church apologists, yet the converts' ardor also veiled insecurities and defensiveness about their faith, given both their tiny numbers and Catholicism's long history of persecution. Here again, the case was entirely different in the U.S. By the late 1940s and early 1950s, American Catholics numbered in the tens of millions and had become one of the groups that Hollywood producers, eager to attract that huge audience, apotheosized as the incarnation of patriotism—personified by the likes of James Cagney and Pat O'Brien.

American Catholics could overlook Orwell's hostility to religion because he was seen as a man with a clear moral compass, one whose ethic was essentially Christian. He sympathized with the poor and victims of oppression throughout the world, including the British Empire, and he and his writings exemplified decency and fair play. Moreover, he was honest enough to admit that the decay of religion in the modern world had left a spiritual void, one that was filled by totalitarian ideologies like Nazism and Communism. Orwell believed that Christianity had fostered a genuine sense of altruism, and he lamented "the decay of religious belief" because the Christian ethos had encapsulated the best of the Western tradition, especially in its emphasis on human dignity and the concept of free will. This self-styled unbeliever was someone with whom American Catholics could posthumously establish, as it were, a cordial ecumenical dialogue. It also didn't hurt that Orwell happened to share the Catholic view on some hot-button issues. For example, he opposed abortion and despised what he called "birth control fanatics."

According to various scholars, such as Thomas McAvoy, the prominent place of well-bred, highly educated English Catholic families who assimilated easily into the U.S. is the crucial link between the history of the Catholic immigrant and that of the native Protestant. That history has its roots in some of the founding colonial families, especially in Maryland, and represents another distinctive feature of American Catholic culture. *Commonweal* drew on this tradition, and its editors and editorial board were also heavily connected to the Ivy League. Members of the early editorial boards almost all possessed an Ivy League background, with graduates from Harvard, Yale, and Princeton predominating. George Shuster was from a Catholic college, Notre Dame, but was receiving his doctorate from Columbia (where Carlton Hayes, president of the American Catholic Historical Association and an influential *Commonweal* board member, taught history). The single exception was Michael Williams, a maverick autodidact who never graduated from college.

Certainly the prevailing orientation toward Albion by the educated, literate American Catholic community generally and *Commonweal*'s board members specifically predisposed its editors to be attentive and receptive to a writer such as Orwell, particularly given his growing reputation for "Englishness." So too did the magazine's stable of English reviewers and the Ivy League affiliations of its staff and advisory board contribute significantly to the influence that it exerted on Orwell's reputation far beyond Catholic circles.

A Religious Fellow-Traveler?

Commonweal's review of *Animal Farm* in September 1946 was a *tour de force*, easily the most insightful and comprehensive notice that the fable received on either side of the Atlantic. The review was written by Adam De Hegebus, a Hungarian-born British citizen, and it reflected his experience of living in England for years. De Hegebus knew Orwell's writings far better than did American intellectuals, having read much of his work still unpublished in the U.S. He argued that *Animal Farm* was not just a parody using farm animals to allegorize the tragic and horrific regress of the Russian Revolution. De Hegebus believed that an aggressive nationalism had almost destroyed European civilization in World War II, and he saw *Animal Farm* as Orwell's commentary on the disease of nationalism. Furthermore, he recognized that Orwell's emphasis in *Animal Farm* demonstrated Lord Acton's "immortal thesis according to which power corrupts and absolute power corrupts absolutely."

Placing *Animal Farm* within a Catholic context, De Hegebus associated the fable with "man's craving for the absolute, which is the most powerful basis of nationalism"—an obvious reference to the French Personalist philosopher Leon Bloy. Here De Hegebus is implying that Orwell is one of Bloy's "pilgrims of the absolute," someone who recognizes that the spiritual dimension of life is ultimately far more important than the political or the ideological. De Hegebus actually calls *Animal Farm* a "parable," noting that Orwell "is an artist who knows precisely how effective it can be not to say explicitly what he means, and this little tale of 120-odd pages has more explosive energy and actuality than a five-hundred page carefully documented report on Russia." It is "poetry … the type of journalism that stays news." Shrewdly and accurately, he observes that Orwell is "angry with Russia because Russia is *not* socialist," but that Orwell himself is "not a real socialist but a well-meaning and intelligent radical liberal" much like Dickens. His review concludes with a short discussion of Orwell's first collection of essays published in the U.S., along with observations on *Burmese Days* and *A Clergyman's Daughter*, updating and elaborating on the judgments in *Commonweal*'s 1937 review. De Hegebus even shows a familiarity with Orwell's other work, including *Down and Out in Paris and London* and *The Road to Wigan Pier*, which he describes as "the best books about poverty in England."

In the decade following his death in 1950, *Commonweal* promoted Orwell even more enthusiastically. The magazine's subsequent writing about Orwell went far beyond *Animal Farm* and *Nineteen Eighty-Four*, spotlighting his affinities with Catholic ideas and ideals. Looking back in a 1964 *Commonweal* essay on the first postwar decade, Andrew Greeley wrote, "The big change in the Catholic intellectual climate apparently happened toward the end of the ten-year period [*sic*] which began with [the] G.I. Bill and ended with *Sputnik*." This was precisely the period—13 years (1944–1957), to be exact—when *Commonweal* successfully championed Orwell within the Catholic intellectual community.

Commonweal featured Orwell in a dozen substantial essays and reviews in the decade after his death. In December 1950, Richard Weaver, author of *Ideas Have Consequences* and already recognized as an influential conservative voice in America, greeted him in a review of a new collection of Orwell's essays, *Shooting an Elephant*, as a "good humanist" who in *Animal Farm* and *1984* condemned the mania of the age: ideology. Its maniacal "consequence," Weaver noted, was totalitarianism of the Right and Left.

Commonweal found this self-proclaimed hater of Catholicism close to its views on many issues. In 1951 the English critic Geoffrey Ashe pondered in a comprehensive review essay why Orwell's work should appeal to Catholics. Despite being a convinced unbeliever who sought material progress for the working classes, Ashe told *Commonweal* readers, Orwell also longed for a "reign of kindness, brotherhood, beauty, truth." *Animal Farm* portrayed the impossibility of reconciling these two goals and the inevitable spiritual crisis to which the vainglorious dream of revolution leads. To Ashe, *Animal Farm* was nothing less than a rejection of the utopian delusion—and the anti-utopian nightmare that must follow. Moreover, revolutions become perverted for moral rather than political reasons. Ashe argued that Orwell's socialism was essentially a Christian ethic—do no harm to others—and that toward the end of his life, Orwell transcended socialism, for though he proved unable "to budge an inch towards Christian orthodoxy, he clung to Christian values."[6]

Later in the 1950s, *Commonweal* touted Orwell's importance in the magazine's lead essay. In "Orwell's Secular Crusade," Richard Voorhees, who wrote the first academic book on Orwell's ideas (*The Paradox of George Orwell*, 1960), devoted four full pages to the central preoccupations of what he called Orwell's "philosophy"—the danger of nationalism, the problem of power, the dignity of the common man, and the role of religion in society. Like Chesterton, Voorhees observed, Orwell possessed common sense, loved nature, and cherished the common man. One of Orwell's observations about the modern world—that "it is a restless, cultureless life … in which children grow up with an intimate knowledge of magnetos and in complete ignorance of the Bible"—would have appealed to Chesterton's love of paradox. Where they differed, of course, was on the question of religion. Voorhees argued that Orwell was "just not interested in religion except as an *institution* which seemed to him an impediment to socialism." Even in *Animal Farm*, Orwell found the opportunity to express his hostility to organized religion (specifically, the Russian Orthodox Church) in the form of the raven, Moses, a clever homilist who preaches about Sugarcandy Mountain, where all obedient, submissive animals will go to their reward.[7]

But Orwell's derision of religion in general and Catholicism in particular did not negate the political force of his appeal for Catholics. Instead, Orwell's loathing of communism fortified Catholics, whose own anticommunism had rendered them suspect in American intellectual circles. *Animal Farm* and *1984* were openly and explicitly welcomed as support for this Catholic stance. Orwell vindicated Catholic opposition to communism and the cult of Stalin among progressives during the war. Voorhees and other Catholics pronounced him one of Chesterton's "good agnostics," even a *homo religiosus*—just as did Catholic Conservatives in England such as Christopher Hollis, as we saw in Chapter 2. Whereas Hollis generated controversy and provoked accusations of seeking to "press-gang" Orwell "for the papists," however, liberal Catholic admirers of Orwell aroused no ire among secular leftists, probably because of their shared political outlook with most non-Marxist American liberals. That the English Catholic Church in general and London Catholic intellectuals in particular represented a small, often embattled presence within cultured British society—in contrast to the powerful, populous American Catholic Church and the rising stature of educated American Catholics—doubtless also contributed to the divergent receptions.

Literary Reception as Ecumenical Outreach?

So if *Animal Farm* shaped the American public's view of the Soviet Union and its interpretation of the Cold War, it was *Commonweal* that played a key role in that development, for it drew attention to Orwell's work long before any other American journal, including *Partisan Review* and *politics*. It took tolerance, insight, and independence of mind for a Catholic journal to praise a figure with such a strong antipathy to religion and perceive him "on our side." It is noteworthy that no other Catholic journal— not *America*, not the *Dublin Review*, not the *Tablet* or *Month* in England—gave more than passing attention (if even that) to Orwell until after his death, when almost everyone (including even the chastened *Nation* and *New Republic*) jumped aboard the Orwell bandwagon. Apart from all the aforementioned historical and sociological factors, such attention testifies to the generosity of spirit and moral courage displayed by *Commonweal*'s long-time editor, Edward S. Skillin.

Furthermore, whereas other Catholic publications gave Orwell merely brief or belated recognition and viewed him even in the 1950s and early 1960s mainly through Catholic spectacles, *Commonweal* not only sought to spotlight Orwell's similarities to the Catholic tradition and his fundamentally Christian values but also made strenuous and successful efforts to see Orwell in his own terms, even fully acknowledging his sharp differences both with Catholic views and with the magazine's own editorial stance—and never aiming either to convert him or to rewrite (and rationalize away) his anti-Catholic venom (as Christopher Hollis did). Years before the sea change inaugurated by Vatican II (1962–1965) turned the Church decisively toward the world, *Commonweal* exemplified a stance of liberal tolerance and openness toward the modern secular age that fully respected Catholic morality and tradition. The once-familiar phrase "*Commonweal* Catholic" dates from this period and proudly proclaimed this fresh, new, liberal Vatican II vision. The magazine's reception of George Orwell expresses this vision, and it serves in microcosm as a revealing case study of *Commonweal's* history and values—and also of the ecumenical spirit that imbued the Second Vatican Council.

If *Commonweal* was sometimes on the defensive and was even castigated within official Church circles as insufficiently "Catholic," it was also ahead of its time as more "catholic"—and its pioneering, idiosyncratic "*Commonweal* Catholic/catholic" sensibility both anticipated and animated the modern Church's assertive counterculture outreach toward the world and separated the wheat from the chaff of Church dogma and doctrine. Both Orwell and *Commonweal's* editors turned out to be prescient in their visions of where the postwar zeitgeist would go.

Without skirting the fact of his adamantly avowed atheism and litany of grievances against Catholicism, the magazine presented "*Commonweal* Catholic" Orwell as a man of conscience and a "good agnostic" whose best virtues represented a worthy example for American Catholics. As a believing Catholic myself, I fully endorse that verdict. Today, more than ever, it warrants reaffirmation by Christians and non-Christians alike.

FIGURE 12. Even before the plethora of allusions to *Nineteen Eighty-Four* and "Big Brother" that accompanied the presidency of Donald Trump, President Barack Obama and his Democratic administration were associated with the same derisive terms by political opponents—from the Left as well as the Right. The frequency of such rhetoric multiplied after leaks by self-declared whistleblowers such as Edward Snowden in 2012. Documents stolen by Snowden revealed (among other disclosures) that the NSA had been snooping on tens of millions of American citizens (not to mention the leaders of foreign allies).

CHAPTER 11

"Orwellian" Warfare:
From Cold to Cyber

The Orwellian Future?

As everyone knows, *Nineteen Eighty-Four* is a satirical anti-utopia that features a horrific and tyrannical dictator, Big Brother, whom Orwell imagined to be a Janus-faced totalitarian bogeyman figure, a hideous and fearful amalgam of Hitler and Stalin. It is a caricature of what Orwell feared the Western democracies could become in his time. And what about in our time, more than three full decades beyond his novel's title year, a four-digit profanity that the postwar zeitgeist—in an incomparable feat of negative branding—has forever darkened?

The Cold War has passed, but the cyberwars are upon us. (Are "Star Wars" far behind?) The postcommunist New World Order of the twenty-first century has already witnessed "Orwellian" developments—rogue states, drones, government-sponsored cyberattacks, and on and on—that make the bugaboos of midcentury seem by comparison as medieval as the rack and dungeon. The spectre of terrorism and its offshoots, along with the far-reaching, digitalized tentacles of both government and private industry, imperil our right to privacy and freedom of expression far more pervasively and insidiously than the thuggish hardware of the past. Not to mention today's sophisticated psychoterror. Old-fashioned physical torture has been supplemented and extended by "enhanced interrogation techniques"—a Newspeak locution for "methods" such as waterboarding, mock executions, "deep cold" exposure, "rectal rehydration," nakedness in total darkness and isolation, and "extraordinary rendition" (i.e., transportation to a succession of secret "black-site" prisons).

During the McCarthy and Stalinist eras, that was the stuff of dystopian fiction. Nowadays—as in Room 101—"they" *can* "get inside you." *Mutatis mutandis,* the so-called Free World faces "totalitarian" threats formerly unknown, indeed almost unimagined, except in Orwellian horror scenarios. Yes, fiction is fast becoming fact, leaving many of us feeling less free *and* less secure than ever before.

Will our technology outflank our technical capacity—and our moral will—to safeguard civil liberties?

The danger is there: Big Brother is watching us.

The Techno-Tree of Ignorance

Big Brother is an invisible, apparently mythic, presence in Orwell's novel whose very name—in fact even his mere initials, "B.B.," which are shouted at the regularly orchestrated spectacles of collective hysteria known as the Two Minute Hates—strikes terror in the hearts of the citizenry to the extent that they become willing zombies who give up their civil liberties in exchange for state protection.

Yet do not we too collude in our insecurities—and our unfreedoms? The seductive Baconian proclamation "Knowledge Is Power" mesmerizes us with its macho promise that Mother Earth is ours to dominate. As we succumb to this sadistic lure of technological omnipotence, however, our glistering hardware and magical software entrance us like a spellbinding utopian dream.

Our Eden with its shiny techno-Apple! The blasphemous four-letter word deep in every heart is: "More!" More and more scope and speed! More and more power!—at the cost of a click. Our powerlust proves insatiable—and disempowering.

"Freedom Is Slavery!"

As we embrace the Faustian bargain, our miraculous gadgetry processes and perverts us into obsessive control freaks. Cozily ensconced inside the Matrix, we too, like Oceania's zombie-like proles, reflexively surrender our leisure, our health, our social lives, and our physical senses to the hypnotic screen. The (virtual) reality today is that the dream has turned nightmarish, inverting "Knowledge Is Power" into the culminating worshipful slogan to Big Brother: "Ignorance Is Strength!"

Our ersatz "strength" (like the Nazis' *Macht durch Freude* ["Strength Through Joy"]) makes it easy for propagandists to colonize our minds and spirits. "We shall squeeze you empty," O'Brien declares to Winston, and "we shall fill you with ourselves." As we cruise and surf and scan and click, the Telescreen—the Apple of Our I(phone)s—"unpersons" us, with no need for primitive terror contraptions like cages of rabid rats against our faces. We check ourselves into Room 101 as we text and tweet, all the while luxuriating in the tonal bath of the I-tune Telescreen Lullaby: "We shall drain you of your identity—and we shall fill you with our hype." All this is not MAD but SAD (*Self*-Assured Destruction).

In light of these realities, a former contractor for the FBI wrote me that he is even more worried by domestic security alarmists than by international terrorists, fearing the possibility of federal overreaction "to the threat of violent acts" in the United States. "I do not think it improbable that most citizens would exchange their civil liberties for promises of security and social benefits," he noted. "There is no shortage of real enemies the government must legitimately defend against.... Focusing on one threat to the exclusion of others is a real danger. Also not realizing how these threats interact and relate to one another is dangerous as well."[1]

The Spectre of Cool War

Beyond the "conventional" (or neo-conventional) terrorists facing us, Orwellian forecasters surveying the cyberscape fret about the ever more imaginable nightmare of possible cyberwar, a form of engagement distinguished by warhead-type code or digital worms deployed to decimate infrastructure and even murder human beings.[2] These mega-viruses infect rival networks, causing them to self-destruct or implode/explode. Orwellian voices argue that a cyber arms race is well underway. Michael Hayden, a former CIA and NSA director, has characterized such code as "a new class of weapon, a weapon never before used" that possesses the "whiff of August, 1945."[3] The only question is whether this future conflict will be "hot" or "cold." Will it be Cyber World War III or the Cyber Cold War? One expert has predicted that it will be a "cool war," "a little warmer than cold because it seems likely to involve almost constant offensive measures that, while falling short of actual warfare, regularly seek to damage or weaken rivals or gain an edge through violations of sovereignty and penetration of defenses."[4]

Of course, in one key respect, cyberwar is utterly unlike conventional terrorism. Cyberthreats are invisible and surreptitious, whereas terrorist groups such as ISIS thrive on sensation and spectacle. And yet, as former president Barack Obama acknowledged, both kinds of terrorism, whether in the form of endless rendition and physical torture or drone attacks and surgical cyberattacks, "raise difficult questions about the balance we strike be-

FIGURE 13. In the early 1980s, even as the feverish countdown to 1984 heated up, a prole like Ziggy was hardly an object of concern for Big Brother. But we have come a long way from the pre-Internet Age, during which this cartoon appeared in 1982.

As we enter the third decade of the twenty-first century, it is indisputable that, in fewer than four decades, Western society has morphed into a world of digital communication in which Big Brother (whether in the form of a government agency like the NSA or in his corporate guise as Facebook or Amazon) collects data on everyone, high and low.

Surveillance is the norm because in the Digital Age, when bombings and mass murders are almost quotidian events, everyone is a potential "terrorist."

tween our interest in security and our values of privacy."[5] Arguably, ever since the terrorist attacks of September 11, 2001, the "balance" has fallen heavily on the side of limiting liberty in the name of security. In fact, numerous critics contend that the professed differences between the Bush and Obama administrations

FIGURE 14. In the years following the Orwell centenary in 2003, as the American invasion of Iraq that spring descended into a guerrilla war against the occupying army, left-wing cartoonists delighted in lampooning President George W. Bush and his "Orwellian" administration (and its supporters). Typifying the confusion between and conflation of the author George Orwell and the bogeyman "Orwell," Bush is satirized here as "Orwell Man," supported by his handpicked troika of Inner Party ministers.

At the Ministry of Peace, Secretary of Defense Donald Rumsfeld was the moving force behind the invasions of Afghanistan and especially Iraq, thanks to his notorious "shock and awe" assault strategy that aimed to test the power of America's new military weapons. At the Ministry of Love, Attorney General Alberto Gonzalez crafted the administration's legalistic rationale for (or rationalizations of?) waterboarding and other questionable procedures of interrogation (or torture?). At the Ministry of Truth, Fox News commentator Bill O'Reilly (or O'Brien?) boasted that viewers had entered the "no spin zone" when they tuned into his show, which spun reports of America's conduct in the military invasions rightward at high velocity.

FIGURE 15. Peeking out from Orwell's eye socket are the beady little all-seeing eyes of the Thought Police. This cartoon, which appeared in late 1983, exemplifies how the Orwell portrait gallery showcases depictions of "Orwell" and mindscapes of *Nineteen Eighty-Four*—rather than the writer Orwell and his other work. The gallery treats the author as a mere sideshow to the avatar of the numerical nightmare 1-9-8-4, whether the chimeras appear in the form of spectral Big Brothers or sadistic O'Briens or zombie-like proles bellowing Two Minute Hates.

(continued)

The last panel of the cartoon comes full circle in its critique of President Bush as "Orwell Man"—or what should be called "'Orwell' Man" (another instance of the conflation of the creator with his creature). In the caricature, the Big O—President Bush, outfitted as Superman—targets scapegoats such as Osama bin Laden to energize his Two Minute Hate campaigns.

Cartoonist Andy Singer contributes his self-syndicated *No Exit* cartoon to numerous publications. This cartoon appeared in February 2006, as American soldiers' injuries and deaths in Iraq were escalating precipitously and the military situation was deteriorating into near-chaos.

on national security were rhetorical, leading the *Economist* to dub Obama "W's Apprentice."[6] Other observers have branded him "Big Brother Obama," chanting mockingly, "Yes We Scan" (a derisive pun on his popular 2008 campaign slogan, "Yes We Can").[7]

Admittedly, both the stagecraft and substance of the Trump administration's foreign policy are quite different from those of Barack Obama and even George W. Bush. If anything, however, civil liberties seem under siege to an even greater extent today. And whatever one writes about the topic is soon hopelessly dated. Exposés uncovering the skullduggery of Cambridge Analytica, the misuses of Facebook data, and the Soviet and Chinese governments' officially sponsored hacking programs reveal vertiginous quantum leaps in technotyranny on an almost weekly basis. Given the current state of affairs, in which incursions into and even abrogations of our personal freedoms are so frequent as to render them a casual, matter-of-fact norm of contemporary life, I believe that Orwell would voice anew his anxieties of yesteryear. Whether applied to state torture or techno-trespass, his novel's cautionary warnings are unfortunately evergreen—or as we have noted, ever-ebony.

Of *Un*lessons and Isms

Cautionary warnings? Yes. For I do not believe that history yields explicit "lessons." That applies equally or even more to serious fiction.

Maybe "*un*lessons"?

If so, one germane warning (or "*un*lesson") in *Nineteen Eighty-Four* is that a visible external threat—such as both Eurasia and Eastasia represent for Oceania, or Emmanuel Goldstein's dissident underground "Brotherhood" signified for the Inner Party—makes it much easier to achieve national unity and consensus on geopolitical goals. For decades, the *bête noire* of communism (especially the so-called Red Fascism of Stalin's rule) served the West well in this regard—so well in fact that the West—the purported Cold War victor—seemed rather disoriented or even demoralized by its "victory" in 1989–1991. In the absence of a common enemy, its leaders could not forge consensus and cohesion. In a certain sense, peacetime was more difficult than wartime in the 1990s, putting a new twist on the Oceania slogan "War Is Peace." "Islamicism" (an "ism" designed to distinguish terrorist activity from Islam) and al-Qaeda/ISIS have served partially since the disappearance of the USSR in 1991 as the West's substitute bogeymen—though Vladimir Putin and Russia are undeniably making a comeback as "contenders" for that dubious distinction.

Can we not do without an enemy scapegoat? For all his hatred of Stalinism, Orwell did not regard the USSR or Bolshevism as a Two Minute Hate rallying cry for the West. In his essays of the 1940s on James Burnham's *The Managerial Revolution* and *The Struggle for the World*, Orwell argued that the ex-Communist Burnham, a belligerent anti-Stalinist, exaggerated the durability and might of Stalin's tyrannical regime. In doing so, Orwell contended, Burnham overemphasized the likelihood that a bureaucratic-technocratic elite of party functionaries would arise and furnish one-party dictatorships in totalitarian states with both dynastic stability and quasi-permanence.

I suspect that Orwell probably would also have looked skeptically on Burnham's efforts in the 1950s, directed on the political front by Republican leaders such as John Foster Dulles, to win support for an "offensive" strategy aimed at reversing the territorial gains of Soviet communism—even if "rollback" meant dropping a nuclear bomb.[8] Much as Orwell obviously deplored the "evil empires" of Oceania, Eurasia, and Eastasia in *Nineteen Eighty-Four*, it portrays a stalemate after the nuclear wars of the 1950s—which probably reflects Orwell's pragmatic preference for an enduring Cold War rather than the confrontational stance urged by Dulles in 1952, when he declared that the United States must abandon "treadmill policies" and adopt "aggressive" tactics.

By implication, Orwell broadly shared the outlook that guided the main architects of American postwar diplomacy during the Cold War: containment. His geopolitical worldview resembled George Kennan's in this crucial respect: Orwell too was a "realist." [9] He was a rebel and a gradualist, not a fundamentalist ideologue and revolutionary. As R. J. Stove has pointed out:

> Before the Spanish Popular Front, he sought no democratic crusades inside or outside Europe. He never called for an invasion of, or even sanctions against, Mussolini's Italy. Of non-Italian and non-Nazi rightist dictators, he abhorred Franco alone. If he ever denounced Chancellor Dollfuss, General Metaxas, or Admiral Horthy, it has escaped his editors. Toward Marshal Pétain and Pilsudski he showed subdued aversion rather than loud anger. (He made one neutral reference, in 1944, to Dr Salazar's rule of Portugal.) ... Also, he resented those Zionists who blew up the King David Hotel.[10]

Orwell's realism made him skeptical about bellicose initiatives for "regime change" or the kind of adventurism that would be involved in remaking the world safe for democracy. Nor did he advocate that the atom bomb be employed to roll back the Soviet army from occupied Eastern Europe or that first-strike capability in atomic weaponry—let alone a policy of mutually assured destruction—was essential. Instead he took a pragmatic view that, with qualifications and ambivalences, clearly sided with America and a version of *realpolitik*.[11] Given Orwell's refusal to support aggressive military options in the Cold War, it seems most unlikely that he would have sanctioned such responses in a (still comparatively) lesser conflict such as the War on Terror.

Certainly Orwell also retained a sense of historical scale that allowed him to recognize that a politics of equivalence was, as it were, spatial presentism—and itself misconceived. Distinctions—both political and historical—need to be drawn here. To equate McCarthyism (or the anticommunist extremism that Orwell called "hundred percent Americanism" in pre-McCarthy days[12]) with Stalinism—or, for that matter, East German "*Stasi*sm" with Nazism—elides the distinctions within each pair in turn. We too need to maintain such balance, which includes the judicious use of political and historical analogies. That is to say, equating the War on Terror with the Cold War is also misconceived. No "Big Brother" totalitarianisms exist on the globe today. Even North Korea is, at worst, an example of "Little Brother." It belittles the historical experience of the Cold War, not to speak of World War II, to equate the terrorists of today with the totalitarian regimes of the last century. For example, the all-too-casual comparisons between murderous Islamist terrorist cells and Bolshevik genocide—the latter a "demos-cide" against huge segments of The People accounting for 100 million twentieth-century corpses—insult the victims of the latter.[13]

Despite these glaring discrepancies between totalitarian nation-states and terrorist networks, however, might the vision and views of Orwell the Cold Warrior still speak to our present circumstances? Might the "realist" sensibility of Orwell's anti-utopia and anti-Burnham essays possess practical contemporary relevance? That is to say: Might some version of Cold War containment furnish American policymakers today a cogent strategy—absent any recourse to fundamentalist theology[14]—for a patient, long-term antiterrorist campaign on multiple fronts? Like Soviet communism, might "Islamicist" terrorism eventually implode as a result of its own fatal self-contradictions? Might the West "contain" international terrorism through limited measures in the long term, without recourse to large-scale military operations, monitoring it closely in the conviction that it will eventually subvert itself?

Watching Big Brother Watching Us

Whether or not such a containment strategy could succeed—or even gain support as a new Western consensus—concerned citizens need all the while to practice with vigilance a form of "containment" of our own. *We* need to "monitor closely" our own governments (and corporations)—to keep "Watching Big Brother"—ever on the alert for abuses by our own government and our own geopolitical "side." Yes, we need to keep watching Big Brother even as he (or it) watches us. We need to keep our eyes on *them* as their panoptical telescreen eyes us. If we value the freedoms that form the cornerstone of democracy, watching Big Brother is indispensable. Only then can we expose the perils to those freedoms—before we lose them.

The ultimate "*un*lesson" of Cold War surveillance excesses in general and the warnings of *Nineteen Eighty-Four* in particular is a stern and challenging one. It comes down to this for twenty-first-century America: The best means to combat those forces that would conspire to destroy our liberties is not to curtail these liberties in the name of national security. Rather, it is to champion and cradle humane values as the proper counterforce.

And ultimately it is, if necessary, not that alone. For it is also to insist that these values be maintained and defended even in the face of sadistic acts of mass violence—and to hold firm to the position that those who cherish democracy will not sacrifice the fundamental principles on which both our civic integrity as a nation and our basic human dignity rest.

CHAPTER 12

Why I Am Not a Socialist

> Yes, surely! and if others can see it as I have seen it,
> then it may be called a vision rather than a dream.
> —William Morris, *News from Nowhere* (1890)

Confessions of a Recovering Utopian

I address in this final chapter a topic that has animated my own intellectual life—just as it did George Orwell's: the dream of utopia and nightmare of anti-utopia. Yet my meditations here not only mark the elective affinities between us, but also highlight where and how I depart from, or dwell beyond, Orwell's lengthy shadow. I thank my readers for allowing me to indulge in this personal turn in the hope that you may identify with my musings. Perhaps you too possess an intellectual big brother or sister to whom you acknowledge a notable cultural (and personal) debt that warrants sustained reflection.

For years I taught university courses with titles such as "The Utopian and Anti-Utopian Imagination." As a young man, I embraced a radical politics and utopian aspirations. The dream of utopia resounded much more powerfully in my ears than did the warnings of anti-utopia. In my classes on the utopian imagination, I would play John Lennon's "Imagine" and talk about the utopian commune in rural Virginia in which I'd briefly lived. I would bang the drum loudly for utopian classics usually neglected by literary critics and scholars, such as Condorcet's *Esquisse*, Edward Bellamy's *Looking Backward*, and H. G. Wells's *Men Like Gods*. I was also an enthusiast for experiments such as Esperanto, the artificial world language that envisioned a communitarian utopia possessed of socialist ideals. By surmounting the Tower of Babel, universal peace and global harmony would supposedly reign.

In my high-minded idealism I maintained that the possibilities discussed in all these visionary proposals were indeed within human reach. We only needed to design communities that would "make it easy to be good." I believed that the obstacles of building the "Good Society" lay in the unjust social structures and economic disincentives of the social polity that we ourselves had made, which virtually demanded that men and women be nothing less than figures of heroic virtue. We could reconstruct social reality toward ends that would facilitate the means to reach them.

None of this was utterly misconceived or fundamentally askew. As I studied the course of twentieth-century politics and culture closely, however, I came to see that it was unrealistic. It was not where most human beings and most human institutions found themselves; it was beyond our present state of development. The twentieth century had registered that fact with terrifying clarity. The nightmare of anti-utopia had left its indelible, uniquely horrible imprint, forever marking and staining the century. The terrible expressions of Dionysian dystopianism—the rise of totalitarian tyrannies and abject leader worship, the occurrence of two horrific world wars accompanied by a diabolical Holocaust and a demonic gulag, mass genocides across several continents, and the advent of weapons of mass destruction imperiling the survival of so-called *homo sapiens* altogether—all testified that the dire warnings of the anti-utopians were timely. The "Black Book" of socialism—whether we allude to right-wing "national" socialism or the left-wing "Union of Soviet Socialist Republics"—recorded a dark criminal history just beneath the story of the "glittering Wells-world," in Orwell's sardonic phrase. For many Marxian, Fabian, and National Socialists, "socialism" was a fantasy future of techno-ease and mass liberation.

In 1990, while visiting a collapsing East Germany, the erstwhile proud showcase of "really existing socialism," the self-professed GDR, aka German "Democratic Republic," I saw firsthand how Marx was wrong. With hundreds of thousands marching in the street demonstrations led by Lutheran pastors and churchgoers, religion was not the opiate of the masses. It was the elixir of a rejuvenated *Volk*, who were taking back their country from the Party, its ruling pigs, and *der Grosse Bruder* at last.

And (uncomfortably) closer to home, I realized too: idealism is the opiate of the *apparatchik*—and the academic bourgeoisie. For the spellbound ideologue, revolutionary terror may be part of "the necessary murder," in Auden's notorious phrase.[1] After all, from inside the Third Reich or Stalin's USSR or the GDR, the true believer imagines—entranced by the perverted utopian imagination—that the ends justify all means. ("If the ends don't justify the means, what does?" Shaw once bantered. Never a jester, the deadly serious Lenin outdid G.B.S. as a wiseacre—and with deadly consequences. "You can't make an omelet," Lenin remarked about the murderous, lawless Cheka, his secret police, "without breaking a few eggs."[2])

Like Aldous Huxley and George Orwell, I soon realized that my utopian visions must bow to the grim and alarming material facts of twentieth-century history. Given such bracing reality checks, my visions were little more than willful hallucinations. That is, they amounted to naïve utopian illusions (or delusions) that needed to give way to anti-utopian admonitions. In the order of my temporal priorities, if not in the hierarchy of my political values, the warnings of the anti-utopians began to take precedence over the vision of the utopians. I learned to respect Alexander Herzen, who felt uplifted by the utopian impulse yet was ever aware of how utopian dreams descend into nightmares. I came to agree with the political philosopher Michael Oakeshott that the Tower of Babel represents the *locus classicus* of the failed utopian experiment.

Into Reality!

I am still inspired by the moral courage and intellectual integrity of many radicals and democratic socialists—especially writers such as George Orwell. Unlike them, however, I am not a socialist, but a social democrat. I am wary of fixing my gaze on dazzling communitarian ideals that are beyond me and my fellow citizens. Better to honor "where people are" in their lives—and to legislate from there—rather than to mesmerize them with a vision that is far beyond their moral reach. And perhaps this is why socialism, as a public policy, is misconceived. It locates its aims at an altitude too high for the general public. In so doing, it embraces Unreality.

The problem is in part an issue of scale. In a small group, such as my Virginia commune, which aimed to combine the best of both B. F. Skinner's *Walden Two* and Hawthorne's *Blithedale Romance*, face-to-face interaction and negotiation made possible small-group consensus and intermittent unity of moral and political vision. (Nevertheless, even in such utopian experiments, such as those described in the aforementioned pair of novels, countless conflicts and difficulties inevitably arise.)

Far more difficult to achieve, however, is this kind of unity—even on a provisional, intermittent basis—on a large scale. This is true for all groupings that grow larger and larger—whether nations and societies, or even companies and monastic communities. Apple Computers tosses out the charismatic Steve Jobs for a "pragmatic" successor, though Jobs manages later to come back. The Franciscan monks, after the death of Francis of Assisi, elect a series of monks skilled in administration and organization to succeed him. Of course, in recent political history, Lenin is followed as leader of the Bolsheviks by the Party "Secretary" Joseph Stalin, not the stirring orator and general of the Red Army, Leon Trotsky. To an extent, this issue of scale prompts those antipragmatic "purists," the "fundamentalists" adamantly committed to the dazzling vision, to institute totalitarian measures in order to bolster political unity or the "party line," a form of ideological (and even at times ethnic) cleansing practiced whenever mass resistance or counterrevolution occur.

The fact is this: fundamentalist socialism, as a public policy, is a form of Unreality, because most people will not cooperate with or respond to incentives that are several steps beyond them. Or, to quote Yeats's magnificent poem "The Circus Animals' Desertion," "I must lie down where all the ladders start /In the foul rag-and-bone shop of the heart." To begin—not end—with realistic, individualistic economic incentives before advancing to versions of communitarianism is to honor the hierarchy of human needs. As the airlines say, "Put on your own oxygen mask first—before trying to assist others, even loved ones." Otherwise, feelings of deprivation, failure, and indignant entitlement ("Enough of this!") will soon overwhelm your high-minded intentions.

As this train of thought evolved and my ideological ardor cooled, I found myself pondering how the insights of Piaget, Erik

Erikson, Robert Coles, and other developmental theorists might have a broadened application to social psychology and political science. I drew one immediate conclusion: it's useless and dangerous to dangle ideals above people that they can't get close to reaching. That is what leads to the cynical abuses of socialism, the self-righteousness of the people who promote these ideals, and so on. The ideal becomes a forced, hated abstraction—there is no gentleness, no pleasure, no real understanding of limits and the need to downscale the idea to something reachable and work upward step by step. As Newman's tombstone proclaims: "Out of Unreality into Reality."

To Dream the Possible Dream?

All that is why I am no longer a radical or a socialist—but rather a gradualist, a parliamentary social democrat. On a public policy level, that position embraces reality. And reality is the diet on which all growth of the body politic must feed—a nourishing, health-supporting diet. It is pointless and even alienating and debilitating to urge people to embrace a strict, self-denying diet—it may not be suited to them, and, regardless of how healthy it may be in the abstract scientific sense, it may represent a level of virtue that they cannot attain given their current habits. People feel discouraged if they keep failing at an ideal. But they feel encouraged if they make a couple of small steps forward ("Onward and upward!") on a regular basis—and then consolidate those steps into lived practice as they go.

So the neocons and leftists are both right—and wrong. Yes, choose the best of available options, as the neocons urge, but do not fix your gaze on them. The radical humanist is right, too: aspire to something higher. But it is wise to pursue immediately not the distant ideal, not what exceeds both our grasp and our reach—but rather something within our grasp or at most within our reach.

Likewise, I value the skeptical, anti-utopian politics of the conservative British philosopher Michael Oakeshott, who bemoans that the architects of utopian states of mind dwell in impossible dreamworlds. I too spent time in these Never-Neverlands of Grand Theory, getting mired in every *nouvelle* Slough of Abstraction. Yet I worry that Oakeshott sets the bar of human aspiration *too* low. On the one hand, he rightly warns that, "like Midas," the utopian is "always in the unfortunate position of not being able to touch anything without transforming it into an abstraction; he can never get a square meal of experience."[3] Utopian thinkers are, that is, the architects of System who flee the concrete and particular for the abstract and universal, victimized by the Edifice Complex that lures them into utopian delusions of grandiosity. Certainly, in recent centuries, they have tended to be progressives, whom the traditional conservative recognizes as immense dangers to the conduct of life. They inflate politics, forgetting, as Oakeshott wrote, that "politics is the art of living together & of being 'just' to one another—not of imposing a way of life, but of organizing a common life."

All this is well taken and bracing. Yet, unlike Oakeshott, I disagree that "the conjunction of dreaming and ruling creates tyranny." Dreams and ideals are part of what it means to be human, and they have their place in politics, just as in ethics, aesthetics, erotics, and other realms of experience. To be a social democrat means to start from reality and yet to aspire to realistic ideals. It is right to aspire to something higher, but not to the stratospheric. Flights of fancy into the realms of Grand Theory veer disastrously, calamitously off-course into Never-Neverland ("second star to the right, and straight on 'til morning, Tinkerbell!"), then nosedive into the Slough of Despond—or much worse. The immature, tragic pride of what I call "nosebleed idealism" is the bracing, ever-relevant lesson of Icarus. I have tempered that idealism and embraced earthbound realities as a result of learning a very elementary, difficult, and invaluable lesson: lasting social transformation is possible only with a broad consensus of the citizenry. Visions are wonderful—but they can also be entrancing hallucinations, forming mirages that undermine consensus and the capacity to attain goals. Yet if many radicals err because they insist on striving for the best possible option, many conservatives and neoconservatives do so too in their insistence on choosing the best available option. We need to weigh the latter's practical considerations against the former's uplifting call to dream the not-yet-possible dream.

That means, I now realize, that we must look just beyond our immediate horizons and affirm aspirations that are straightforward, widely understandable, and above all attainable. The step-by-step realities of implementation must be balanced against the speculative leaps of creation. An "attainable" challenge leverages the aspiration so that it inspires and motivates us but does not prove so challenging as to strain us. A good stretch is healthy; strained muscles and ligaments signal injury. To move beyond our "complacency zone" and out of our "comfort zone" into our "challenge zone" represents a good stretch, but let us remain attentive and stop before we hit our "crisis zone."

Goals that lie far beyond the immediate horizon—and therefore "out of sight" of many of us—are futile, even if they inspire a minority. An attainable goal entails getting down to work and into the trenches to tackle those hands-on tasks crucial to achieve measurable progress.

I can now admit the plain truth that most people need to experience the gratifying feeling that their efforts are paying off.

They need to feel that they are making headway toward a realistic finish line. As Yeats expressed it in "Easter, 1916," "Too long a sacrifice / Can make a stone of the heart." If we strain people beyond their capacities, they will reject not just the ultimate vision or the immediate goal, but, sooner or later, everything associated with both the process and the product.

Here again, I am not saying that the utopian thinker is somehow "wrong." Insofar as goals need to be inspirational and challenging—and given that no progress or headway can be sustained without motivation—ideals too possess a certain pragmatic ethos. We need to keep our eyes on the stars as well as on our shoestrings. The guiding polestar is our beacon, but let us not trip ourselves up by failing to watch where we are planting our feet. Beware the impatient utopian's mistake of dismissing "possible" goals because they seem too obvious and too clear—and therefore boring.

Can we foster the patience and self-trust to temper our idealism yet sustain our ideals? To become lucid social dreamers?

To dream the possible dream?

Yes! "To dream the *attainable* dream ..." Let *that* be our theme song!

Parting Company with Orwell

Let me place these comments on what could be termed "developmental social psychology" within a wide historical frame. My position is that we do not need to wait any longer for the so-called forces of History to pronounce a verdict on the choice between socialism and capitalism. Clio has already delivered her verdict. Witness the sad record of socialist regimes, a mind-numbing saga of despotism, the somber centenary of which recently passed with much breast-beating and head-shaking in 2017–2018. Extending from the former Soviet Union to the failed Eastern European states to present-day communist nightmares such as North Korea (and even the "lesser" tyrannies of China and Cuba), Clio's anguished cry is a piercing scream of suffering under torture.

Yes, Clio has indisputably vouchsafed her answer to us, and—unsurprisingly—that answer represents an affirmation of human nature generally and developmental psychology in particular. It turns out, ironically, that Marx and Engels were entirely right in one respect: their critique of "utopian" socialists, who are indeed typically idealists and enthusiasts for such radical experiments as state collectivism. What Marx and Engels neglected to do was to include themselves under the rubric of "utopians." In retrospect, their presumed "scientific socialism" has proven equally utopian, because human beings simply do not possess the intellectual and political maturity to live as socialists. That is, we—the crooked timber of humanity—do not yet possess the developmental maturity to align with a utopian program. For we do not have the requisite consistent awareness of holistic-minded beings, of "systems" thinkers who remain conscious of the intimate, symbiotic relationship between part and whole—between individual and society. We do not possess the maturity to understand that the whole is greater than the sum of its parts, and that the highest calling of individuals is to contribute to the welfare of the whole, indeed to sacrifice themselves for the ultimate benefit of the whole.

Or, as I might say to Orwell: "George, here is the Rubicon. Here, after the fall of the Berlin Wall, after the collapse of the USSR, after the other failed 'socialist' experiments beyond your day from the Albanias to the Zimbabwes—here we part company."

Like Orwell, that is to say, I am a "recovering utopian" who acknowledges that the utopian dream must yield to the dystopian warning. We both reluctantly accept that the latter's admonitory vision is *the* lesson of the twentieth century. But Orwell, upon his death at midcentury, had witnessed the historical development of just a single corrupted experiment in socialism: the USSR. He could die in 1950 still believing, not unrealistically, that the socialist idea might be realized, that state collectivism did not at all mean oppressive oligarchy. He could die as a democratic socialist *and* a utopian skeptic. History had not signposted—not yet—that the collectivist ethos detours into Room 101. Seven decades beyond Orwell, Clio speaks to me differently, with new and diverse evidence. I must draw conclusions based on it—that is, conclusions suitable for my own, still-young, century. In light of all these factors, I part company with Orwell. I extend my hand to him across the Rubicon. Unlike him, I am not a socialist—democratic or otherwise.

And yet, I still feel that I can—and must—learn from visionary liberal thinkers in the tradition that Orwell and I share. In fact, as I ponder how and why humankind lacks the "maturity" to embrace socialism authentically, I advert to the genius of a nineteenth-century British liberal forbear.

Dreamweaving in the Margins

I stand with John Stuart Mill, that brilliant exponent of British liberalism whose prophetic insights in *Principles of Political Economy* (1848) about the importance of sober statesmen cherishing personal liberty stand as enduring lessons still pertinent today, arguably more so than ever. Equally important and relevant are his warnings about the dangers of high-flown naïfs drugged on nosebleed idealism espousing utopian doctrine. Mill admonished against trying to imagine the ideal commonwealth that the abstract "best form" of capitalism or socialism might produce. The case for or against a political system should be based on an assessment of comparative advantages, he averred, which in fact History alone can make—or, in his words, "which futurity must determine." My own argument is that "futurity"—Mill's alias for Clio—has repeatedly, desperately voiced a compelling answer— and her answer humbly respects our limited condition of human maturity. "We are too ignorant," Mill wrote, for solo flights of passage to Socialist Utopia. History evinces that our revolutionary ideals inevitably "revolve" full circle, accelerating as they nosedive, only to crash and burn in the form of concentration camps, (psycho)terror, holocausts, and gulags. Mill, of course, witnessed none of that; but he realized that "ignorant" as we humans are, "the evils which now bear down humanity" are most unlikely to be alleviated by the prophets of rigid utopian dogmas.

> The question of Socialism is not, as generally stated by Socialists, a question of flying to the sole refuge against the evils which now bear down humanity; but a mere question of comparative advantages, which futurity must determine. We are too ignorant either of what individual agency in its best form, or Socialism in its best form, can accomplish, to be qualified to decide which of the two will be the ultimate form of human society.[4]

Nonetheless, Mill tentatively advanced a speculation based on the bedrock value of liberalism: freedom, animated by serendipity. Or, as he phrased it: "liberty and spontaneity."

> If a conjecture may be hazarded, the decision will probably depend mainly on one consideration, viz. which of the two systems is consistent with the greatest amount of human liberty and spontaneity. After the means of subsistence are assured, the next in strength of the personal wants of human beings is liberty; and (unlike the physical wants, which as

civilization advances become more moderate and more amenable to control) it increases instead of diminishing in intensity as the intelligence and the moral faculties are more developed. The perfection both of social arrangements and of practical morality would be to secure to all persons complete independence and freedom of action, subject to no restriction but that of not doing injury to others: and the education which taught or the social institutions which required them to exchange the control of their own actions for any amount of comfort or affluence, or to renounce liberty for the sake of equality, would deprive them of one of the most elevated characteristics of human nature. It remains to be discovered how far the preservation of this characteristic would be found compatible with the Communistic organization of society.

Mill added an important caveat. An indispensable criterion for choosing a preferable political order, he said, must be its respect for "individuality of character" and its acceptance of "eccentricity." Here again, we in the twenty-first century can see that most socialist states (and literary utopias) have proven hostile to the latter and discouraging to the former. I find it refreshing that Mill, who was so often (like Orwell) hoisted on the petard of his own virtue—and thereby dismissed by political adversaries as a secular saint ("a saint of rationalism," in Gladstone's disparaging phrase)—explicitly urged the polity to make room for the quixotic and the quirky and the quizzical (and the "queer"), for unconventional and unorthodox behavior, for a style marked by nonconformity, for an "untamed" independence of mind. He wrote:

But it is not by comparison with the present [rev. ed., 1852] bad state of society that the claims of Communism can be estimated; nor is it sufficient that it should promise greater personal and mental freedom than is now enjoyed by those who have not enough of either to deserve the name. The question is whether there would be any asylum left for individuality of character; whether public opinion would not be a tyrannical yoke; whether the absolute dependence of each on all, and surveillance of each by all, would not grind all down into a tame uniformity of thoughts, feelings, and actions....

No society in which eccentricity is a matter of reproach can be in a wholesome state. It is yet to be ascertained whether the Communistic scheme would be consistent with that multiform development of human nature, those manifold unlikenesses, that diversity of tastes and talents, and variety of intellectual points of view, which not only form a great part of the interest of human life, but by bringing intellects into stimulating collision, and by presenting to each innumerable notions that he would not have conceived of himself, are the mainspring of mental and moral progression.

"Individuality of character," "multiform development," "manifold unlikenesses," a "diversity of tastes and talents," a "variety of intellectual points of view," and a "stimulating collision" of minds in which we can learn and grow into our best selves—that is the "liberal" social democracy of my dreams today. Dwelling just beyond the horizon, it is a "utopia" within our reach, if not our grasp, to paraphrase Mill's Victorian-era colleague, the poet Robert Browning, in his beautiful verse in "Andrea del Sarto": "Ah, but a man's reach should exceed his grasp, / Or what's a Heaven for?"

Those are my political convictions—or rather, my personal confessions. I grant that these stances doubtless mark my outlook as eclectic (and, I hope, "eccentric"!). But I take solace from the fact that my idiosyncratic, Pickwickian politics places me in good company with many writers and thinkers of the past. For we must refuse to sacrifice critical thinking for Grand Theory or totalistic ideology, refuse to renounce subtle perception and intellectual integrity in exchange for the comforts of tidy consistency or neat coherence.

Might Orwell have concurred? Might he have evolved in a similar direction? Might he—oh, so wisely!—have come to agree with me?

Having criticized other scholars and intellectuals for indulging in precisely such fantasies, I won't flatter myself by imagining that he would have done so. (But my ego repeats, as Hemingway's Jake Barnes says, "Isn't it pretty to think so?")

In any case, I will probably long remain a "recovering" utopian. Yet like Irving Howe, another of my intellectual "big brothers," I retain "a margin of hope" for a democratic socialist future.[5] "Hope dies last," as Alexander Dubček proclaimed during the brief, abortive Prague Spring of 1968. Call me today a chastened dreamweaver, downsized to fit the reduced margins afforded by the lesson book of dystopia. Perhaps one day, the human species might evolve sufficiently to embrace a politics ("the art of the possible") capable of democratic socialism.

Might a society inspired by visionary pragmatists and hardheaded utopians emerge? Might a fully mature citizenry find present-day "utopian" socialism within its reach, perhaps even within its grasp?

Let us preserve—and affirm—our margin of hope that it one day may be so.

CONCLUSION

Whither Orwell—and "Orwell"?

Importance Versus Immediacy

When I published my first book on Orwell, *The Politics of Literary Reputation* (1989), public interest in his work stood near its peak. The fateful year of 1984 had just passed, and it had occasioned much discussion among academics and ordinary readers alike. Many of Orwell's old friends, colleagues, and early American supporters at *Partisan Review* were still alive, and their own stature in Anglo-American culture was also at its height. Meanwhile, major biographies of Orwell by Bernard Crick and Michael Shelden were either already out or forthcoming, and Peter Davison was hard at work on his exhaustive, (presumably) definitive *Complete Works of George Orwell*.

Now that another three decades have passed since I first started writing about Orwell, let me return to a query that I broached in the Introduction. In any serious reflection on Orwell's pertinence to contemporary politics and society, the question inevitably arises: Are George Orwell and his work—or rather "Orwell" and the Work—still as important today as they were in the closing decades of the twentieth century?

My answer is this: Yes, at least in the case of the latter pair. Timely? Same answer. Increasingly so in the developing postcolonial world, if perhaps not so obviously in the West. Overall, I believe that the latter pair are just as important today, even if they are not as burningly contemporary as in 1984, when the frigid Cold War era of Reagan and Yuri Andropov still prevailed. Our distance today from the geopolitical faceoff of the two Cold War superpowers and their respective capitalist and communist camps should remind us of the relatively narrow, monochromatic Cold War caricature of "Orwell"—the crusading anticommunist "St. George"—that predominated throughout the post–World War II age. That was the case above all in non-English-speaking Europe, where the looming spectre of "Orwell" and the Work (especially the vision and catchwords of his dystopia) were paraded in Western propaganda campaigns, with nary an acknowledgment or even awareness of the man and writer Orwell.

Two key historical differences account in large part for my answers. The first has to do with the very ubiquity of Orwell's catchphrases in anglophone culture, for the ceaseless droning of *Nineteen Eighty-Four*'s language in all sorts of ideological (and commercial) campaigns has inevitably dulled and lowered their decibel level on the 13-tone dystopian terror scale. Their shock value is largely gone: "Room 101" no longer hits the screeching, ear-splitting high note that once rent the air(waves) of postwar Britain and America, which encountered Big Brother and the tortures of Room 101 when Stalin still ruled (and Hitler and the Holocaust lurked in the shadowy recent past).

The second historical difference is an "accident" of history, namely the contingent, fortuitous publishing history of Orwell's work. It is easy for readers in Britain and the United States to forget that Orwell's books were not published elsewhere in the sequence in which they appeared in English. Rather, *Animal Farm* and *Nineteen Eighty-Four* appeared first. That is, his books were published beginning with those written at the very end of his career, so that foreign-language (and British Commonwealth)

readers encountered a (soon-to-be posthumous) figure sensationalized by the Cold War media. Most American readers did so
as well, given that the U.S. editions of *Dickens, Dali, and Others*
and *Animal Farm* did not appear until mid-1946, 11 years after
Orwell's previous book in America, *Burmese Days*. So theirs too
was the image of a clamorous anticommunist prophet whom I
might dub "Jeremiah Jeremiad"—with little or no knowledge of
Orwell's literary-political background as a democratic socialist,
champion of popular art, and gifted essayist. It was only after his
death and the enormous success of his last two books that his
other writings interested foreign publishers. Even in France, where
some of his writing appeared in the 1930s, his early work sold
meagerly and gained little critical notice.

This different order of publication has had enormous importance in the foreign-language media. It helped establish Orwell
as the West's leading literary Cold Warrior at the very moment
when the battle lines between East and West were being drawn.
During the early Cold War period, *Animal Farm* and *Nineteen
Eighty-Four* were institutionalized in curricula in Germany and
throughout the British Commonwealth as well as in American
schools. "St. George" Orwell was cast as a paladin of liberal (and
often capitalist) Civilization and became probably the most quoted
representative of Western cultural and political values, a Joan of
Arc of the "Free World."

Today the geopolitical vision of rival superstate confrontations
in Orwell's dystopia is not as timely as it once was, because the
Cold War nuclear standoff between the U.S. and USSR is over.
(On the domestic scene, however, the media circus accompanying each new viral malapropism by the Trump administration
["alternative facts," "truth isn't truth"] evinces that the relevance of
Newspeak, *Minitru*, and *Nineteen Eighty-Four*'s profound themes
connected with language—whether political propaganda [double-

think, doublespeak], the rewriting ["rectification"] of history, or philosophical relativism ["2 + 2 = "]—are just as timely as ever.)

So the current international scene little resembles the Cold War epoch, especially not the Stalinist era of Orwell's time. To younger generations, it probably seems as if an incommensurable gulf exists between the 1940s and 1950s and the early decades of the twenty-first century. Fascism and even to a great extent communism are no more, with the latter nowadays seeming more like a defunct experiment. "Really existing socialism" now (really?) exists in just six countries around the globe. Even in China, which has risen to dominance not only in Asia but also throughout the world, it is so mixed with capitalism and concessions to free enterprise that it is nothing like the communism of Mao Zedong.

In the immediate post–World War II epoch, however, the temptation to combat state socialism by using (and abusing) Orwell's catchphrases from *Animal Farm* and *Nineteen Eighty-Four* was extremely attractive for two related reasons. The first was historical timing; the second, "free license." Remember that Orwell died less than one month before Joseph McCarthy came on the scene in the United States and the so-called Red Scare ensued. Ripeness is all: the arsenal of slogans was available, ready to be battle-tested. The lure was irresistible. During the next four years, the anticommunist fever was most intense in the United States, but it also prevailed to a less extreme extent in Europe, and the film and television adaptations of *Animal Farm* and *Nineteen Eighty-Four* helped elevate it. So too did their translation into at least five dozen languages and many dialects.

After all, a dead man cannot object—which leaves the field open to the numerous ideologically motivated would-be spokespersons eager to pontificate on his behalf. This is just what happened with Orwell's work—and soon gave rise to the spectral "Orwell" and the doomsday Work. Although the vehemently pro-American, jingoistic, anticommunist agenda—what Orwell labeled in the pre-McCarthy era "hundred percent Americanism" —had received no support from him during his lifetime, ideological grave robbers and political body snatchers could now ransack his legacy at will.

Nevertheless, despite our lack of historical immediacy in relation to the Soviet gulag and the American Red Scare, comparisons between *Animal Farm* and *Nineteen Eighty-Four* and present-day geopolitical issues are still made and are still compelling. One only needs to google "Orwell" or "Orwellian" to see this. You will get tens of thousands of hits, encountering references in the English-language and foreign press to Orwell's work and breaking international news (e.g., Syria's chemical weapons, North Korea's nuclear testing, Russia's conduct in the Ukraine or Crimea) and pervasive surveillance by other governments, even ostensible allies (as the Obama administration experienced to its embarrassment when leaked documents disclosed extensive spying of western European leaders' private communications). And those reference totals are dwarfed by the digital hit parade for google searches pairing Orwell's coinages with domestic headliners such as Donald Trump, Edward Snowden, Facebook's Mark Zuckerberg, and so forth. Time and again, reporters and pundits commandeer "Orwell" and "Orwellian" to describe transgressions of privacy, infringements of civil rights, and government encroachments into the lives of private citizens.

Orwell's reputation as a masterful prose stylist is also limited to his English-language audiences. The literary "St. George" image—as Prose Laureate and Defender of the King's English— does not travel well, given that other languages often have very different rhetorical traditions. Nor, I believe, can any translator do full justice to Orwell's stylistic gifts. Both factors account for why he has never been celebrated outside the English-speaking world for his essays, journalism, and reportage, except in special circumstances, such as the warm respect accorded *Homage to Catalonia* by Catalans, especially in the province of Huesca, located in northern Aragon,[1] and in Barcelona, where a city square is named after him.[2] Elsewhere abroad, save for a select group of his German readers who prize a few of his political essays, Orwell is neither admired nor derided as a man and writer.

It is true, however, that a small minority of more sophisticated and informed foreign readers do value Orwell as a stylist. That perception is contingent on the fact that their level of English is skilled enough to appreciate the clarity and simplicity of Orwell's prose. (This is preeminently so within his sizable German-speaking audience.) Here again, the point is that Orwell possesses a more circumscribed reputation outside the anglophone countries.

Thus Orwell and certainly "Orwell"—the work and the Work—generally remain as important today as in the past, even if the geopolitical vision of *Nineteen Eighty-Four*—essentially a scenario of an interminable Cold War stalemate—is less pertinent in our age of terroristic cadres, rogue states, digital hackers, and global (even extraterrestrial) cyberwar. His catchphrases and governing themes, however, have unfortunately lost none of their relevance, and I believe these trends will continue indefinitely. Orwell and his work will increasingly be valued in the next 20, 30, or even 50 years as a warning and as a historical landmark. In the latter case, it will be remembered by literary and political historians as an invaluable compass that, as much as any other twentieth-century expression of the creative imagination, steered the course of history true north in the direction of democracy and against tyranny. To put it simply, it will be remembered that *1984* led to 1989—that is, to the fall of the Berlin Wall and the collapse of communism—and not to Room 101.

As the forgoing chapters demonstrate, that tendency has already had decisive political implications for Orwell's reputation and legacy. Orwell never championed capitalism and free enterprise, but some of his conservative and neoconservative admirers have shifted his coffin decisively to the right, claiming him as an ally of capitalism. Despite his receding profile as a culture hero, it is possible that—just as in the 1950s and 1960s, when his work was exploited to attack communism and sometimes even democratic socialism—his intellectual authority may be exploited again: Orwell the socialist attacking socialism. That sham may reemerge as the simplistic caricature of his career and legacy, with the implication being that Orwell swerved rightward at the end of his life, turning into a conservative or premature neoconservative, and abandoned socialism.

Yet historians with intellectual integrity will instead observe that Orwell's work possesses far greater credibility than that of most of his adversaries of the late 1940s. He avowed himself a socialist—albeit a "democratic Socialist"—willing to castigate the shortcomings and abuses of state socialism and hold his own side to a very high standard. In this he was protecting not just equality, but also liberty. In fact, he was insisting on a semantics that mirrored his politics, as it were, on a grammatical heresy that matched his left-wing ideological heterodoxy: the lowercase adjective should really modify the uppercase noun. Liberty and its defense not only precede but should also exceed concerns about equality. I believe he would say the same thing today in the ongoing battle waged between freedom and security in the long shadow of September 11, 2001. Yes, these two values need to be carefully balanced, but when it comes down to the painful choice of which to prioritize: freedom first, freedom first.

Historiography, Iconography, and Scholarship: A Personal Statement

Telescoping history through the "Orwell" lens in a series of books that address the author's reputation and impact, I have taken an in-depth look at considerable swathes of twentieth-century culture in order both to tell the fascinating tale of his unfolding reputation and to generalize about some of the historical processes and social mechanisms involved. It may appear ironic that such a large project should become connected with Orwell, a man who distrusted system-building and adopted contrarian positions throughout his life. Yet such a historiography became possible *because* his literary work developed into the legendary, catchword-crazed Work. It became possible *because* Orwell morphed into "Orwell"—as if the righteous father had metamorphosed into his monstrous albeit well-intended brainchild—Dr. Frankenstein mutating into his grotesque creation.

"The face of Orwell is the face of the mid-twentieth century," wrote the London weekly newspaper *Picture Post* in the early 1950s. Three decades later, during the countdown to 1984 in the early 1980s, I began to scrutinize the "Orwell" physiognomy and unveil a "portrait gallery" of these faces. The portraits were limned from a variety of perspectives on both Orwell and the cultural phenomenon "Orwell." They included separate case histories of Orwell's reputation in Germany and the Soviet Union, of his standing among Jews and Catholics as well as nondenominational Christians (despite his atheism), of his adoption by various groups of writers, including those at little magazines and intellectual quarterlies (such as *Partisan Review*, *Commentary*, *Dissent*, and *Tribune*), and on and on.

So it became possible to treat "Orwell" as a looking glass through which to behold Western culture since midcentury, precisely *because* the writer George Orwell had metamorphosed into the historical talisman "Orwell" with which pea-and-thimble charmers of the Right and Left conjured. As the twenty-first century has proceeded, numerous other images in this "portrait gallery" have emerged, and Orwell's reputation has become ever more multifaceted. Today his unique reputation continues to serve as a lens through which to illuminate the culture he both reflects and formed. "Orwell" provides us with an illustrated biography of the last seven decades, showing how the posthumous reputation of a writer sheds light on the intricate interconnections between biography and history.

By presenting dozens of case histories in literary reception across nearly four decades of research in numerous studies about reputation-building, I have sought to convey how the reception history of a writer can vouchsafe us an accessible and even revelatory view of cultural and social history. I have referred elsewhere to this approach to literary historiography as "reputation history." I am presenting not merely a history of reception, a chronicle of those moments in which audiences have responded to a writer, but my own guided tour of the "Orwell" gallery: my own self-curated exhibition of mindscapes ("reception scenes") featuring "Orwell" profiles in the form of dramatic narratives that envisage literary reception as historical portraiture and "art" history. The show's collection of exhibits on display is my own imaginative reconstruction, distinctive and inevitably subjective. Yet it is, I hope, also much more than that: a public—not a private—tour, my biases and blind spots notwithstanding.[3]

The Orwell/"Orwell" bifocals are ingeniously designed by Clio, with variable high- and low-resolution features (e.g., the windowpane prose of England's Prose Laureate and the screaming slogans of *Ingsoc*). Above all, they possess a telescopic power nonpareil. Hence the phenomenal vistas and endless procession of modern history that this Sartrean singular universal, "Orwell," empowers us to survey.

The study of a figure such as Orwell/"Orwell" is, therefore, ideally suited to the large aims of reputation history because it unfurls a stupendous pageantry of scenes portraying the life and times (and "afterlife" and times) of a writer and his age. Reputation history is a personalizing of the historical and a historicizing of the personal. Just as Orwell was a witness of his time, I have used him as a far-seeing witness to events since his death, aiming to make public a history visible only through the eyes of his ghostly presence. As the story progresses beyond the brief, embattled life into the ever-lengthening, wondrous, yet terrifying afterlife, it moves beyond literary biography into cultural thanatology.

Indeed this study informally inaugurates a new branch of cultural studies that could be termed "thanatology studies," [4] namely a serious, interdisciplinary inquiry into the postmortem existence of persons and phenomena (e.g., institutions, ideas, artifacts). The cultural thanatologist probes the forensic aspects of these afterlives, not excluding mutations, pathologies, degenerations, regenerations, and related social mechanisms and processes of change.[5] As our "case histories" of the dark spectre "Orwell" illustrate, all of these developments and dimensions are present in the scenes of Orwell's afterlife.[6] The writer George Orwell became, within a few short years after his death, the behemoth "Orwell," a bogeyman figure recognizable on every continent of the globe and form-fitted, as it were, for "thanatology studies" of all kinds, ranging from intellectual inheritance disputes and ideologically motivated accusations of parricide to psychosocial autopsies and ceaseless partisan reports of resurrection followed by descent into hell or ascension into heaven.

Beholding Mount "Orwell"?

Was *Nineteen Eighty-Four* a "game-changing" book that altered the course of history, in the phrase of William Steinhoff in *George Orwell and the Origins of 1984* (1973)? Yes.[7] As we have discussed in connection with various concepts in our sociology of reputation (e.g., moments of entrance and exit), the "temper of the times" must be propitious. Unusual circumstances must arise to trigger tectonic shifts in the cultural terrain to occur, such as happened within five years of the novel's publication and Orwell's death. That period witnessed the media Big Bang that generated "Orwell" and sent the writer's work into the "statusphere," where it continues to orbit as the Work. That is to say, in the mid-1950s, new, ultimately decisive shaping forces elevated the posthumous George Orwell beyond the status of writer and literary figure into the world-historical phenomenon "Orwell."

Yet the prevailing temporal conditions enabling such cataclysms are inevitably set in motion decades or more earlier. These massive, accumulating forces represent a sociodynamic that generates seismic epistemic tremors and displacements (or "paradigm shifts") that alter the cultural cartography. For instance, among the higher-order historical developments was, of course, the establishment of the English language itself as the global *lingua franca*. The importance of the rise of English as a factor contributing to Orwell's own international reputation cannot be overestimated. Would an author of "Politics and the Burmese Language" (in Burmese, let us add) likely be known worldwide today as a distinguished political essayist and prose stylist? Would his dystopia's catchwords be translated and tweeted and blathered and brayed in dialects on every continent? Orwell happened to write his now-famous essays and novels precisely at the historical moment when English began to be taught to hundreds of millions of adults as the world's "second" language. Because it was alphabetic (unlike Chinese), uninflected (unlike the Romance languages), and the official language of North America, it had both a linguistic simplicity and a newly dominant social power base— as well as a literary-cultural prestige—indispensable to the circulation of Orwell's work.[8] The (apparent) simplicity of Orwell's own literary style dovetailed perfectly with the relative pedagogic simplicity of English itself.

And so, conditions fully ripened for the world-historical "Orwell" to burst forth by mid-decade. The emergence of "Orwell" in the 1950s was due not just to the cultural climate of the Cold War, Red Scare, and McCarthyism, but to larger, amorphous forces in process, among them a kind of linguistic imperialism that ironically witnessed the rise of English coincide with the decline of England, that is, the global conquest of English at precisely the historical moment when the sun was setting on the British Empire. As we saw in Chapter 9, a single event in Orwell's reputation history triggered the emergence of "Orwell": the BBC-TV production of *Nineteen Eighty-Four* in December 1954. Remember that in 1953 the NBC-TV *1984* enjoyed high viewer ratings and received positive reviews in America but aroused no controversy —even though the Red Scare and McCarthyism were near their peaks. The seething Cold War atmosphere in America fomented necessary yet not sufficient conditions to seed a "perfect storm" of contention that would assemble "an ideological superweapon" out of the materials of *Nineteen Eighty-Four* and launch them into the political statusphere. By contrast, the BBC's adaptation did exactly that, attracting the largest audiences ever accorded a program to that date in British history, occasioning a month of debate in the British media that spilled over into the House of Commons, and even prompting British programming changes that included the legislation of a new public television channel within months—not to mention immortalizing a "quintessentially English," recently deceased native son.

As we have seen, this perfect storm was electrifying, and its aftershocks enduring. Orwell's coinages entered the public domain, and from then on "Big Brother Is Watching You," Newspeak, doublethink, and even "Orwellian" were daily patter in political culture chat. From the vantage point of Orwell's publishers and the Orwell estate, however, a "perfect rainbow" thereby appeared. Suddenly the sales of Orwell's books briefly zoomed from 150 per week to more than 50,000 per month. *Animal Farm* and *Nineteen Eighty-Four* entered school curricula and became institutionalized in English classrooms at the elementary and secondary levels. What I have termed the "Orwell legend" was born.

To come full circle: as the "countdown to 1984" approached and passed, after exactly three decades of "Orwell," I stood at a historical palisade from which the cultural cartographer could survey this now-worldwide mythos from a variety of locations: national, generational, political, cultural, and on and on. As I discuss in *The Politics of Literary Reputation* and later books, I beheld a literary skyline emblazoned with numerous Orwell "faces" sculpted by Clio. My task became to chart the limits and survey the terrain of this mammoth literary Mount Rushmore, a colossus consisting of a vast range of social formations, complete with ideological fault lines, political eruptions, and historical craters—all of which have given rise in turn to new cultural (trans)formations since my geo-sociological investigations began decades ago.

Puzzling Out the Puzzle: A Latecomer's Endeavor

In "Esthétique du Mal," Wallace Stevens speaks of "the lunatic of one idea." The phrase reminds me of Isaiah Berlin's distinction between the hedgehog and the fox, the man who knows one thing versus the man who knows many things. I myself may be guilty of being a "one idea" man, blessed or burdened by the energy of a lunatic in his zeal to follow Orwell and "Orwell" in whatever directions they may lead.[9] Although they ostensibly move in an endless multiplicity of directions—a rather fox-like tendency—at bottom they are still part of the "one idea" of Orwell/"Orwell."[10]

For Orwell's example inspired me to become a writer, and in this book, as in all my previous work on Orwell, my aspiration resembles that of James Boswell in his great biography *The Life of Samuel Johnson*, namely that Orwell "will be seen as he really was; for I profess to write, not his panegyric, which must be all praise, but his Life; which, great and good as he was, must not be supposed to be entirely perfect." That is exactly the note on which I closed Chapter 1, with a nod to the "adamantly unsainted," unsaintly "St. George." So I hope that Orwell emerges here, as does Johnson in Boswell's biography, as a "good great man," his flaws notwithstanding. I admire George Orwell, but I do not hesitate to acknowledge his weaknesses, while sternly insisting that we beware the seductions posed by both historical hindsight and the tyranny of the present, whereby our moralistic myopia smugly induces us to condemn the prevailing behaviors of the past while deceiving ourselves that we are not dwelling within our own limiting horizons.

So much for my experience of Orwell's personal and literary example, with its sometimes heady, sometimes bracing cocktail composed of the inspiration of the heroic laced with the anxiety of influence. By contrast, the complex, checkered heritage of "Orwell" has gifted me with a rare intellectual treasure: a concrete instance enabling me to conceive an inductive, evidence-based approach to the issue of reputation. While he did make things difficult for his biographers (he specifically left instructions that he wanted no biography), his uncooperativeness and reticence inadvertently furnished me with the materials for the central intellectual-speculative project of my life. How? Because the fact that he made things difficult for biographers also made it easier for legend-builders to generate the outsized reputation that eventually raised much larger questions compelling to a historian of reputation like myself. That is to say, the biographical "difficulties" paradoxically contributed to the mutation of the writer Orwell into the spectre "Orwell." Or rather: to Orwell "becoming" the unbecoming "Orwell." With so few established facts, and amid all the mantle-snatching and ideological controversies swirling around his name, legends quickly multiplied to fill the vacuum.

Orwell's friend Cyril Connolly, the editor of *Horizon* and his classmate at both St. Cyprian's and Eton, wrote in his essay "Reputations":

> Since Homer, a major consolation of literary life has been the belief in reputations. "Not all of me shall die"—"*non omnis moriar.*" If I were in a position to advise a writer who was so ambitious as to desire recognition both in his lifetime and after his death, I would say: "Set posterity a puzzle. The living dislike puzzles, the unborn worship them. Keep your contemporary success within bounds. Above all, beware not to deprive posterity of all speculation, of its right to model you in its own image."

This is an utterly remarkable and prescient observation if we consider it (as Connolly did not) in relation to Orwell. Connolly wrote this essay in early 1950, perhaps just days after Orwell's death that January. But Connolly could have had no idea that within half a decade it would soon apply so exactly to his oldest literary friend. Before Connolly's eyes Orwell would mushroom into "Orwell," the cultural phenomenon that bore only traces of resemblance to the man and writer whom Connolly had known so well.

Orwell's death in 1950 thus left posterity with a puzzle—and his allies and adversaries vied to put the pieces together in a self-flattering and nonetheless plausible way.[11] Yet putting the pieces of the puzzle together meant in fact scattering them in all directions and then attempting to reassemble them according to the political agenda of the puzzler. As a latecomer, my aim became to disassemble these puzzles of the dissembling puzzlers, and then to reassemble it all in some understandable order, trying to make coherent the processes of reputation-building. Without fantasizing that I could be "objective," I declared my own vision of it all (or "color filter"), as far as my awareness allowed, seeking to make some sense of the elusive figure-making process in figures of my own, variously derived from art history, astronomy, architecture, geology, geography, and optics.

I have aspired further in the present book to capture, however partially, the properties of reputation-building through an eclectic, selectively applied collection of tropes. Approaching the literary figure and phenomenon of Orwell/"Orwell" through such a miscellany of metaphors reflects my conviction that the process of making and claiming reputations is fundamentally metaphorical and that its dynamics are often illuminated by a figural vocabulary.[12]

Whither Orwell—and "Orwell"

Where might scholars—myself included—go from here in their study of both Orwell and "Orwell"? Is there really much new and worthwhile still to be said about the author? Or even about the apparition?

The answer to the latter question should already be clear: a resounding "yes." So long as newly emerging events across the globe continue to feature such (quotidian?) "Orwellian" iniquities as privacy invasion, media manipulation, historical "rectification," political Newspeak and doublespeak, leader worship and personality cults, and Big (or pint-sized) Brothers—which is to say: so long as we humans continue to be all too human (and fall short of utopia)—the nightmare visions and rhetorical arsenals of *Animal Farm* and *Nineteen Eighty-Four* will pervade the public consciousness, called forth and canted at every turn. And because their circulation breathed life into the spectral "Orwell," this apparition will "cut a figure" for a long time to come. Ironically, it is as if—through an act of literary metempsychosis—the spirit passed from dying author to dormant avatar. Thereupon "Orwell" drew its breaths from the tubercular father of *Nineteen Eighty-Four*, whose own breaths became ever fewer and fainter as his swaddling *doppelgänger* grew, that is, as the life force passed to the afterlife.

And so then: What about the prospects for further study of Orwell himself?

Let me address this question via two very different examples. The first is an ongoing Western controversy—the infamous "list"— that both has provoked much debate about Orwell's personal character and Cold Warrior status and has become linked to (ostensibly) unrelated current political disputes, thereby conflating and entangling biographical issues with news headlines. The second addresses Orwell's largely unexamined connection to Asian political developments, including the Asian context of much of his work. (I could well have added a chapter devoted to the latter in my book, *The Unexamined Orwell* [2011].)

In 2013, Edward Snowden, a former employee of the U.S. National Security Agency, began to reveal classified information regarding mass surveillance of international telephone and Internet communications, revelations that once again occasioned a flood of references to George Orwell in the international press. Around the same time, new accusations of Orwell's own alleged McCarthyite (or Big Brother-ish!) behavior surfaced. The airwaves once again blared that in the late 1940s, he had compiled a list (in a private notebook) of people who were in his opinion "crypto-communists, fellow-travelers or inclined that way." The significance of this much-debated "list" is an element of the controversy still enveloping Orwell more than a decade after the list was unsealed by the U.K. government in 2003.

The controversy was soon yoked to the Snowden scandal, with some observers viewing Snowden as a whistleblower not unlike George Orwell, and others, especially Orwell's Marxist critics, seeing them as quite dissimilar, insofar as Orwell allegedly betrayed the Left by exposing communists to government harassment, whereas Snowden dared to risk imprisonment by releasing evidence of Big Brother's Thought Police villainy. Whether or not Orwell would have defended and praised Snowden as a courageous whistleblower, he would have liked his underdog status. Snowden was a little guy, a small fry—no high-ranking official in the intelligence services or even an Outer Party member like Winston Smith, but just a 20-something government contractor. Yet he possessed audacity.

I do not mean to imply that Orwell would surely have endorsed Snowden's actions, which have been widely condemned as irresponsible and threatening to U.S. national security interests. Snowden is not necessarily lily white, morally speaking, though he is also no Winston Smith, a corrupt bureaucrat fully willing to scream the slogans of the Two Minute Hates and revel in a public execution during Hate Week. Winston Smith is as much an antihero as a hero. To commend his rebellion against the Inner

Party—or to sympathize with Snowden's campaign to expose the surveillance of private citizens and purported allies—is not to lionize them as unvarnished heroes.

As far as the notorious "list" is concerned, Orwell did keep a private list of suspected communist fellow-travelers. In 1949, on his deathbed, he shared this personal notebook with Celia Kerwin, a friend who had begun to work for the Information Research Department (IRD), which had recently been formed by the Labour government under Clement Attlee to counter Soviet propaganda.

News of this allegedly deplorable notebook first exploded into the headlines in 1996, occasioning criticism of Orwell from the Left as a hypocrite and "snitch." In 2003, during his centennial year, the list was made fully public. Waves of controversy ensued, fueled by Marxist and neo-Stalinist critics of Orwell on the Left. Keeping the issue of "the list" alive both reinvigorated their criticism of his Cold War positions and gave them a new line of attack. Moreover, it furnished them with a specific, complicated issue to use against him rather than just general complaints of *ad hominem* derision.

As I put it in *Every Intellectual's big brother*, the critics who twisted the issues involved in Orwell's notebook exemplified the "ethics of detraction." In reality, the publication of the list in 2003 was already warmed-over news.[13] I myself had first written about it in the 1980s, and Bernard Crick mentioned it in his Orwell biography in 1980. It is true that the George Orwell Archive did not make it available for quotation or publication to me, Crick, or anyone else until much later. But Orwell was not in this list snitching on fellow writers. He was simply advising the IRD, which never became a powerful, octopus-like organization comparable to the CIA or J. Edgar Hoover's FBI,[14] not to employ those whom he regarded as Soviet sympathizers or fellow-travelers to represent the British government or be trusted to participate in pro-Western propaganda. At no point did he advocate infringing on their civil rights or curtailing their freedoms. He simply advised that such people were not to be depended on to represent British interests faithfully. It was not much different than a negative letter of recommendation or an editor advising his colleagues that a particular reviewer was not appropriate for a certain book.

Nevertheless, the controversy over "the list" does have significant contemporary implications. It is not just much ado about nothing or a matter of dated "fake news." Orwell grasped the tradeoffs of the spying game. He was no champion of unfettered freedom, which runs the risk of jeopardizing public policy and civil rights. Every nation has geopolitical interests and must balance its commitments to both national security and civil liberties.

Since 9/11 the balance in the United States has swung excessively toward national security, as the so-called Patriot Act of the Bush administration, the drone policy of the Obama administration, and the immigration proposals (e.g., to build a wall along the Mexican border) of the Trump administration exemplify. Yet the fact remains that the tradeoffs are real and the search for balance crucial and never-ending. When Stalinism was in the ascendancy in 1949 and the Red Army was occupying half of Europe, Orwell's concerns about security were well taken. But he wrote a stern letter to the Duchess of Atholl when she asked him to represent a conservative, pro-imperialist group in 1945, and he always refused to write for Lord Beaverbrook's right-wing press, except on some whimsical cultural matter like brewing a pot of good tea (another example of his commitment to patriotism and his hostility to nationalism and jingoism).

Our prose laureate, "St." George Orwell, the much-honored Defender of the King's English, assumed that self-appointed role on the self-imposed condition that he become the scrupulous, unabashed critic of his own side—especially his own political side. His conception of this knightly role demanded a rigorous self-criticism, which Orwell regarded as a test of civic duty and intellectual integrity.[15] Do we forget that the hymn in *Animal Farm* sung by the animals is called "Beasts of England"? Or that in *Nineteen Eighty-Four* the Party name is *Ingsoc* (English socialism)? Or that the Party currency is dollars, and the Party members smoke Victory cigarettes?

Here too, first and last, Orwell's position was in effect always: "Let us hold our own side to the highest standards. It can happen here too." The corruptions of state socialism in the USSR were not attributable chiefly to the culture or society of Russia and the Soviet Union, but rather to the dangers of excessively concentrated political power—dangers to which all nations and leaders are susceptible.

"Orienting" Orwell? The Asian Connection

A second, entirely different, non-Western subject is suggestive of the future directions in which discussion about and interest in Orwell's heritage will lead: the Asian reception of and background for his work. I myself have developed a strong interest in these topics. In 2014 *Concentric*, a literary quarterly based in Taiwan, published a special number entitled "Orienting Orwell: Asian and Global Perspectives on Orwell." (A "George Orwell in Asia" conference at Tunghai University in May 2011 addressed the same theme and was the impetus for this issue.)

Serious study of the Asian cultural contexts of Orwell's work and legacy is original, important, and quite timely. It comes at a moment of heightened global awareness regarding the rise of Asia and the meeting of East and West in a sense beyond most Westerners' Cold War preoccupations of the mid-twentieth century. To them, "East versus West" meant Eastern Europe versus Western Europe, or the communist world versus the capitalist world, or free enterprise versus state socialism. A new global understanding of the relationship between East and West has emerged with the decline of European state socialism and the end of the Cold War. Paradoxically, the People's Republic of China, which is still a one-party communist state, is the great Asian power that is spearheading and dominating this new consciousness.

Orwell's work gained significance partly because of the ever-relevant application of his work on totalitarianism to developments in communist Asia since the official founding of the Chinese Communist state in October 1949, just four months after *Nineteen Eighty-Four* appeared. Yet the novel also fully applies to the history of authoritarianism in Taiwan up to the 1980s (and elsewhere still today, such as to North Korea). Moreover, our discussion in Chapter 3 about Orwell's "A Hanging" and its haunting, enduring relevance to the frequent use of the death penalty in my home state of Texas could certainly be extended to capital punishment in Singapore, whose claim to having one of the highest number of executions in the world never ceases to amaze Americans and Europeans.

Another Asian topic ripe for further exploration bridges the life and afterlife: Blair/Orwell's long-term relationship to India. Before World War II, Orwell considered whether to pursue an offer to join the staff of the *Lucknow Pioneer* in India. Behind the scenes, however, British authorities in the India Office advised the *Pioneer* against it. (Probably Orwell's poor health would have ruled out the possibility anyway.) Instead he maintained his connection to India by signing on with the BBC as a producer for the Indian section during the war. His close acquaintance and friendships with old India hands (Muggeridge), fellow novelists interested in the subcontinent (E. M. Forster), and expatriate Indian writers in London (Mulk Raj Anand) kept him in near-constant contact with Indian affairs. A compact biographical portrait thematizing Orwell's connection to the Indian subcontinent would be a worthy addition to the literature. That connection spanned his full lifetime, from cradle to deathbed. In January 1949, when he was sick in hospital, he composed one of his best and most memorable essays, "Reflections on Gandhi." Both as an essayist, writing about capital punishment and "social saints" like Gandhi, and as a novelist, addressing British imperialism in *Burmese Days*, Orwell on numerous occasions lent his considerable literary talents to Asian topics.

Allies and adversaries have long debated how the posthumous Orwell would have judged Asia's development. Pundits have never ceased to ask: "If Orwell were alive today," what would he say about events in the Korea of the 1950s? Vietnam of the 1960s? Africa and Asia of the postcolonial age of the 1970s and later? Would Orwell's anti-imperialist stance toward British policy in Asia have persisted? Would he have voiced doubts about the "America First" policy of the Trump administration—just as he inveighed against "hundred percent Americanism" in the pre-McCarthy Cold War climate? After all, Blair came to hate his life in Burma in the Indian Imperial Police. The idea of a British or any other empire, including an American or Soviet one, became anathema to Orwell.[16]

In all these respects, it will be fruitful for both Asian and Western scholars to consider Orwell from the perspective of his Asian interests, political positions, and social sympathies. More broadly, I believe that the topic of Orwell's international reputation and relevance will dominate future discussion about his work. If so, it may well be that Orwell's reputation did not at all reach its final high-water mark with the arrival of the Donald Trump administration. As the Orwell estate's literary agent, Bill Hamilton, reports with delight: "Interest in Orwell is accelerating and expanding practically daily.... We're selling in new languages—Breton, Friuli, Occitan ..."[17]

Shakespeare, Goethe, and ... Orwell?

And what about the much larger questions of import and impact? As the twenty-first century advances, will George Orwell continue to be a public habitation and a name in contemporary culture? Or will his influence and reputation dwindle, rendering him no more than the property of academic specialists?

Orwell's *oeuvre* has been examined from a staggering range of perspectives by literary scholars, political scientists, linguists, philosophers, gender critics, and cultural historians. All of them have brought their specific orientations and methods to his work. I do not anticipate any radical new perspectives in scholarship on Orwell, but I fully expect ever new perspectives to emerge in the scholarship on "Orwell," that is, on the legend and legacy, rather than on the life and letters, whether biography or exegesis.

Another way of putting it is that Orwell's life and writings have been exhaustively studied. No breakthroughs are likely. On the other hand, the posthumous story continues to acquire new afterlives as it enters new scenes of reception, and it therefore offers endless possibilities. The Asian context is a good example.

So however doubtful it is that George Orwell and his work will occasion fresh new perspectives, "Orwell" is certain to do so. This certainty will prevail so long as Orwell's language, themes, and vision serve to encapsulate and express higher-order historical developments that have forged and fashioned "Orwell," such as the ubiquitous presence of bureaucratese and official government euphemisms, the trespasses against privacy by both government and industry, and the unceasing fear of authoritarian (and even totalitarian) power structures leading to state tyranny. Yes, so long as these historical developments remain in process, new perspectives on Orwell's Work will emerge as examples of Newspeak, two-way telescreens, Room 101, and doublethinking.

The opportunity for fresh perspectives does not necessarily mean, however, that interest in both Orwell and "Orwell" will not wane. Inevitably, it will do so, at least in the West. Might levels of attention comparable to the four peaks of his reputation attained in the first seven decades after his death be reached again? The mid-1950s (with the BBC *Nineteen Eighty-Four*), the so-called countdown to 1984 (during the years 1982 to 1984), the centennial of Orwell's birth (in 2003), and the Trump presidential campaign and administration have witnessed sustained, worldwide interest in both Orwell and "Orwell."

At least this much can be said: notable blips or new bounces upward in sales of Orwell's books and commentary on the work and Work are likely to happen; not only the Trump election and presidency, but also the aforementioned Snowden case, which gave rise to thousands of Internet hits for "Snowden and Orwell," is an example. The Prologue addressed how the Trump phenomenon boosted sales of *Nineteen Eighty-Four* (and a few other classic dystopias) to best seller status in 2016–2017—and those record totals of citations and sales may be matched or even topped if a major political crisis arises. New anniversary dates, such as the sesquicentennial in 2053 (or the centenary of his death in 2050), will also invite renewed reflection on George Orwell and his legacy.

And yet, even if the literary historian with an eye for the long view concedes that the high-water mark may have passed for good, Orwell will remain in orbit, overshadowed yet visible, in the celestial statusphere. Hovering above (and partly enveloping and obscuring) him will be his ghastly-ghostly *doppelgänger*, the unicum "Orwell," the canonical mainstay of school curricula and Big Brotherly spectre in the ether whose subjects' Two Minute Hate chants muffle the music of the spheres.

The twin peaks of the 1954 BBC-TV broadcast and the 1984 countdown generated a propulsive two-stage "lift-off" effect, whereupon Orwell's reputation ascended to a statuspheric height beyond the downward gravitational pull exerted by the onrushing daily tide of information. As a result, the position of Orwell in the literary firmament—thanks to the Work of "Orwell"—became fixed at a cultural altitude in the West occupied only by world-historical figures possessing the stature of a Shakespeare or a Goethe.

At least for the foreseeable future, I believe it will remain there.

Notes

In order to streamline the text and with an eye toward the general reader, I have dispensed in this book with most reference notes to document textual citations, unless a source is obscure or difficult to identify. Cited below are primarily substantive notes that clarify or elaborate upon points discussed in the main text.

Prologue

1. Yes, Mr. President, there are 13 of them.
2. One could argue, as I pointed out in interviews, that the groundswell of demand for *Nineteen Eighty-Four* and other dystopias began months before the week of January 20. Various political leaders and celebrities had already associated Trump with "Big Brother" in the months leading up to Inauguration Day, pushing *Nineteen Eighty-Four* into the top slot in the political fiction category on the Amazon list. The skyrocketing sales of the novel also had lifted *Animal Farm* into the top 10 on the same list.

   In fact, the Trump administration inadvertently boosted sales of numerous books within the anti-utopian genre. For instance, Aldous Huxley's *Brave New World* also cracked Amazon's top 10 best seller list in late January 2017 and continued to hold its place throughout the spring. Far more surprising, in November 2016 Sinclair Lewis's anti-utopian *It Can't Happen Here* (1935) jumped to No. 1 on Amazon's best seller list. Long out of print in the United Kingdom, Penguin did not bother to print a new edition of the novel until the week of the inauguration, during which it quickly sold 11,000 copies. The largely forgotten satire features a charismatic, demagogic jingoist, who pledges to restore American greatness—very much in the spirit of Mussolini's Rome and Hitler's Germania—and proceeds to lead the nation into fascism. "My one ambition," claims the new president, "is to get all Americans to realize that they are, and must continue to be, the greatest race on the face of this old Earth."

   Another brisk seller in 2017 was Margaret Atwood's *The Handmaid's Tale*, originally published in 1985. It too briefly occupied Amazon's top spot for fiction in spring 2017, thanks above all to Hulu's TV series adaptation of the work, which premiered on April 26 and starred Elizabeth Moss (with a cameo appearance by Atwood herself). The novel tells the story of a woman in New England after an oppressive religious regime takes over power.

Meanwhile, publishers of classics in political science, science fiction, and socially aware realist fiction were twittering with glee as Hannah Arendt's *The Origins of Totalitarianism*, Ray Bradbury's *Fahrenheit 451*, and John Steinbeck's *Of Mice and Men* also enjoyed revivals of interest.

But *Nineteen Eighty-Four* remained the biggest international best seller of the dystopian genre. It was the only classic among Spain's 50 best-selling books of 2016 and topped some European fiction lists in 2017.

3. Eighteen months later, another choice example of Newspeak—this time by the president's lead lawyer, Rudy Giuliani—drew countless references to Orwell and may even have "trumped" Conway's howler. "Truth isn't truth," said Giuliani, replying to an interviewer's comment that the president should just "tell the truth" if he met with the special prosecutor investigating the president and other Trump administration officials about their connections to Russia and its alleged interference in the 2016 presidential campaign. Giuliani made the statement during a Sunday morning *Meet the Press* television appearance (August 18, 2018) in the course of explaining that he was advising his client not to testify before the special prosecutor since the president might make a statement that could lead to a perjury charge.

The outcry from both the media and political liberals about Giuliani's "Orwellian" line was loud and immediate. Analogies were drawn between the disappearance of "objective truth" in Orwell's Oceania and life in "Trumpland." Headlines such as *New York Magazine*'s "Giuliani Goes Full Orwell" were also common—here again conflating and confusing Orwell with his "Orwellian" *doppelgänger*, "Orwell."

As much as the political pundits enjoyed the hilarity of Giuliani's blooper, book publishers took less delight in it, for unlike the case of Conway's blunder, Giuliani's remark had no discernible effect on sales of any books, including *Nineteen Eighty-Four*.

4. As a result, *Nineteen Eighty-Four* was among the top 100 of Amazon's books from the beginning of the Obama administration to the time of the writing of this book, in the third year of the Trump administration. Virtually every new political scandal involving the degradation of language, destruction of truth, intrusion on privacy and personal liberty, and spectacle of leader worship has occasioned countless references to *Nineteen Eighty-Four* and reignited sales explosions. For instance, the book sold at six times its nor-

mal rate in 2013 after Edward Snowden revealed the extent of the National Security Agency's (NSA) surveillance programs, when many newscasters compared the agency to the Ministry of Truth. Former NSA contractor Snowden leaked details of the U.S. surveillance program to news outlets.

5. While American print and broadcast media have preoccupied themselves since 2016 with the question, "What would Orwell say about Donald J. Trump?" it is also worth asking, "What might Donald Trump say about a crotchety Orwell upbraiding Trump for one of his diatribes about 'fake news' or 'crooked Hillary' or 'shithole countries'?" One can imagine a Trump tweet against him: "A total loser! Not a clue! Park yourself in Room 101 and open the rat cage."

6. In the second impression of the first edition of *Nineteen Eighty-Four*, published in March 1950, the equation "2 + 2 =   " appeared, rather than the more famous "2 + 2 = 5" (printed in June 1949). The "5" was omitted in all British and Commonwealth editions thereafter until 1987, when it was restored to all editions. That decision was based on the argument by Peter Davison, editor of *The Complete Works*, that its disappearance had been the result of a typesetting error. The "5" had already been restored in the Secker & Warburg Uniform Edition published in December 1950, and this (third) impression thereafter became the standard for all American editions, creating an odd discrepancy between the British and American editions on this crucial detail.

   Which impression(s) should be treated as authoritative? The second or the third (which coincides with the first)? For more than three decades, textual scholars and bibliographers have followed Davison, but allegiance to his view has been shaken by the skillful sleuthing of Dennis Glover, an Australian scholar. Based on his consultations with book historians specializing in midcentury production technologies and printing practices, Glover argues that the blank space was deliberate and that the "5" was mistakenly restored to the third impression, contrary to Orwell's dying wishes, since Orwell himself authorized the deletion just weeks, or even days, before he died, when the proofs for the second impression were being checked. (No surviving historical or biographical evidence exists to support this claim.) If true, this would have been the last significant literary decision of his life.

   Glover makes his case not only as a scholar but also as a prose fiction writer. In his excellent historical novel *The Last Man in Europe* (2017), which takes its name from the working title for *Nineteen Eighty-Four*, Glover reimagines the history of Orwell's creative process from the dystopia's conception to completion across a 14-year period, dramatizing in his epilogue how

Orwell struggled with the novel's ending and particularly the "2 + 2" equation that Winston Smith traces in the dust of his table in the Chestnut Tree Café after being tortured and brainwashed in Room 101 of the Ministry of Love.

In his introduction to an edition of *Nineteen Eighty-Four* published in Australia (where Orwell's novel is in the public domain) by Schwartz Publishing in July 2017 to accompany the release of *The Last Man in Europe*, Glover shares his research regarding the second impression of *Nineteen Eighty-Four*. He also contends that the "2 + 2 = " equation possesses immense significance for the novel's ending, because it preserves a ray of hope that Winston can still dissent, still commit seditious thoughtcrime—and thus find a space for resistance even in a totalitarian dictatorship. By contrast, Glover interprets "2 + 2 = 5" to mean that *Miniluv* brainwashing leaves Winston nothing more than a shell, one of T. S. Eliot's "hollow men," bereft of any independence of mind ("He loved Big Brother") or even personal identity, as O'Brien predicted in Room 101 ("We shall squeeze you empty and we shall fill you with ourselves"). Glover adds that his biographical argument is compelling in light of Orwell's remarks about the novel in a few letters and conversations in 1949. Orwell expressed regret that his "ghastly" illness had led to a darker conclusion than he had planned, which Glover contends may suggest that the open-ended "2 + 2 = " equation represented a small, subtle, yet decisive step to restore his original intention by inflecting the ending's tone and message.

INTRODUCTION: Orwell, My "Orwell"

1. My main title for this pair of chapters draws attention to Orwell's special "French Connection," and that connection is a leitmotif of this book, extending far beyond his affinities with Malaquais and Camus. Orwell was well informed about the Parisian intellectual scene and steeped in the French literary tradition. Scattered throughout his journalism and correspondence are references to numerous French authors, especially novelists, whom he was already reading (in the original) during his Eton schooldays and whose attainments he acknowledged, if not always admired.

2. See the chapter "Doubles" in Max Saunders, *Ford Madox Ford: A Dual Life*, vol. 2 (Oxford: Oxford University Press, 1996), esp. 392. I am indebted to this analysis of Ford's late fiction for stimulating some of my own reflections on Orwell and "Orwell."

3. Saunders, "Doubles," especially the section "Doubles and Biography," 396.

4. Saunders makes a similar point about Ford's *The Good Soldier*.

5. I am reminded here of a cautionary warning voiced by Paul Valéry. In his essay "Descartes," he wrote: "My own view is that we cannot really circumscribe a man's life, imprison him in his ideas and his actions, reduce him to what he appeared to be and, so to speak, lay siege to him in his works. We are much more (and sometimes much less) than what we have done." Any literary historian or biographer must ponder this insight, for it should weigh heavily in any assessment of a person's conduct and achievement, especially in those cases (such as that of Orwell) in which posthumous history seems vastly at odds with the life that was lived.

6. See A. N. Wilson, *Hilaire Belloc: A Biography* (London: Atheneum, 1984).

7. The casual observations of numerous political journalists and social commentators implicitly support my claim. For instance, although in his bestselling *Churchill and Orwell: The Fight for Freedom* (London: Penguin, 2017), two-time Pulitzer Prize winner Thomas E. Ricks gives Churchill top billing, he remarks: "In recent years, [Orwell] may have even passed Churchill, not in terms of historical significance but of cultural influence." If not Orwell, I would contend, "Orwell" has certainly done so—in fact, decades ago and on both counts.

8. Or so I would maintain. I conducted an informal poll that turned up suggestions quite varied. But virtually all of them are largely unrecognizable beyond a literary-minded audience versed in Anglo-American poetry, fiction, and drama. For example:

1. "I have measured out my life with coffee spoons." ... "Do I dare to eat a peach?" (Eliot, "The Love Song of J. Alfred Prufrock")

2. "We are the hollow men / We are the stuffed men." (Eliot, "The Hollow Men")

3. "This is the way the world ends / Not with a bang but with a whimper." (Eliot, "The Hollow Men")

4. "The past is a foreign country." (L. P. Hartley, *The Go-Between*)

5. "If you really want to hear about it, the first thing you'll probably want to know is where I was born, and what my lousy childhood was like, and how my parents were occupied and all before they had me, and all that David Copperfield kind of crap...." (J. D. Salinger, *Catcher in the Rye*)

6. "I am an American, Chicago-born...." (Saul Bellow, *The Adventures of Augie March*)

7. "They endured." (William Faulkner, "Appendix: Compson," *The Sound and the Fury*)

The question continues to fascinate me, and I have subsequently pondered other candidates—yet none of them strike me as contenders, for they too are all quite "literary," not part of the wider public's lexicon of cultural literacy. I considered only full literary lines or sentences, excluding those originating in movies and speeches as well as mere catchwords, phrases, or book titles such as doublethink, thoughtcrime, Catch-22 (Joseph Heller), "the necessary murder" (Auden), "White Man's Burden" (Kipling), "blood consciousness" (Lawrence), and "brave new world" (Huxley via Shakespeare).

Among other nominees of my own are the following dozen lines (in no particular ranked order):

1. "Two roads diverged in a wood, and I— / I took the one less traveled by ..." (Robert Frost, "The Road Not Taken")
2. "But I have promises to keep, / And miles to go before I sleep" (Frost, "Stopping by Woods on a Snowy Evening")
3. "Isn't it pretty to think so?" (Ernest Hemingway, *The Sun Also Rises*)
4. "... [A]ttention must be paid." (Willy Loman in Arthur Miller, *Death of a Salesman*)
5. "Things fall apart; the centre cannot hold" (William Butler Yeats, "The Second Coming")
6. "I am a camera...." (Christopher Isherwood, *Goodbye to Berlin*)
7. "The horror! The horror!" (Kurtz in Joseph Conrad, *Heart of Darkness*)
8. "Whoever you are, I have always depended on the kindness of strangers." (Blanche Dubois in Tennessee Williams, *A Streetcar Named Desire*)
9. "I think that I shall never see / A poem lovely as a tree." (Joyce Kilmer, "Trees")
10. "Love means never having to say you're sorry." (Erich Segal, *A Love Story*)
11. "Do not go gentle into that good night. / Rage, rage against the dying of the light." (Dylan Thomas, "Do not go gentle into that good night")
12. "Hell is other people." ("*L'enfer, c'est les autres*"; alternate translation: "Hell is the Other.") (Garcin in Jean-Paul Sartre, *No Exit* [*Huis clos*])

Yet perhaps even more broadly known and frequently quoted than any of these proposals is another famous Orwell sentence, the Seventh Commandment in *Animal Farm*: "All animals are equal, but some are more equal than others." Notably, Orwell is the only twentieth-century author with two references in "The List" in E. D. Hirsch's best-selling *Cultural Literacy* (1987; revised and expanded, 1988). The only other writers active since 1900 with even a single mention are Conrad and Dylan Thomas, both of whose lines I have already cited above. (I include *Heart of Darkness* on my own shortlist even though the novel's date of publication was 1899.)

The inclusion of two literary lines of Orwell (from two different works, moreover) represents further evidence of his rhetorical prowess and "literary bandwidth," a topic that I discuss at length in Chapter 6, "England's Prose Laureate."

See E. D. Hirsch, *Cultural Literacy: What Every American Needs to Know* (New York: Vintage, 1988 [1987]), esp. "The List" in "Appendix: What Literate Americans Know," 152–225.

9. The widespread confusion between the man or writer (Orwell) and the "bogeyman behemoth" ("Orwell" or "Orwellian"), which serves to blur or completely efface any distinction between them, bears comparison with the widespread confusion between Dr. Victor Frankenstein and his mutant monstrosity. Among those who have never read Mary Shelley's *Frankenstein*, "Frankenstein" is the monster—not unlike the case with Orwell and Big Brother (or "Orwellian" and "Ingsoc-ian," to coin a jarring Newspeak-ism!)

It is worth noting that Dr. Frankenstein's Promethean creation—which he variously refers to as "creature," "being," "thing," "spectre," "wretch," "fiend," "ogre," and "demon"—remains nameless in the novel. In a passing remark, the monster does address himself to Dr. Frankenstein as "the Adam of your labors," imputing godlike power to his creator.

CHAPTER 1: The Quixotic, Adamantly Unsainted Life He Lived

1. A rent of "7 and 6" (seven shillings and sixpence) is equivalent to £19 or $25 (in 2020 currency).

2. Among Orwell's friends to memorialize him as Don Quixote for both his scraggy appearance and his amusingly "quixotic" behavior were Pritchett, Muggeridge, Anthony Powell, George Woodcock, and Paul Potts. Orwell biographers such as Bernard Crick also devote attention to the analogy.

The hilarious topic of Orwell's feet (and boots) warrants further comment. When Orwell was transferred outside Alcubierre to a newly formed ILP unit within the POUM, his company commander, Bob Edwards, was astounded by the size of Orwell's feet and his size 12 boots. "He wore huge boots," Edwards told BBC Radio listeners in a memorial broadcast in 1960. "I've never seen boots that were so large."

Scholars and biographers have devoted dozens of pages, and even book chapters and articles, to Orwell's physical features, personal habits, and psychological makeup. They have scrutinized his sunken tubercular face, his nose (i.e., his "pathological" sense of smell), his moustache, his voice, and

his tubercular lungs. They have analyzed his humor. They have psychoana-
lyzed his sadistic urges, "morbid" fear of rats, and (purported) autism (specifically Asperger's syndrome).

I believe a separate, quite entertaining chapter could also be written about
Orwell's feet, highlighted by his lifelong quixotic (and often desperate) pursuit of boots. One would include anecdotes about how the entire POUM
could not outfit him with boots (he instead hired a cobbler to custom-make
a pair) and how numerous postwar friends and colleagues (e.g., Muggeridge, Warburg, David Astor, Dwight Macdonald, and even his Harcourt
Brace editor in New York) were commissioned to find suitable boots in the
United States (which turned out, when Orwell received the transatlantic
shipment at last, to be an *American* size 12—and therefore too small).

Of course, as generations of his intellectual successors have attested, it is
in more than just a physical sense that the author of *Animal Farm* and *Nineteen Eighty-Four* had big shoes to fill.

Ex pede Herculem! "From the foot [we may gauge the size of] Hercules!"
(i.e., infer the whole from the part), the classical maxim of proportionality
attributed to Pythagoras.

So might we jest about the outsized reputation of Orwell today.

3. Quoted in Michael Barber, *Anthony Powell: A Life* (London: Duckworth,
2004).

4. Not only his publisher, Fred Warburg, but also numerous friends of Orwell
canvassed London to find a typist willing to travel to Jura and type the manuscript there. All efforts failed. Certainly the tubercular Orwell was well
aware that undertaking the task of typing the manuscript himself might
shatter his fragile health completely—and thus kill him. Yet had he not for
years been heedless of his physical well-being? Had he not almost defiantly
been risking his life for decades? Indeed his decisions to both fight in Spain
and semi-retire in remote Jura far from any medical facility typified his
reckless disregard for his failing health. To complete *Nineteen Eighty-Four*,
his *chef d'oeuvre* and (perhaps sole) claim to fame, might have entailed sac-
rificing the man Blair for the writer Orwell.

Yet that very tradeoff had been in progress for two decades, and if he
intuited that such a price would have to be paid, he could at least console
himself with the fantasy that he had exited in triumph and martyred himself
for a great cause: the possibility that Blair's death would grant Orwell life,
perhaps even literary immortality. Can one perhaps conclude, as does a sympathetic reader of Edgar Allan Poe, who also suffered a lifetime of debilitating illness and died young, that Orwell "paid dearly for immortality, gave
his whole life to attain it. But in his terms it was probably worth the cost"?

Finis coronat opus? Did "the end crown the work"? Or just spawn the "Work"?

E. M. Forster told BBC Radio listeners just months after Orwell's death: "*1984* crowned his work, and it is understandably a crown of thorns." Nonetheless, it needs emphasis that Blair/Orwell did not *want* to die. He still wanted to live, passionately so. He had just remarried, had new literary projects underway, and had still others in mind. He yearned both to live and to complete what might become his lasting memorial. His death was a misfortune, not a conscious, affirmed act of will. *Nineteen Eighty-Four* did not represent Orwell's deliberate "parting testament," I believe, just his last book.

The observation about Poe is by Philip Van Doren Stern, cited in J. R. Hammond, *A George Orwell Chronology* (London: Palgrave, 2000), xi–xii. For Forster's BBC address, see "The Listener," November 2, 1950, reprinted in E. M. Forster, *Two Cheers for Democracy* (London: Abingdon, 1951). Forster was discussing Orwell's dystopia and its satiric themes, not his life or death, let alone the possibility of his (half-deliberate?) self-martyrdom.

5. Asked once if he had ever considered changing his name officially, he replied waggishly: "Ah yes, but then I'd have to write under a different name, you see."

6. Admittedly, as a mere toddler of 70, *Nineteen Eighty-Four* has a long, long way to go before Orwell can echo Horace's proud boast.

   Exegi monumentum aere perennius, declares the poet as he closes the first three books of his *Odes* (III, 30). "I have erected a monument more lasting than bronze." Horace has often been mocked for his braggadocio. Given that his *Odes* are well past 2K on the endurance clock and still widely quoted, however, his boast doesn't sound so empty.

7. From the opening line in the preface of my *The Politics of Literary Reputation: The Making and Claiming of "St. George" Orwell* (New York: Oxford University Press, 1989), xvii.

CHAPTER 2: Frenemies at Fisticuffs?

1. See my foreword to the recent reprint of the biography in Christopher Hollis, *A Study of George Orwell: The Man and His Works* (New York: Racehorse Publishing, 2017). For a nuanced, comprehensive assessment of Orwell's engagement with religious matters, see Michael G. Brennan, *George Orwell and Religion* (London: Bloomsbury Academic, 2016).

2. "I was of poor parents and only able to go to the school," recalled Hollis, "because of the charity of the headmaster," who never mentioned his largesse to Hollis either during Hollis's schooldays or later. Even Hollis, whose

parents were staunch Conservatives, was taken aback by the reactionary political and cultural views of Dr. Williams and his top assistant master (and eventual successor), Hugh Alington. "I am against all change, even change for the better," Williams once declared. Or, as Hollis summed it up: "From their general habits of mind, they were two Tories of a hard and conventional school." See Hollis, *A Study of George Orwell*, chapter 1; Hollis, *Along the Road to Frome* (Oxford: Hollis & Carter, 1958), 17, 45, 51.

3. I have discussed this letter and the circumstance's surrounding Blair's marriage proposal in Chapter 17, "The Life Orwell Never Lived," in *The Unexamined Orwell* (Austin: University of Texas Press, 2011).

CHAPTER 3: The Literary Breakthrough, or When Blair Became Orwell

1. Like other opponents of the Texas death penalty, I have been gratified that there are "only" 221 inmates on death row in the state (according to official data for 2019), which is a sharp decline from the total of 451 in 1999. Moreover, 2018 witnessed "only" 13 executions in Texas, a steep drop from the high of 40 in 2000. Probably the law enacted in 2005 that introduced a sentence of life in prison without parole as a third option in capital cases (in addition to the death penalty or parole after 40 years in jail) has contributed to a reduced number of death sentences. The figures are from the nonprofit, Washington-based Death Penalty Information Center, March 2019.

2. Alex Woloch, *Or Orwell: Writing and Democratic Socialism* (Cambridge, MA: Harvard University Press, 2016).

CHAPTER 4: Orwell's Twin Masterpieces, *Animal Farm* and *Nineteen Eighty-Four*

1. Eliot's decision to decline *Animal Farm* may be regarded as the worst blunder in publishing history, especially in light of the revenue that it has earned for Secker & Warburg and its publishing partners. The misjudgment is rivaled only by the rejection of Marcel Proust's opening volume of *In Search of Lost Time* by André Gide at the publishing house of Nouvelle Revue Française, which is arguably the most egregious mistake in literary history. (Two other publishers also turned this work down before Grasset accepted it, with the humiliating condition that Proust pay all printing costs.) Yet at least Eliot read Orwell's submission and respected him sufficiently to send a personal note of explanation and regret, not a mere form letter. By contrast,

Gide seems to have done nothing more than glance over the page-long sentences in Proust's (admittedly massive and intimidating) 712-page typescript before casting it aside.

2. For this reason and related concerns, I devoted an entire book to the matter of *Animal Farm*'s satirical aspects and relationship to contemporary history. See John Rodden, ed., *Animal Farm in Historical Context* (Englewood Cliffs, NJ: Greenwood Press, 1999).

3. That famous statement is frequently attributed to Danton, especially because Georg Büchner's widely performed play about the French Revolution, *Dantons Tod* (*Danton's Death*), features an impassioned Danton declaring, "Like Saturn, the revolution devours its own children" ("Die Revolution ist wie Saturn, sie frisst ihre eignen Kinder"). The quotation is also attributed to Jacques Mallet du Pen (1749–1800), a French journalist who took up the Royalist cause during the French Revolution. In a widely circulated essay, he wrote: "A l'exemple de Saturne, la revolution devore ses enfants." This essay first appeared in his book *Considérations sur la nature de la révolution de France* (London and Brussels: Flon, 1793), 80.

4. Or Harriet Beecher Stowe? Even more so than in the case of *Animal Farm*, it was remarkable that the writer heralded by leading Western intellectuals for his uncannily realistic, gripping vision of a totalitarian world—what Orwell called "that special world created by secret-police forces, censorship of opinion, torture and frame-up trials"—was an Englishman, a fact that was no less remarkable than that Harriet Beecher Stowe had been a white woman. Orwell himself had observed that only writers such as Malraux, Borkenau, Silone, Victor Serge, and his friend Arthur Koestler had been able to re-imagine such a catalogue of horrors and craft it into "concentration-camp literature" because they were continental Europeans who had experienced it: "There is almost no English writer to whom it has happened to see totalitarianism from the inside," he noted. For an Englishman to write *Darkness at Noon* would be as unlikely, he added, as for a slave trader to write *Uncle Tom's Cabin*. So it was an amazing achievement that the Englishman George Orwell managed the feat of writing his own "*Uncle Tom's Cabin* of our time"—not just once, but twice.

5. When Orwell's agent, Leonard Moore, submitted *Animal Farm* to Dial Press, it was politely declined because "it is impossible to sell animal stories in the USA." Surely the editors' fatuous letter of rejection must rank as one of the all-time boners in the history of publishing.

6. Quoted in Jeffrey Meyers, *A Reader's Guide to George Orwell* (London: Thames & Hudson, 1975).

7. Was Orwell "guilty" of failing to prevent the political hijackings and mantle snatchings of his work? Such a veiled accusation betrays an ignorance of the nature of fiction in general and political satire in particular. One critic has accused me of holding that "Orwell could and should have made his position clearer, by somehow writing *Nineteen Eighty-Four* as unmistakably pro-socialist and anti-capitalist" in order to avoid any misunderstanding about his intentions and prevent "monstrous" right-wing claims to his mantle of Decency and Democracy.

I do nothing of the sort. Instead, I merely point out that *Animal Farm* and *Nineteen Eighty-Four*, a pair of incomparably powerful cultural bombshells, inevitably trade political accuracy for literary throw-weight. That is, the greater the ideological power possessed by an artwork—especially a political satire—the greater the likelihood that its reception will be marked by imprecision of targeting—that is, that its audience(s) will misconceive (deliberately or unawares) its referents and targets—and that it will suffer gross misapprehension and even outright distortion, bowdlerization, and hijacking. The devil can and does quote Scripture to his purpose. Or, to cite Orwell's famous opening line of his essay "Charles Dickens," "Dickens is one of those writers who is well worth stealing." That charged trade-off—political power or aesthetic precision (and satirical "accuracy" of aim)—has in the case of Orwell galvanized stormy trade winds of confusion and controversy through which I have sought to navigate across three decades of discussion about the politics (and ethics) of reception. I do not advance the simplistic notion that Orwell should have "pre-empted the misunderstanding" by writing *Nineteen Eighty-Four* (and *Animal Farm*) to avoid literary theft— which in any case, no matter how one writes, is impossible to avoid completely. See David Ramsay Steele, *Orwell Your Orwell: A Worldview on the Slab* (South Bend, IN: St. Augustine's Press, 2017).

8. And let us not forget that Orwell himself is credited (according to the Oxford English Dictionary) with coining the phrase "Cold War" in 1945. (He did not seem to consider the conflict a post–World War II phenomenon, for he first used the term even before the war had formally ended.)

CHAPTER 5: A "Utopian" Edition of a Dystopian Classic

1. The line ("*Les mots ont une âme*") expressed Maupassant's homage to his revered master, Flaubert, who extolled *le mot juste*. See Guy de Maupassant, *Flaubert, ou l'âme des mots*.

2. Publishers such as Harcourt, Penguin, and Signet have no strong motivation to issue critical editions of Orwell's novel—which would, of course, expand its length and raise the price of any print edition. Might a practical solution to our problem be an online critical supplement? Such material could be issued without concern for length (and price). Of course, it could also be directly incorporated into ebook and Kindle editions. (Unfortunately, readers of print versions who do not have easy access to online material would not benefit at all from this circumvention.)

3. That explains why, for example, no Norton Critical Edition of *Nineteen Eighty-Four* has ever appeared—or is likely to do so in the foreseeable future. Generally speaking, the Norton editions of other British and American classics have been affordably priced, substantive, "critical" editions, providing valuable background information and featuring excerpts from reviews and other criticism of the work itself. (Regrettably, some Norton editions in recent decades—such as Twain's *Huckleberry Finn* and Conrad's *Heart of Darkness*—have been so ideologically skewed by the critical apparatus as to make balanced interpretation impossible.)

4. As I explained in an endnote to the Prologue, an Australian edition of *Nineteen Eighty-Four* has been available from Black Inc. in Melbourne (an imprint of Schwartz Publishers) since July 2017, introduced by Dennis Glover and timed to coincide with the appearance of his historical novel dramatizing Orwell's creative struggle to complete it. Schwartz obviously determined that the publication of *Nineteen Eighty-Four* was justified economically, perhaps both because any success for Glover's historical novel might send readers back to the original and because the arguments in Glover's introduction about the equation "2 + 2" are fresh and compelling. Glover believes that Orwell preferred "2 + 2 = ," with the answer left blank, not the far better-known (and now-standard) equation "2 + 2 = 5." Glover's introduction makes an interesting case, which the novel reimagines, that Orwell altered the ending as he proofed the second impression of the first edition (March 1950) just a few weeks before his death on January 21—and that the alteration is significant for our interpretation of the book's ending and Orwell's message.

The decision to publish in the tiny Australian market shows that it is possible to issue a new edition of *Nineteen Eighty-Four* in those countries where the novel is already in the public domain, even if the print run is very small and does not reach either of the major markets (the U.S. and UK, although it is important to note that the Australian edition will soon be available in the UK market, where Orwell's dystopia will enter the public domain after January 2020). It also demonstrates that such an edition can include a substantial new introduction that would assist readers.

Glover's introduction is the only substantial one currently on the market. Unfortunately, it too possesses limited value for many readers, given its narrow focus on a single textual detail. It restricts itself to Glover's argument about issues in textual scholarship related to the equation "2 + 2" and includes no supplementary material useful to readers uninformed about the novel's historical context and satiric referents.

5. See Chapter 9, where I discuss at greater length both the national ruckus in Britain over the BBC *Nineteen Eighty-Four* and these subsequent three apogees of repute.

6. For example, I adverted earlier in this chapter to the conspiracy-minded, far-right John Birch Society (JBS) and have long maintained that the organization "defaced" Orwell's reputation by adopting "1-9-8-4" as the last four digits of its national office's phone number in Washington and suggesting that its outlook dovetailed with Orwell's own. ("Call 202-659-[pause]1-9-8-4 … NOW!" proclaimed the old JBS ads.) The JBS has long been a dead issue, but the issues raised by its "borrowings" are not, and that topic has been especially prominent in Orwell's multichromatic reputational history. One recent critic, David Ramsay Steele, has taken me to task for my use of the terms "septic treason" and "poisonous betrayal" in describing the selective quoting of Orwell by right-wing admirers in general and by the JBS in particular. "Just what's so bad about it?" he asks. "Are you debarred from quoting a writer sympathetically on one topic if you don't share all his views?"

My answer is: No, not at all. One topic? Just the reverse: the much-advertised "1-9-8-4" phone number (which uneasily evokes the Oceania Two Minute Hate chants) and frequent citation of Orwell's coinages by JBS representatives sent the subliminal message that they *did* "share all his views." Or rather: Orwell shared all *their* views. I've argued throughout my work that the "ethics" and "politics" of reception are inextricably connected. That means that even when we do not "share all his [or her] views," we explain where we part company from another person. Otherwise we distort (or "deface") the image of the cited figure. To describe such an act as "defacement" entails an awareness that some "portraits" of Orwell are more equal than others. That is, some interpretations better fit or are at variance with available factual material—literary, biographical, and otherwise—than others. The fact that the JBS has always expressed a "preference for democracy over dictatorship" and for "capitalism to collectivism," as did Orwell, does not mean that the JBS did not "shamelessly exploit" *Nineteen Eighty-Four*.

Steele asks: "Why should anti-Communists be ashamed of utilizing an anti-Communist work in support of their anti-Communist message?" Answer: the JBS should be ashamed that in making claims of Orwell's patrimony, it *omitted* such relevant facts as these: that it opposed the Civil Rights Act of 1964 and the civil rights movement itself as Communist infiltration projects, denounced the United Nations as an international conspiracy to destroy American sovereignty (e.g., the "Get USA Out!" campaign for UN withdrawal), awarded thousands of dollars in prize money to college students for essays promoting the impeachment of Chief Justice Earl Warren, and accused President Dwight Eisenhower of "deliberate treason." For these reasons and more, the JBS was disavowed by conservatives ranging from Barry Goldwater to William F. Buckley for its "paranoid and idiotic libels" (in Buckley's phrase).

To imply (by omission) that Orwell's anti-Communism would have extended to support for such positions (among numerous other extremist JBS conspiracy theories) is indeed an example of "septic treason" and a blatant violation of "the ethics of reception." I suspect that if members of the John Birch Society had ever bothered to read Orwell's *CEJL* in the late 1960s or 1970s, they might well have changed their phone number. In fact, they might have lacerated the Cold War champion as "soft" on communism and the Soviet Union. Certainly no faithful JBS supporter—nor any of the vociferously anti-Stalinist ex-Trotskyists among Orwell's *Partisan Review* colleagues in New York—would have characterized Stalin's USSR in such positive terms as "the real dynamo of the socialist movement in this country and everywhere else." Would not architects of the "rollback" position in the mid-1950s such as John Foster Dulles have blanched at Orwell's statement that "if the USSR were conquered by some foreign country, the working class everywhere would lose heart.... I wouldn't want to see the USSR destroyed and I think it ought to be defended if necessary"? During the post-Stalin "thaw" of the late 1950s, many American conservatives and liberal anticommunists—and most JBS members—were even willing to risk nuclear war for the possibility of "regime change." (Orwell quotations are in David Ramsay Steele, *Orwell Your Orwell: A Worldview on the Slab* [South Bend, IN: St. Augustine's Press, 2017], 229.)

7. Written by the Canadian poet John Macrae, "In Flanders Fields" gave voice to the public outrage over the waste and futility of the Great War.

> We are the Dead. Short days ago
> We lived, felt dawn, saw sunset glow,

Loved and were loved, and now we lie
In Flanders fields.

8. See Jeffrey Meyers, *A Reader's Guide to George Orwell* (London: Thames & Hudson, 1975); and Bernard Crick, *Nineteen Eighty-Four; With a Critical Introduction and Annotations* (London: Clarendon, 1984).

CHAPTER 6: England's Prose Laureate

1. Largely unknown are the similarities between how the two men conducted their personal lives. (Was this resemblance part of what could be called Orwell's unconscious identification with Dickens?) Just as Dickens's long-term intimacy with Ellen Ternan (whether consummated or not) was completely unknown to virtually everyone until more than seven decades after his death, Orwell's numerous affairs, as well as his marriage proposals to at least four women within months of his first wife Eileen's death in 1945, were unknown until the publication of the first full-length biography of him, by Bernard Crick, in 1980. Furthermore, both Dickens and Orwell not only led private lives that included hidden affairs, which are common enough, but also carefully compartmentalized their circles of relationships.

For at least the last 13 years of his life, between the mid-1850s and his death in 1870, Dickens constructed a life of sealed units that rarely overlapped. He structured his life into "cells" in several different locations. Among them were his official residence (the "family fortress"), where he sought to shield his children from his encounters with 18-year-old Ellen Ternan after his estrangement from his wife Katherine; his paramour's quarters (the "love hideaway"), where he set up his young mistress, supplemented by various holiday locations for assignations in France and outside London; and his business office (the "work headquarters"), where he edited his weekly magazine, conducted his professional affairs, and did much of his own writing. Each location featured one (or two) close relationship(s)—his family's nanny/caretaker, his love interest, and both his publisher and his administrative assistant for public readings and other trips. His busy professional schedule of publishing commitments and reading tours served as a cover for meeting Miss Ternan in still other locations. Was Dickens aware that he externalized his inner compartments in this remarkably well-defined physical and material fashion? It is impossible to say.

Orwell did much the same—absent the externalizations. Orwell did not possess Dickens's financial resources or any easy cover (e.g., public readings in far-flung places), nor did his long-term affair with Inez Holden in London necessitate such arrangements. Nonetheless, he externalized what must have been segmentations in his inner life with comparable ruthlessness. Although Orwell did not live within the confined social constructions of middle-class Victorian England, he too must have concluded that his romantic arrangements required some form of concealment. (Possibly they also became even more erotically charged as a result of that concealment.)

Orwell did not go so far as Dickens in conducting what amounted to a double life. Dickens's choice to live two lives—one public, one secret—fits latter-day Stracheyean caricatures of duplicitous Victorian mores. In the case of both men, it should be emphasized that the habit of secrecy preceded the necessity of secrecy. In fact, the former facilitated the latter and perhaps even led to it or made it inevitable. For reasons likely obscured even from themselves, both Dickens and Orwell were loath to reveal (or rather expose) their personal lives. They wanted acquaintances as well as readers to accept the public image that they projected. I have discussed some of these aspects of Orwell's personal behavior elsewhere. See, e.g., John Rodden, "'Permanent Outsider' among Friends: Orwell's Compartmentalized Life," in *The Politics of Literary Reputation*, 181–191.

2. See Mark Thompson, *Enough Said: What's Gone Wrong with the Language of Politics?* (New York: St. Martin's, 2016).

3. Yet even England's Prose Laureate nodded. The masterful polemicist of *Animal Farm* and *Nineteen Eighty-Four* sometimes coined phrases that proved rhetorical duds. Consider, for example, the title of his early novel, *Keep the Aspidistra Flying*. What on (or in!) earth is an "aspidistra"? Does it really fly? The title suffers from the obvious fact that most people today do not even know that such a word exists, let alone that it is a sturdy (usually potted) houseplant that was often mocked for its dowdiness and (rather like plastic flowers now) once possessed bourgeois connotations. (Gracie Fields did a send-up in a rollicking music-hall song, "The Biggest Aspidistra in the World.") Non-British readers—as well as highly literate, politically informed British readers with whom I have spoken—are unaware that Orwell's title jokingly alludes to an old socialist hymn, "The Red Flag" ("Though cowards flinch and traitors sneer, / We'll keep the red flag flying here"). That includes even Labour Party members and supporters, who know full well that "The Red Flag" is their own party anthem yet fail to register that the novel's title alludes to it. Nor is this ignorance probably attributable to the (inevitable) decay of cultural memory, or what I might term the "lost allusions" of history, for not a single book reviewer of *KAF* mentions the party anthem.

So Orwell "nodded" and the task of titling his novel was turned over, as it were, to Gordon Comstock and his fellow admen. Of course, as we have just seen in Chapter Five, the problem of "lost allusions" is common with satire. Unlike *Nineteen Eighty-Four* or *Gulliver's Travels*, however, which are great works of art that induce (at least some) readers to invest effort in recovering the forgotten references and reconstructing the context, a slight novel such as *Keep the Aspidistra Flying* will seldom elicit (or warrant) such exertions. Only a handful of scholars will trouble themselves to establish its satirical references and clarify its latent meaning.

An equally poor title—due to blandness rather than obscurity—is *Critical Essays* (1946). Fortunately, unlike *KAF*, the volume's quality easily compensated for its ho-hum title (though the enduring acclaim accorded the collection may well owe more to its American edition, published under the eye-catching title *Dickens, Dali, and Others: Studies in Popular Culture*).

4. See T. A. Shippey, *J.R.R. Tolkien: Author of the Century* (Boston: Houghton Mifflin, 2000), xix.

5. Anthony Burgess, *Observer*, November 26, 1978, and quoted in Shippey, *J.R.R. Tolkien*, xx. Burgess's stance is representative of a not-infrequent view. It warrants emphasis that not only ideologically motivated critics, especially Marxists and other radicals who stand opposed to Orwell's heterodox or dissident Left politics, have dismissed or vilified him. Numerous literary figures, some of them "FAMOUS AUTHORS" in their own right, have also derided his plain, simple prose as simplistic or merely popular, sometimes linking it to his allegedly sensationalist fiction. For instance, on hearing that his novel *Invitation to a Beheading* was being compared to Orwell's *Nineteen Eighty-Four*, Vladimir Nabokov scoffed during the 1960s in his new foreword that his own work was instead "a real description of a fantastic world," not a "fantasy" of the future. Nabokov added that "G. H. Orwell [*sic*] or other popular purveyors of illustrative ideas and publicistic fiction" were no "kindred soul" for him. Quoted in Mel Oettinger, "Vladimir Nabokov: The Novelist as Musician," *Dialogue* 11, no.1 (1978): 89.

6. And yet, ironically and surprisingly, "Politics and the English Language" was rejected by the editors of *Contact*, George Weidenfeld and Philip Toynbee, evidently on the grounds that it did not meet their editorial criteria. (Weidenfeld subsequently lamented his "sacrilegious mistake.") Orwell published the essay in his friend Cyril Connolly's *Horizon*. Like *Animal Farm*, therefore, which was turned down by at least four leading London publishers, "Politics and the English Language" is paid homage today as a canonical work of enduring distinction despite the "sacrilege" committed by London

editors against it. Peter Marks discusses the episode of PEL's rejection in his excellent study, *George Orwell the Essayist: Literature, Politics, and the Periodical Culture* (London: Continuum, 2011), 158.

7. See *What Orwell Did Not Know: Propaganda and the New Face of American Politics*, ed. Andras Szanto (New York: Public Affairs, 2007). It is indeed ironic that this group of left-wing critics and theorists would invoke Orwell's name and pedigree for the very purpose of chastening him for his liberal, empiricist naïveté and politically regressive ideological outlook, all of which resembles the faint praise of earlier generations of British Marxists such as Raymond Williams. Even the conference title ("There You Go Again: Orwell Comes To America")—which draws on a famous Ronald Reagan zinger in a presidential debate against Democratic nominee Walter Mondale—makes it sound as if paleo-Reaganite George Orwell had "come to America" and was spreading his lies and obfuscations here again. This confusion exemplifies how Orwell and "Orwell" are regularly blurred and even inverted. Perhaps the *locus classicus* on the Left of this tendency is the judgment pronounced by Williams himself, then nearing 60, to the younger editors at *New Left Review* about "the figure of Orwell." This nightmarish presence, like a politically reactionary, finger-pointing Ghost of Christmas Past, supposedly haunted Williams and his cohort throughout the decade following the man's death: "In the Britain of the Fifties, along every road that you moved, the figure of Orwell seemed to be waiting. If you tried to develop a new kind of cultural analysis, there was Orwell; if you wanted to report on work or on ordinary life, there was Orwell; if you engaged in any kind of socialist argument, there was the enormously inflated statue of Orwell warning you to go back."

Could not every reference to Orwell in the above paragraph be placed in quotation marks—"Orwell"? Williams's entire statement about this omnipresent "figure," this "enormously inflated statue" can be read as a projection of his own massive anxiety of influence—which Thompson (and numerous other Marxists) evidently shared. Echoing Thompson's line in his essay "Outside the Whale," Williams adds: "Down into the Sixties political editorials would regularly admonish younger radicals to read their Orwell and see where all that led to." All of them have recoiled before their "Orwell," their "intellectual Big Brother"—which I deliberately uppercase here. See Raymond Williams, "Orwell," in *Politics and Letters* (London: New Left Books, 1979), 42–43.

8. E. P. Thompson, "Outside the Whale," in *Out of Apathy* (London: Stevens & Sons, 1960); Salman Rushdie, "Outside the Whale," in *Imaginary Homelands* (London: Granta, 1991).

9. Broadcast internationally in numerous versions and languages, the *Big Brother UK* franchise was canceled by Britain's Channel 5 after its nineteenth season ended in November 2018. Both the original *Big Brother* series and the spinoff *Celebrity Big Brother* show continue to run in the U.S. and several other countries.

10. Quoted in Steele, *Orwell Your Orwell.*

11. And yet I strongly suspect that the author of "Politics and the English Language" would have found the prose style of Raymond Williams, the acknowledged founder of British cultural studies, jargon-laden and would have charged such literary-cultural theorists with having succumbed to what he called (in a 1937 review about Ortega y Gasset) "the lure of profundity," that is, of "avoiding thoughts" by "thinking too deeply." (He might have seconded Geoffrey Wheatcroft, who remarked about the turgid prose of Williams: "He will be read when George Orwell is forgotten—but not until then.")

It is in this context, as an attack on the seductive "lure of profundity," that Orwell's calls for clear writing and plain speaking recur. He was well aware, especially during his stint as a BBC broadcaster, of the dangers of the "Big Lie," what Burckhardt referred to as the mystifications of the "terrible simplifiers." So it is misplaced for a critic such as Denis Donoghue to condemn Orwell for his statement in "Why I Write": "Good prose is like a windowpane." Donoghue bemoans that "the shoddiest part of Orwell was his determination to link plain English to freedom and truth-telling." Not at all. For Orwell rightly saw that the obfuscations perpetrated by bureaucratese and academese, which constantly prove susceptible to pretentious, empty profundities, mire people in the infernal coils of status anxieties that invite compensatory euphemisms, legalisms, and elitist twaddle. Donoghue is quoted in John Sutherland, *Orwell's Nose: A Pathological Biography* (London: Reaktion Books, 2017), 228.

CHAPTER 7: French Connection, Part 1: Jean Malaquais, a "French Orwell"?

1. Trotsky's review in English appeared in the New York communist journal *The Fourth International.* He included the review, titled "Un Nouveau Grand Ecrivain: Jean Malaquais," in *Litterature et Revolution de Trotski* (Paris: UGE, 1938), 333–346. Malaquais told André Gide that he was "extremement flatteuses" by Trotsky's comments. See Pierre Masson and Geneviève Nakach, *André Gide-Jean Malaquais Correspondance, 1935–1950* (Paris: Phebus, 2000), 88. Grateful for the review as he was, however, Malaquais came by

the mid-1940s to despise the Trotskyists too, regarding them as politically expedient and foolishly romantic. Malaquais was an ideological purist who characterized his politics in later years as anarcho-syndicalist. Whatever his affiliation, however, he was always an ultra-leftist and anti-Bolshevist who proudly viewed himself as an independent radical and revolutionary Marxist.

2. The seven books were *Down and Out in Paris and London* (1933), *Burmese Days* (1934), *A Clergyman's Daughter* (1935), *Keep the Aspidistra Flying* (1936), *The Road to Wigan Pier* (1937), *Homage to Catalonia* (1938), and *Coming Up For Air* (1939). The first two were published in the United States by Harpers; Gollancz published six of the seven in England. He rejected *Homage to Catalonia* because of its criticisms of communism. It was eventually published by Secker & Warburg.

3. The letter that Malaquais wrote to Gide has been lost, but years later Norman Mailer reconstructed the key passage as he recalled Malaquais explaining it to him in the 1940s: "You ought to get down on your knees and pray to that God you occasionally pretend to believe in that he has let you be a comfortable bourgeois so you can make your art."

4. Characteristically, in the lines following this phrase from "Looking Back on the Spanish War" (1943), Orwell immediately injects a human element, noting that he once had a clear shot at an enemy soldier running "along the top of the parapet in full view. He was half-dressed and was holding up his trousers with both hands as he ran. I refrained from shooting at *him*.... I had come here to shoot at 'Fascists.' But a man who is holding up his trousers isn't a 'Fascist,' he is visibly a fellow-creature, similar to yourself."

5. Isaac Rosenfeld, "Man from Nowhere," *New Republic*, April 12, 1943, 288–290. Rosenfeld bemoaned Malaquais's "aloofness" that never rose to "detachment." But Malaquais's "sincerity," above all his willingness to show "the mind's failure to understand the heart," rendered his book a valuable document of personal testimony. Is this failure—which is far more a "moral" than a "literary" matter—simply the occupational hazard of the intellectual turned witness and journal keeper? It was, in any case, a failure of Malaquais's own, and it damaged or destroyed many friendships throughout his life.

For his review of *Les Javanais*, see Lionel Trilling, "The Lower Depths," *Nation*, April 24, 1943, 602–603. Malaquais would probably have sneered at the plaudits from literary ex-radicals associated with *Partisan Review* such as Rosenfeld and Trilling. Even before the onset of the Cold War, he would likely have regarded them, at best, as armchair intellectuals in retreat—and as hypocritical sellouts at worst.

6. Victor Serge was a former communist intellectual and author who fled France for Mexico in 1942. He and Malaquais fell out over the proper policy toward the war for *engagé* radicals to support.

7. Quoted in Jean Luc Douin, "Jean Malaquais: Revolutionnaire d'instinct," *Le Monde*, December 26, 1998, 7.

8. Numerous essays and even a book-length study have addressed Orwell's "Englishness." See Robert Colls, *George Orwell: English Rebel* (New York: Oxford University Press, 2013). On the larger issues, see also Linda Colley, *Britons: Forging the Nation 1707–1837* (New Haven, CT: Yale University Press, 1992); Jeremy Paxton, *The English* (Woodstock, NY: Overlook Press, 1998); and Peter Mandler, *The English National Character: The History of an Idea from Edmund Burke to Tony Blair* (New Haven, CT: Yale University Press, 2006).

9. Claus-Dieter Krohn, *Intellectuals in Exile: Refugee Scholars and the New School for Social Research* (Amherst: University of Massachusetts Press, 1993); Peter Rutkoff, *New School: A History of the New School for Social Research* (New York: Free Press, 1986).

10. Alfred Kazin, "The Trouble He's Seen," in *Critical Essays on Norman Mailer*, ed. J. Michael Lennon (Boston: G. K. Hall & Company, 1986), 60–61.

11. Steven Marcus, "Norman Mailer: An Interview, 1964," in *Conversations with Norman Mailer*, ed. J. Michael Lennon (Jackson and London: University Press of Mississippi, 1988), 85; Christopher Hitchens, "Norman Mailer: A Minority of One," *New Left Review*, March/April 1997, 115, 119.

12. Quoted in Benjamin Ivry, "A Rebel Reviewed by Trotsky," *Jewish Forward*, February 15, 2012.

13. Carl Rollyson, *The Lives of Norman Mailer* (New York: Paragon House, 1991), 50. Malaquais also derided both Mailer's pursuit of notoriety and his fascination with popular culture as signs of a lack of seriousness. A few years before his death, Malaquais had a bitter argument with Mailer over his alleged failure to become a serious writer. Malaquais accused him of being "just a commodity" whose pursuit of television celebrity status revealed his "infantile malady." The truth was that Malaquais scorned with increasing intensity every tawdry "success" of Mailer's that brought him higher and higher in the literary *demimonde*. Mailer once described his colleague as "an intellectual Sultan" and by the 1980s had grown tired of Malaquais's patronizing attitude. He told the convicted murderer Jack Abbott that he was moving away from Malaquais's influence because "I found it unendurably arid."

14. Mailer even chastened the younger self of his 20s, admitting that he hadn't liked the book when he first read it and in fact had been aghast and found it disappointing. On a second reading, he now saw it more positively: *The*

Joker had appeared 20 years too soon, but now the world was ready to understand it. What looked like fantasy in 1953, Mailer wrote, stood forth in the 1970s as prophecy.

15. Norman Mailer, "A Preface to *The Joker*," 11–25, in Jean Malaquais, *The Joker* (New York: Warner, 1974). Mailer once offered an explanation for why Malaquais abruptly stopped writing fiction that resonates with my own conjectures in this chapter. Mailer's fanciful prose notwithstanding, his speculation is that the failure of *The Joker* to win even a small following was Malaquais's final experience of disillusionment and ushered forth his literary death. "Just as it is the human fate to die, so it may be the novelist's fate to stop writing—it comes finally out of the baggage of disappointment in one's life, a species of cumulative nothingness, and Malaquais' fictional talents have indeed been [since 1953] silent."

16. From the outside, the mystery of why Malaquais turned to Kierkegaard remains. Indeed it is almost as if the subtitle of his dissertation, "Faith and Paradox," is self-referential or at least indicates his veiled relationship to the philosopher—for it is surely a paradox that this avowed atheist and abstract thinker who embraced a materialist version of Hegel's metaphysical system should dedicate several years of his life to an intensive engagement (that even included learning Danish) with a man of burning faith. Yet these paradoxes point toward an explanation: self-analysis, even self-disclosure. From the inside, the specific choice of Kierkegaard, the proud "individualist," possesses a certain biographical or psychological *raison d'être*. Doubtless some part of "*Malaquais rebelle*" identified with the recalcitrant, defiant Dane.

17. Perhaps one factor that accounts for Malaquais's decision to stop imaginative writing is that, in the end, he was far more an abstract, theoretical thinker than a creative writer possessed of a mind that dwelt in particularities—which is to say that he was far more an intellectual at home with Marxist dialectics than a born novelist à la Gide, let alone Flaubert. In this light, the trajectory of Malaquais's writing, which finally arrives at the academic treatise, is an intelligible, even inevitable evolution. And the selection of a subject such as "faith and paradox" in the existentialist philosophy of Kierkegaard is a (failed?) attempt to resist icons of Abstraction and the totalistic god of System, and instead to preserve some margin of psychic space for particulars and the literary imagination.

18. Mailer once described him as "a man locked in chains when it came to writing." He elaborated:

> Only a soul paying in this life for outrages it had performed in another could pass through such suffering.... He would sit at his desk for ten or

twelve or fourteen hours a day, every day. It was his boast that he would not get up, not pace around, not break for a meal, no, he would sit, contemplate his page, and would write ... to the tune of two or three hundred words a day. Two hundred words in ten hours! It is twenty words an hour, or a new word every three minutes. Can any torture be more horrifically designed for a man who could deliver an extempore lecture complete in thought, example, and syntax, a work of seven or eight thousand words in less than an hour.... How could he dare to write about anything? Given his profound contempt for authors who rushed to place their shoddy artifacts into that small temple where only a few perfect works ought to be installed, how could he presume to add to the excrementa?

Malaquais described his own writing process as *pisser le sang*. That is to say: every drop of ink that trickled from his pen in composing *The Joker* was like pissing blood. It may possess biographical significance that Dr. Babitch thrills when state authorities honor him with a vial of ink, and he dreams of the day when he soon will also be awarded an inkpot.

19. Jean Malaquais, "George Orwell: *La Route de Wigan Pier*: mineurs et chomeurs au pays de galles," *Le Débat* 9, no. 16 (November 1981): 118–128.

20. The publication of the Gide–Malaquais correspondence, edited by Pierre Masson and Geneviève Millot-Nakach, was part of the French publisher Phebus's effort to revive interest in Malaquais.

21. The line is from Victor Hugo's epic poem, *La Légende des siècles* (*The Legend of the Centuries*), in *Les Grandes Lois*, Chapter LV.

CHAPTER 8: French Connection, Part 2: Camus and Orwell, *Rebelles avec une cause*

1. The narrator even goes so far as to muse at length on certain Scriptural stories in the course of extended, brilliantly original meditations, pondering (for example) how Jesus of Nazareth coped with his presumably lifelong "guilt" upon learning of his "responsibility" for the deaths of the Holy Innocents of Bethlehem, whom King Herod had ordered his soldiers to butcher in a vain hunt to murder the Baby Jesus himself, the future "King of the Jews."

2. In a ceaseless, dizzying, book-length monologue that consists of a torrential rant of confessional prose, Clemence alternately pleads desperately for "clemency" for his offenses and brusquely reasserts his pride.

3. The 24-year-old Dean died instantaneously in the head-on collision that occurred on September 30, 1955, in Northern California.

CHAPTER 9: How and Why Orwell Became "A FAMOUS AUTHOR": Surfing the Tides of Time

1. The following six paragraphs are derived from my lengthy discussion of the BBC-TV adaptation in Chapter 5 of *The Politics of Literary Reputation*.

2. See also Sutherland, *Orwell's Nose*. Just weeks earlier, Churchill had suffered a near-fatal heart attack, which the government hushed up and kept secret until after his term in office ended in 1955.

3. Because it was a teleplay and not a film—that is, a drama on stage that was simply being filmed for a television audience—the production was no taped broadcast but rather a second fresh, live performance.

4. What gave rise to this phrase of Forster? I believe it had to do with the concept of the "middlebrow," which arose in Britain in the mid-1920s. "Middlebrow-ism," better known as "Midcult," stood between high culture and low culture. It was derided by the advocates of high culture—such as Forster, his fellow Cambridge Apostles, and the Bloomsbury crowd—as simply a dumbed-down version of Highcult that oversimplified complexity and stood only a few steps above the vulgarity of Lowcult, the province of the *demos*. A world-famous, highly prosperous author of the day often dismissed as a Midcult favorite (and openly envied as an international best seller) was W. S. ("Willie") Maugham. Forster's phrase is likely a satiric reference to Maugham.

5. See Sutherland, *Orwell's Nose*, 52.

6. I should clarify that this conjecture, which I have ventured since the mid-1980s (and most extensively in *The Politics of Literary Reputation*), pertains exclusively to the contingencies of repute bearing on his cultural afterlife. I don't at all believe that it was "good for Orwell to die when he did," as one scholar misconstrues. When I speak about Orwell having arguably died at the "right historical moment," I am speaking about the effect of his "moment of exit" on his posthumous reputation—not about his life or the integrity of his legacy. I do not hold that *Orwell* would have been "compromised" by having to take sides on political issues in the 1950s and 1960s, but rather that Orwell's *reputation* would have been tarnished (or "compromised") in the eyes of some of his followers on both the Right and the Left. They would no longer have exalted him so uncritically as their intellectual hero and champion of their cause. Nor would they have been so ready (or able) to claim his legacy. See Peter Marks, "Reputations: George Orwell," *Political Quarterly* 70 (1999): 84–85.

7. And what if, in May 1937, the Falangist bullet had not missed his carotid artery by millimeters? Or if weeks later the manhunt by the Spanish police

(under orders from Stalin's NKVD) to capture and execute him had succeeded (as it did with Orwell's colleague, the POUM leader Andrés Nin)? Dead at the age of 33, Orwell would have left not just his political fantasias but even *Homage to Catalonia* and all his greatest essays forever unwritten. Then George Orwell would have gone down the memory hole just as surely as has Jean Malaquais—and far more justifiably.

8. I rather doubt it. The mathematical models developed in cliodynamics and cliometrics may yield valuable insight into some macrohistorical patterns—for example, the rise and fall of empires, the outbreak and course of civil wars, and so on. Yet I suspect that the so-called whirligig represents a sociohistorical mechanism whose complexity will inevitably frustrate efforts to determine precisely its direction of travel and degree of velocity. Even the biggest databases and the most sophisticated quantitative tools may never pinpoint reliable answers because the near-infinite amount of data will overwhelm the capacity of the model to yield fruitful results. No model is likely to ever do justice to the empirical evidence available or likely even to recover the bulk of evidence, much of which will vanish forever into the memory holes of History.

9. Christopher Hitchens, often touted by his admirers as "Orwell's natural successor" and "the Orwell of his generation" of British writers, acknowledged the danger. The urge "to be like him," to be "the next Orwell," he implied, may skew your decisions and deprive you of the opportunity (and responsibility) to live your own life. As he observed in an interview conducted in August 2011, just four months before his death:

> I think it's very wrong to have role models. Imagine how ludicrous it would be if I were to say that I thought of myself as "the George Orwell of my generation." I'd be making a spectacle of myself.... I wrote a whole book on George Orwell [*Why Orwell Matters*, 2002] because I had to get it out of my system. I'd been so [deeply] influenced by him from the very early years of my life, not just because of the stances he took politically and the moral and intellectual courage he exhibited, but also because of the vividness and spareness of the prose that was a reflection of that integrity.

Hitchens explained further that he coped with the temptation to pace in Orwell's footsteps by pursuing a quite different style of living, combined with a conscious effort at *agere contra*.

> I had to try consciously *not* to emulate him. I was so full of admiration that I had to aim off and away from [Orwell's choices]—which, after all,

was easy for me to do because Orwell never had a steady job, never had any money, his health was always bad, and he only lived until he was 46. . . . Whereas I've been quite lucky. I've traveled a lot, made quite a lot of money from journalism, never been persecuted for my beliefs, never been shot at as he was in Spain (from both sides!).

Hitchens concluded that his rather surprising, unsentimental "education" was to "learn how unlike my hero I was." I wonder if Hitchens ever pondered that, in the opening lines of "Why I Write," his hero may have been addressing him regarding their differences, for both he and Hitch "belong[ed] to a . . . minority of gifted, willful people . . . determined to live their own lives to the end. Serious writers are, I should say, more vain and self-centered, though less interested in money." Christopher Hitchens, interview with Charlie Rose, *The Charlie Rose Show*, August 13, 2011.

10. George Woodcock, "Orwell, Blair, and the Critics," *Sewanee Review* 83, no. 3 (Summer 1975).

CHAPTER 10: "Catholic Exceptionalism": Why Catholic America Canonized "St. George"

1. Did Blair's experience as a day pupil at the strict, ascetic school run by the French Ursuline nuns in Henley-on-Thames (1908–1911) spark his antagonism toward the Catholic Church? Or did it cultivate his religious sensibility and help foster a sympathetic outlook toward the social gospel of Christianity? Both are plausible, for the French Ursulines were known widely for their adherence to ecclesiastical authority. And yet, given that this teaching order was founded by and served the progressive vision of Pope Leo XIII, who authored the encyclical *Rerum Novarum* championing the common worker and his campaign for a just wage, the Ursulines also pursued a mission that George Orwell would have endorsed.

2. Quoted in Brennan, *George Orwell and Religion*, 160.

3. Cited in Frances Spalding, *Stevie Smith: A Biography* (New York: Norton, 2002).

4. Orwell might have been amused by the exchange between Nancy Mitford and Evelyn Waugh in which Mitford rebuked Waugh for his rudeness and verbal cruelty despite professing to be a practicing Catholic: "You have no idea," Waugh replied, "how much nastier I would be if I were not a Catholic. Without supernatural aid I would hardly be a human being." The substance of that remark seems to have become for Waugh more or less a standard rejoinder. When his friend Randolph Churchill angrily asked, "Have you ever

noticed that it is always the people who are most religious who are most mean and cruel?" Waugh responded with apparent delight, "But my dear Randolph, you have no idea what I should be like if I wasn't." The first account appears in Martin Stannard, *Evelyn Waugh*, vol. 2: *No Abiding City, 1939–1966* (London: Flamingo, 1993). The second story, which was told by the Earl of Birkenhead, appears in David Pryce-Jones, ed., *Evelyn Waugh and His World* (Boston: Little, Brown, 1973), 139.

5. Geoffrey Stone, *Commonweal*, June 18, 1937, 220. Stone was an assistant editor of the *American Review*, a conservative political magazine with strong ties to traditionalist voices on both sides of the Atlantic. Its stable of distinguished contributors included Anglo-Catholics (Eliot, Chesterton, Belloc, Christopher Dawson), New Humanists (Irving Babbitt, Paul Elmer More), and Southern Agrarians (Allen Tate, John Crowe Ransom, Robert Penn Warren, Randall Jarrell, and Austin Warren).

6. Geoffrey Ashe, "A Note on George Orwell," *Commonweal*, June 1, 1951, 191.

7. Richard Voorhees, "Orwell's Secular Crusade," *Commonweal*, January 28, 1955.

CHAPTER 11: "Orwellian" Warfare: From Cold to Cyber

1. Personal communication, February 2015.

2. On these issues, see the comments of ex-CIA director Michael Hayden in Paul D. Shinkman, "Former CIA Director: Cyber Attacks Are Game-Changers Comparable to Hiroshima," *U.S. News & World Report*, February 20, 2013.

3. Quoted in Shinkman, "Former CIA Director," and John Seabrook, "Network Insecurity," *New Yorker*, May 20, 2013, 70.

4. David Rothkopf in *Foreign Policy*, cited in Seabrook, "Network Insecurity," 70. Ever since the release in April 2015 of the Pentagon's 33-page cybersecurity strategy document, speculations have run rampant that the "cool war" may heat up very quickly. The document is a response to discoveries that Russian hackers swept up President Obama's email correspondence during 2014. Although the breach was apparently limited to the White House's unclassified computers, Washington is no longer just "playing defense," but also now "developing the malware and other technologies that would give the United States offensive weapons should circumstances require disrupting" networks of such adversaries as Russia, China, Iran, and North Korea. More than a dozen other countries are "making similar investments," according to the *New York Times*. The FBI has the role of first response to

threats of cyberaggression, with other government agencies (the NSA, the Department of Homeland Security, the CIA, and the Pentagon) following up with various kinds of offensive cyberoperations. So the Orwellian fear that battles in the near future might shift from the international to the extraterrestrial is no longer sci-fi speculation. A militarized cyberspace is now on the verge of developing into a new war front among rival powers. "Star Wars"—or a sinister *E.T.*—is upon us. See "Preparing for Warfare in Cyberspace," *New York Times*, April 28, 2015, A22.

5. See Lara Jakes and Darlene Superville, "Obama: Spying Legal, Limited," *Austin American-Statesman*, June 8, 2013, A1. The president was backtracking from his much-quoted promise as a candidate in 2007 to reject "the false choice between the liberties we cherish and the security we provide." Instead he pledged: "I will provide our intelligence and law enforcement agencies with the tools they need to track and take out the terrorists without undermining the Constitution and our freedom." Al Lewis, "Dirty Bomb Blows Liberty," *Wall Street Journal*, June 9, 2013, 14.

6. "W's Apprentice," *Economist*, May 18, 2013, 29–30.

7. See, e.g., Jürgen Liminski, "Big Brother Obama," *Kirchenpost*, June 15, 2013, 2; and Stephan Meetschen, "Der Deutsche Traum vom amerikanischen Messias," *Die Tagespost*, June 20, 2013, 9. The German press, which had greeted Obama during his 2008 presidential campaign as a political "messiah," "a miracle worker, peacemaker, and ray of hope for a better world," was bitterly disillusioned by the NSA scandals in 2013 occasioned by Edward Snowden's disclosures. (Since April 2015, when reports surfaced that German intelligence agencies had also snooped on important European allies, especially France—and shared much of their data with the United States—the German media's harsh critiques of such surveillance activities have focused on Berlin.)

8. One of the key intellectual works of the "preventive war school" during the early Cold War era was Burnham's *The Struggle for the World* (1947). In hindsight, however, Burnham erred gravely in his doomsday prophecies, such as his prediction that "if the communists succeed in consolidating what they have already conquered, then their complete world victory is certain.... We are lost if our opponent so much as holds his own." Likewise, his "might is right" ideology of beneficent imperialism, whereby he championed what Orwell disparaged as "hundred percent Americanism," verged itself on the totalitarian. Burnham wrote that in the struggle with communism, "For us, international law can only be what it was at Nuremberg (and what it would have been at Moscow and Washington if the other side had

conquered): a cover for the will of the more powerful." Burnham's language was echoed in the rhetoric of a prominent later voice in the neoconservative movement, Charles Krauthammer, who wrote: "America is no mere international citizen. It is the dominant power in the world, more dominant than any since Rome. Accordingly, America is in a position to reshape norms, alter expectations and create new realities. How? By unapologetic and implacable demonstrations of will." Quoted in R. J. Stove, "British Cold Warriors and the War on Terror," *National Observer*, Summer 2009, 61.

9. Kennan (1904–2005) laid out the case for containment in a famous article in *Foreign Policy* in 1947 that he signed "X." His long-range strategy for blocking the worldwide advance of communism and eventually defeating the USSR proved visionary. Kennan argued that firm containment of Stalinism had "nothing to do with outward histrionics: with threats or blustering or superfluous gestures of outward 'toughness.'" Rather, Kennan saw the Cold War campaign as hinging on patience and on the authenticity and credibility of the West's respect for personal freedom. How true would the "Free" World be to its professed values? "It is the Russians, not we who cannot afford a world half slave and half free. The contrasts implicit in such a world are intolerable to the fictions on which their power rests.... If only one ray of light of individual dignity or human inquiry is permitted to exist, the [Soviet] effort must eventually fail."

10. See Stove, "British Cold Warriors," 61.

11. The author of *Animal Farm* would have likely agreed with another British Cold Warrior and realist, the poet-historian Robert Conquest, who was the first prominent Western intellectual to document the scale of the Soviet gulag in *The Great Terror* (1968). Challenged to defend the legitimacy of Cold War surveillance practices and Western intelligence agencies, Conquest replied: "In a jungle full of totalitarian monsters, liberal democracy needs teeth."

Although Orwell was not in favor of saber rattling, let alone war cries and bellicose threats to unleash deadly weapons, he also did not underestimate Stalin. Here again he would have affirmed (and enjoyed) Conquest's dry wit on being asked whether Stalin was an anti-Semite: "Yes, but it was hardly noticed. He was broadly and generously anti-human."

Conquest was a lifelong admirer of Orwell, saluting him in a poem of the mid-1950s ("George Orwell") as "a moral genius."

12. Because Orwell died less than a month before Joseph McCarthy's rise to prominence in 1950 and the subsequent Red Scare, he never referred to either of them in his work. Orwell used the phrase "hundred percent Americanism" in a post-publication press release of *Nineteen Eighty-Four* that he

dictated from his sickbed on June 15 (just five days after its American launch) to Fred Warburg, his publisher and friend, which they issued to clarify already emerging misconceptions about the dystopia.

The phrase was already in general circulation, having arisen not with the growing anticommunist fervor as the Cold War deepened, but rather 30 years earlier, in the wake of World War I, when it gained currency as shorthand for a loosely organized nativist movement hostile to all non-WASP elements. Anti-immigrant, anti-foreigner, and anti-Catholic, this aggressive pro-Americanism was endorsed by groups ranging from the American Legion to the Ku Klux Klan. Beginning in 1919, "Americanists" (or "hundred percenters") precipitated, promoted, and participated in wave after wave of racial violence (e.g., Negro lynchings), deportations (e.g., of the anarchist agitator Emma Goldman), and antiradical hysteria (i.e., the first Red Scare, long before the McCarthy era).

It was doubtless this sorry chapter in American history that Orwell had in mind when he referred to "hundred percent Americanism." Although he never equated that episode with the horror story of Stalinism and the gulag, he worried about the smoldering *potential* of "hundred percent Americanism" to reignite mass violence, adding in his press statement: "The qualifying adjective is as totalitarian as anyone could wish." By that comment, I believe, Orwell explicitly meant to underscore the fascist tendencies in American nativism and to signal that he viewed the "hundred percenter" movement as a (still-nascent) counterpart to Oceania's *Ingsoc*, an embryonic "American National Socialism" (*Amsoc* or perhaps *Yanksoc*).

We should remember that this press release was directed to Orwell's American readers and dispatched at the specific request of a representative of the United Auto Workers of America after a *New York Post* reviewer likened *Ingsoc* to the British Labour Party. For all his readers, including his American audience, Orwell noted: "The moral to be drawn ... is a simple one: *Don't let it happen. It depends on you.*"

13. Likewise, the nonchalant bandying of Orwellian catchwords in attacks on Donald Trump (or Barack Obama or George W. Bush), is usually misplaced. Trump is no Big Brother—and not even a figure of the malevolence of Napoleon in *Animal Farm*. Like his two predecessors, he is at worst like the bullying village dictator in Orwell's first novel, *Burmese Days*, the native Burmese magistrate U Po Kyin. He is a man-eating crocodile rather than a genocidal pig ruler. "He recalls to me a crocodile in human shape," one character in the novel remarks. "He hass [*sic*] the cunning of the crocodile, its cruelty, its bestiality."

14. See my comments about the rhetoric of the Bush administration's War on Terror campaign, which relied on a language of demonology. Reversing the allegedly timid and conciliatory, even pusillanimous, foreign policy of the Clinton years, the Bush White House relied heavily on the use of enemy scapegoats to marshal and maintain support for its two military invasions and dramatic escalations of national security measures. By contrast, the Obama administration made concerted efforts to "rebrand" rival nations (e.g., Iran, North Korea, etc.) so that there were no longer any "enemies." Of course, if foreign nations deem themselves to be at war with the United States, then it is an idealism of the Panglossian kind not to regard them as enemies. The Trump White House has swung the pendulum back in the direction of the Bush years—if anything, with a much shriller, more blustery, and more verbally aggressive tone. Thus we can see that American foreign policy during much of the last two decades has ricocheted from one extreme to another, from Democratic administrations that see no enemies (only misunderstandings) to Republican administrations that are all too willing to scapegoat rivals and pursue military rather than diplomatic solutions in order to further their political agendas. The polar swings evince how very difficult it is to articulate and execute a balanced, rational foreign policy in a seemingly ever more volatile, perilous geopolitical climate.

CHAPTER 12: Why I Am Not a Socialist

1. See the 1937 version of W. H. Auden's poem "Spain." Auden much regretted his line "the conscious acceptance of guilt in the necessary murder," altering it (to "guilt in the fact of murder") in a later version of the poem, prompted by Orwell's indignant attack in his essay "Inside the Whale." Such a phrase could only be written, said Orwell, either by someone who had no conception of "murder" or by an indifferent spectator to (or apologist for) the crimes of "the Hitlers and the Stalins." "Personally I would not speak so lightly of murder," he wrote. "The Hitlers and Stalins find murder necessary, but they don't advertise their callousness.... Mr. Auden's brand of amoralism is only possible if you are the kind of person who is always somewhere else when the trigger is pulled."

2. In the case of the Marxist-Leninist-Stalinist USSR, with its mass starvation policies and gulags, one might reply to the venerable Vladimir, "OK, I see— and smell—the broken eggs everywhere. But where, pray tell, is the Promised Omelet?"

3. Or, as Ortega y Gassett forewarns: "Create a concept and reality leaves the room." Not always, I believe, but certainly one usually feels the "whoosh" of

its quick rush for the nearest exits—and feels the inrushing arctic blast of Unreality's immediate entrance.

4. John Stuart Mill, *Principles of Political Economy: With Some of Their Applications to Social Philosophy* (London: Longman, Green, Longman, Roberts and Green, [1848–1852] 1865), 261.

5. Irving Howe, *Margin of Hope: An Intellectual Autobiography* (Boston: Mariner Books, 1983). The abiding task for intellectual maturation is to lose one's innocence yet retain one's ideals—and to avoid the precipitous fall from innocence into cynicism. In my view, that means to retain the capacity to raise, as Irving Howe titled his last essay before his death in 1993, "Two Cheers for Utopia." As he wrote four decades earlier: "But if the idea of socialism is now to be seen as problematic, the problem of socialism remains an abiding ideal. I would say that it is the best problem to which a political intellectual can attach himself."

Despite his skepticism about the possibilities of ever achieving a "decent" form of socialism, George Orwell did just that, wrestling with "the problem of socialism" and faintly, hoarsely croaking his own "two cheers for utopia" until his dying day. Orwell never retreated to the cynical view that the world would inevitably witness "the triumph of the crocodile." The tragic failure of the Loyalists to defeat Franco in the Spanish Civil War notwithstanding, Orwell concluded in *Homage to Catalonia*: "Curiously enough, the whole experience has left me with not less but more belief in the decency of human beings." In a subsequent essay, "Looking Back on the Spanish War," Orwell reaffirmed his faith in ordinary people: "No bomb that ever burst / Shatters the crystal spirit." He added: "Shall the common man be pushed back into the mud, or shall he not? I myself believe, perhaps on insufficient grounds, that the common man will win his fight sooner or later, but I want it to be sooner, not later." Certainly books such as *Burmese Days*, *Homage to Catalonia*, *Animal Farm*, and *Nineteen Eighty-Four* hastened the triumph of the "common man" over the crocodiles, large and small, of the Cold War era. The fight goes on, but such passages of Orwell referring to the Spanish Civil War evince that he, like Irving Howe, retained a generous "margin of hope."

CONCLUSION: Whither Orwell—and "Orwell"?

1. See, for instance, the lavishly produced, 300-page coffee table book (jointly funded by the regional government of Aragon and the provincial cultural office of Huesca) to commemorate the eightieth anniversary of Orwell's service in the Spanish Civil War, *Orwell toma café en Huesca*, ed. Victor Pardo Lancina (Huesca: Gráficas Alós, 2017).

The volume was accompanied by an Orwell exhibition in Aragon, and the title ("Orwell enjoys [takes] coffee in Huesca") was intended to voice a Catalan "welcome back" gesture. The editor noted that Orwell had looked forward to drinking coffee in Huesca yet "never had his coffee" because he got wounded and had to leave as Franco's well-armed Nationalist troops resisted the attempted Loyalist siege to capture Huesca in June 1937.

2. It is the Plaça de George Orwell, an *outré* youth hangout, better known to locals as the Plaça del Tripi ("Acid Square").

3. True enough, we all wear our own looking glasses through which we (often darkly) look—and we all tend to forget we are wearing them. Whenever I look through the Orwell/"Orwell" bifocals, that is, I am wearing my own glasses, through which I inevitably see "my" Orwell(s) whom I have sought throughout my work to render sufficiently clear and compelling to be fully understandable to the reader.

An extended word about this self-reflexive conception of reputation history as literary historiography is warranted here. Throughout my work, my aspiration has always been to look not only *through* the panoramic "Orwell" lenses before me, but also *at* my own lenses (and frames too), examining their focal strength, degree of magnification, sharpness of resolution, and more. The reputation historian as self-aware curator must also embrace the role of an assiduous optician or even ophthalmologist of sorts, trying to acknowledge and account (and compensate) for his squint (or the lenses' glare), his myopia (or hyperopia), his sundry astigmatisms, and his limited vision at certain angles, always cognizant of how different scenes or locales (e.g., America in 1946, Britain in 1954, Washington, D.C., in 2017) alter as the lenses change and equally attentive to how his own particular lenses (e.g., my post–Vatican II liberal Catholicism) bring particular scenes into view (e.g., the "*Commonweal* Catholic" Orwell).

However salutary and necessary, such corrective steps do not override the human condition: my own glasses, like yours, are forever shaded and tinted. Even when adjusted for obstructions and deficiencies, they enable partial vision (and thus partial blindness) at most. As a result, the first critical duty of the reputation historian as narrative optician is to stay aware of his (color) filters and share them with the reader.

And so, whenever possible, I have sought not only to document and delineate the kaleidoscopic scenes that the "Orwell" prism miraculously exhibits, but also to inspect how the kaleidoscope's plane mirrors and scintillating colored glass generate new images with each new change of position. Alert to all this, we can appreciate how the process of "becoming Orwell"—

and even more, "becoming 'Orwell' "—is also a process of our own individual and collective self-becoming. For *we*—you *and* I—co-create the "Orwell" gallery, and the portraits on view owe to the "specs" and frames we wear.

4. With this phrase I merely seek to bestow a name on the scholarly inquiry (or inquest!) I have conducted into Orwell's posthumous fame—or "afterlife"— since the 1980s. In contrast to the standard biographical studies addressing the "Life and Times" of influential figures, I have written a series of books about the "Afterlife and Times" of Orwell—and especially his dastardly *doppelgänger* "Orwell."

5. As we saw in Chapter 6, Orwell has been hailed as one of the founders of British cultural studies, a direct forerunner of and "trailblazer" for popcult critics with academic positions such as Raymond Williams and Richard Hoggart. He would appreciate the irony that his *doppelgänger* "Orwell" might be responsible for what I am suggesting could be another branch of cultural studies involving the posthumous lives of people and artifacts.

6. Although I do believe that the idea of a "serious interdisciplinary inquiry into the post-mortem existence of persons and phenomena" holds considerable potential for illuminating important historical issues (e.g., cultural memory, social influence, literary reputation, etc.), I suspect that the phrase "thanatology studies" would be met with a sardonic laugh from the author of "Politics and the English Language." Orwell despised not only jargon, but also the pretensions and obfuscations that invariably accompanied it— perhaps especially in its academic versions. He befriended A. J. "Freddie" Ayer, the founder of logical positivism, though he never bothered to read a line of Ayer's work. Likewise Orwell respected Bertrand Russell without having the slightest interest in Russell's role as the father of British analytic philosophy and author of the famous *Principia Mathematica*.

Nor did Orwell think much of continental philosophers such as Jean-Paul Sartre, whom he dismissed as "a bag of wind" for his 900-page wartime treatise, *Being and Nothingness*, which introduced his philosophy of "existentialism," established his intellectual credentials in Paris, and was treated with immense respect by the European intelligentsia. Ironically, Sartre's close colleague Maurice Merleau-Ponty was the love of his second wife Sonia's life. She especially admired the philosopher's celebrated abstruse treatise *The Phenomenology of Perception*.

Orwell's view of Merleau-Ponty is unknown. (Did Orwell realize that Sonia married him on the rebound after the philosopher, a married man, jilted her?) Nowhere does Orwell mention Merleau-Ponty in his writings or correspondence, though he was surely aware of him as the co-editor (with

Sartre) of the leading literary-political journal in Paris, *Les temps modernes*, as well as an eminent academic philosopher in his own right. Nonetheless, it is not hard to fathom what he must have thought about the author of *Humanisme et Terreur* (1947), in which Merleau-Ponty argues for suspended judgment about the Soviet gulag and castigates Western hypocrisy. As if he aimed to compose an inverted version of *Animal Farm* in nonfiction, Merleau-Ponty reframes and defends events in Soviet history ranging from Stalin's proclaimed "liquidation of the kulaks" campaign to the farcical Moscow show trials of the so-called Old Bolsheviks who had led the Russian Revolution. The philosopher argues, for instance, that the latter exemplify a higher "revolutionary justice." That is his judicial principle for rendering judgments according to the deterministic Marxist laws of History that will soon bring forth the Revolution and make the Moscow trials "inevitably" true, even though their contempt for reigning (bourgeois) truths (e.g., belief in due process) may presently seem to condemn the trials as corrupt. In his memorable formulation, Marxism is not a philosophy of History; it is *the* philosophy of History, the disregard of which digs the grave of Reason in history.

Orwell invariably regarded such dialectical acrobatics as claptrap. He had no interest in meeting with the Marxist intellectual elite when he visited Paris in 1945, whom he dismissed as intellectual scam artists at best (and metaphysical Mafiosi at worst). Instead his convictions ran closer to a fellow writer such as Paul Valéry, who remarked (in a famous put-down of Descartes) that "all systems constitute an undertaking of the human spirit against itself." Even before the vogue for abstruse cultural theory gained sway throughout the Western intelligentsias and academic elite, Orwell had dismissed most literary theorists and philosophers as being guilty of what he called (in a review of Ortega y Gasset discussed earlier) "the lure of profundity," that is, of being so obtuse that they fail to see (as Proust remarks in *Le côté de Guermantes*) that "a work of theory is like an object on which the price tag is left."

7. Of course, as literary and cultural historians readily concede, such contentions, let alone grand claims about "the most influential," are hard to "prove." After all, "influence" is an intricately difficult, often pathless process to trace. What counts as persuasive evidence is often disputed, and so I advance such assertions about Orwell and *Nineteen Eighty-Four* (and certain of his essays) in carefully qualified terms and with a sense of confidence tinged with diffidence.

Other readers have proposed different British authors and novels as the "most influential," the biggest "game changer." For instance, the distinguished publisher David Garnett wrote in *Great Friends* that Forster "influenced events with *A Passage to India* more than any other author has influenced events with a novel in this century. It was read widely and fiercely resented, but nevertheless its influence seeped in and then, acting like a hard frost, it began to break up the mortar in men's minds. It changed the climate. *A Passage to India* qualifies Forster to rank as the most effective propagandist novelist in English in this century."

Garnett, however, neither argues nor presents any evidence for his claims. How "widely" was *A Passage to India* (1927) read outside a narrow segment of the British educated classes? The sales totals for the book were not large, and no film or television adaptations were made until decades after its publication and years after British decolonization in Asia and Africa (BBC-TV, 1965; cinema, 1984).

In my opinion, the historical evidence is overwhelming that if one simply takes Garnett literally, his claim is absurd: *A Passage to India* had far less influence in the twentieth century than Orwell's *Nineteen Eighty-Four*. Nonetheless, if one interprets Garnett as referring only to novels of the twentieth century that had a constructive, positive impact on events, then his contention is more plausible—for *A Passage to India* contributed as much as any other work of the literary imagination to changing attitudes toward imperialism and the status of empire in not only British but also international consciousness. David Garnett, *Great Friends* (New York: Atheneum, 1980), 111.

8. A chagrined Bismarck once said that "the most significant event of the nineteenth century was the acceptance of English as the language of North America." By 1920 English was spoken by 300 million people, was the language of government of 500 million, and had penetrated into more areas of the globe than any other language in history. Moreover, the English language boasted a literary tradition nonpareil, represented by figures ranging from Shakespeare and Milton to Wordsworth, Austen, Dickens, Yeats, Joyce, and far more. On the rise of English, see John Paul Russo, *I. A. Richards: His Life and Work* (Baltimore: Johns Hopkins University Press, 1989).

9. In Stanza XIV of "Esthétique du Mal," Stevens has a much darker prospect in mind in the figure of "Konstantinov," his stand-in for Lenin, "a logical lunatic" for whom "the cause"

> Creates a logic not to be distinguished
> From lunacy ...
>
> ...
>
> He would be the lunatic of one idea
> In a world of ideas, who would have all the people
> Live, work, suffer, and die in that idea....

Lenin's "cause" was Marxism (i.e., Marxism-Leninism), and his "one idea" was revolution, which he stalked obsessively and single-mindedly according to the logical "laws" of historical materialism, all of which led to seven decades of unconscionable tyranny, under which untold millions worked, suffered, and died—but scarcely lived.

10. And it should be noted that Orwell himself was a hedgehog, if not precisely a one-idea man—as his fanatical and obsessive devotion to becoming a clear and compelling writer (and "A FAMOUS AUTHOR") attests. His friend Ruth Pitter observed: "He had the gift, he had the courage, he had the persistence to go on in spite of failure, sickness, poverty, and opposition, until he became an acknowledged master of English prose."

11. Long before his death, as we discussed in Chapter 3, Orwell had begun (inadvertently? deliberately?) to "set posterity a puzzle" (and frustrate his would-be biographers) in his works of "faction." Are "A Hanging," *Down and Out*, "Shooting an Elephant," and "Such, Such Were the Joys" straight autobiography? Veiled autobiography? Stories? Essays? "Sketches"? Believers in their autobiographical authenticity, such as Orwell's second wife Sonia and his authorized biographer Michael Shelden, paired off against skeptics such as Malcolm Muggeridge and biographers Bernard Crick and Gordon Bowker. To this day, no arguments have proven conclusive. Some pieces of the puzzle remain puzzling.

12. Although I believe that recourse to these varied metaphors elucidates the varied character of reputation-formation, such an approach does run the risk of trafficking in mixed metaphors. Given that image-making is so rich and complex, however, I believe a lexicon derived from diverse disciplines is worth the potential clash, for it provides significant advantages in terms of range, flexibility, precision, and accuracy. Equipped with multiple, multiform rhetorical instruments, one can describe the reputation process though quick forays conducted from numerous locations and shifting perspectives.

13. Less well publicized is the revelation in 2015 that Orwell himself was misidentified as a communist during World War II by British government informers—a droll blunder torpedoed by a secret agent whom Winston Smith might himself have fabricated. In 1942, a sergeant of the Special Branch absurdly reported that Orwell held "advanced communist views, and several of his Indian friends say they have often seen him at communist meetings." Soon thereafter an MI5 officer named W. Ogilvie questioned this description. He was apparently aware that Orwell was a heterodox socialist and a staunch anticommunist. Familiar with *The Lion and the Unicorn* and Orwell's contribution to a symposium published by Gollancz under the title

The Betrayal of the Left, Ogilvie wrote: "I gather that the good sergeant was rather at a loss as to how he could describe this rather individual line, hence the expression 'advanced communist views.'"

Yes, it is as if the MI5 had its own "Comrade Ogilvy"! Except that, unlike Winston's creation in the Ministry of Truth, he apparently did not seek to rewrite history and fabricate Newspeak lies—just the reverse. Ironically, this real-life Ogilvie seems to have been responsible for coming to Orwell's rescue and sparing him some headaches from the wartime Home Office during his stint at the BBC. On Orwell and MI5, see Ian Williams, *Political and Cultural Perceptions: British and American Views of George Orwell* (London: Palgrave, 2017).

14. I have discussed the FBI, State Department, and U.K. dossiers on Orwell and his work in *The Politics of Literary Reputation* and in *Scenes from an Afterlife: The Legacy of George Orwell* (Wilmington, DE: ISI Press, 2003).

15. Hence his insistent dissociation of patriotism from nationalism and its other bastard siblings. Hence too his already cited cautionary reminder to readers of *Nineteen Eighty-Four*: "The moral ... is a simple one. '*Don't let it happen. It depends on you.*'"

16. That is not how some Indian public officials see it, however. Dismissing Blair/Orwell as a colonial imperialist, they charge him with having "enslaved India." To an outsider, it is ironic that in recent years Orwell has been portrayed in such terms in Indian news accounts—and even more ironic that the reason has indirectly to do with a controversy involving Mahatma Gandhi, about whom Orwell always felt ambivalent.

The controversy has to do with local efforts to establish the Bengali home of Blair's birth in the village of Motihari as a permanent memorial site. The village is located in the state of Bihar, and several vocal state politicians oppose the plan. Their argument is twofold: First, Eric Blair has a tenuous connection to the village. His presence was "insignificant," given that he resided no more than a year in Motihari before his mother decamped with him and his elder sister Marjorie for England. Second, he became a member of the Indian Imperial Police. Like his father, Richard, therefore, he was an agent of the alien occupation power, a British civil servant. His birth in Motihari was due solely to the fact that Richard was stationed in Motihari to oversee the British government opium warehouse situated near the family bungalow.

No objections were raised in 2010 when members of the local George Orwell Commemorative Committee and the co-sponsoring Motihari Rotary Club lobbied the Bihari state government to declare the bungalow a protected monument and then proceeded to place a marble bust of Orwell nearby. The charges against Blair/Orwell as an imperialist tool of the ruling class only exploded three years later, when his monument interfered with an initiative to honor Gandhi. As it turns out, Gandhi also has a connection to Motihari: it was here that he launched his maiden *satyagraha* (noncooperation, or "soul force") campaign of civil disobedience in the form of nonviolent protest. In 1917, he called on indigo farmers to resist British oppression and refuse payment of government taxes. Although a large statue of Gandhi already stands in Motihari, plans have been drawn up to construct a Satyagraha Park to underscore further the village's special link to this "Indian freedom fighter" who helped "liberate" the nation from British rule.

All memorials are equal, but some memorials are more equal than others?

So it would seem. Although Orwell advocates insist that the village should honor both men, Gandhi partisans maintain that "Orwell contributed nothing" to India. Until 2016, an expansive park plan to memorialize Gandhi was "foiled," as it were, by Orwell. Because the park area would encroach on the Blair family bungalow, influential local residents who were opposed to the complete erasure of Orwell's memory had successfully blocked the park's expansion—an unexpected turn of events that had outraged some Bihari state officials. In June 2016, Orwell supporters discovered that the developers had gone ahead and started to build on the Orwell site anyway. Then a judge stepped in to halt that construction, pleasing Orwell allies, who prophesy that their Orwell shrine will one day become the equivalent of Shakespeare's Stratford-on-Avon or Tolstoy's Yasnaya Polyana. The battle rages on.

On the controversy, see the following: Alice Vincent, "Gandhi Memorial Axed to Preserve Orwell's Indian Birthplace," *Daily Telegraph*, April 18, 2013; Gita Pai, "Orwell's Reflections on Saint Gandhi," *Concentric: Literary and Cultural Studies* 40, no. 1 (March 2014): 51–77; Andrew Marszal, "George Orwell's Birthplace under Threat from Indian Developers," *Daily Telegraph*, June 30, 2016.

17. Quoted in Sutherland, *Orwell's Nose.* Hamilton made this statement in 2015. To explain the remarkable phenomenon of Orwell's growing international fame in the twenty-first century, I would heartily welcome a judicious monograph, perhaps titled something along the lines of *Orwell Abroad*—or rather perhaps *"Orwell" Abroad.*

Illustration Credits

Figure 1. © Jimmy Margulies

Figure 2. Ziggy © Ziggy and Friends, Inc. Reprinted with permission of Andrews McMeel Syndication. All rights reserved.

Figure 3. Andy Singer, www.andysinger.com

Figure 4. A 1962 Herblock Cartoon, © The Herb Block Foundation

Figure 5. Image courtesy of the Orwell Archive, UCL Library Services, Special Collections.

Figure 6. © Vernon Richards's Estate. Image courtesy of the Orwell Archive, UCL Library Services, Special Collections.

Figure 7. (Maurice) Christopher Hollis by Walter Stoneman. Bromide print, 14 April 1948. © National Portrait Gallery, London

Figure 8. Penguin Random House LLC

Figure 9. Public domain

Figure 10. © Henri Cartier-Bresson/Magnum Photos

Figure 11. David Low / Solo Syndication

Figure 12. fine art / Alamy Stock Photo

Figure 13. Ziggy © Ziggy and Friends, Inc. Reprinted with permission of Andrews McMeel Syndication.

Figure 14. Andy Singer, www.andysinger.com

Figure 15. Jim Borgman © *Cincinnati Enquirer.* Reprinted with permission of Andrews McMeel Syndication.

Index